普通高校专业英语教程系列

市场营销专业英语

司爱侠 陈红美 郑聪玲 编著

清華大学出版社
北 京

内 容 简 介

本书按照立体化教材建设思路编写，实现线上和线下的有机结合，非常适合教学。全书共 13 个单元，内容覆盖营销基础、市场营销环境、消费者行为研究、消费者决策、营销模型、市场细分、产品分类、产品决策、产品生命周期、定价策略、零售营销策略、促销策略、广告与营销、服务与营销、网络营销等，主题丰富，选材广泛，兼顾行业发展热点。本书每个单元的案例（Case）可作为课外拓展阅读，读者可扫描书中的二维码下载使用。

本书既可作为高等院校市场营销相关专业的专业英语教材，也可供相应的培训班使用。从业人员使用本书"自我充电"，亦颇得当。

图书在版编目（CIP）数据

市场营销专业英语 / 司爱侠，陈红美，郑聪玲编著. —北京：清华大学出版社，2022.11
普通高校专业英语教程系列
ISBN 978-7-302-60957-5

Ⅰ. ①市… Ⅱ. ①司… ②陈… ③郑… Ⅲ. ①市场营销学—英语—高等学校—教材 Ⅳ. ①F713.50

中国版本图书馆 CIP 数据核字（2022）第 089005 号

责任编辑： 徐博文
封面设计： 子　一
责任校对： 王凤芝
责任印制： 刘海龙

出版发行： 清华大学出版社
网　址： http://www.tup.com.cn，http://www.wqbook.com
地　址： 北京清华大学学研大厦 A 座　　**邮　编：** 100084
社 总 机： 010-83470000　　**邮　购：** 010-62786544
投稿与读者服务： 010-62776969，c-service@tup.tsinghua.edu.cn
质量反馈： 010-62772015，zhiliang@tup.tsinghua.edu.cn
印 装 者： 北京嘉实印刷有限公司
经　销： 全国新华书店
开　本： 185mm×260mm　　**印　张：** 15.25　　**字　数：** 366 千字
版　次： 2022 年 12 月第 1 版　　**印　次：** 2022 年 12 月第 1 次印刷
定　价： 78.00 元

产品编号：080079-01

前　言
Preface

市场营销对企业经营至关重要，是决定企业成败的关键因素。随着市场营销的日益国际化，具备相关专业知识并精通外语的人员往往处于竞争的优势地位，成为行业中的佼佼者。职场对从业人员的专业英语水平要求很高，这有力地推动了从业人员学习专业英语的积极性，许多大学因此开设了“市场营销专业英语”课程。本书是一本旨在提高读者的专业英语能力的行业英语教材。本书的教学理念是理论密切联系实际，遵照理论体系组织结构，按照实际应用展现职场实况，通过案例分析来理解理论、运用理论从而掌握理论。这样可以培养理论知识扎实、能够运用理论来分析实际情况、能够解决职场实况中问题的会计专业人才。

本书主题丰富，覆盖营销基础、市场营销环境、消费者行为研究、消费者决策、营销模型、市场细分、产品分类、产品决策、产品生命周期、定价策略、零售营销策略、促销策略、广告与营销、服务与营销、网络营销等，兼顾行业发展热点。全书共 13 个单元，每一单元包含：篇章阅读——题材广泛、切合实际的两篇专业文章；单词——课文中出现的新词，读者由此可以积累市场营销专业的基本词汇；词组——课文中的常用词组；缩略语——课文中出现的、业内人士必须掌握的缩略语；习题——既有针对课文的练习，也有一些开放性练习；案例——进一步扩大读者的视野；参考译文——让读者对照篇章阅读提高理解和翻译能力。本书还提供了“单词总表”“词组总表”和“缩写词总表”，读者既可复习和背诵，也可作为小词典长期查阅。

本书的内容与课堂教学的各个环节紧密结合，并配有立体化的教学资源，支持教师备课、教学，以及学生复习、考试等各个环节。另外，本书还配套了习题参考答案、教学课件，以及参考试卷（读者可从清华大学出版社官方网站免费下载）。读者在使用本书过程中，如有任何问题，都可以通过电子邮件与我们交流［邮件标题请注明姓名及“市场营销英语教程（清华大学出版社版）”］，邮箱地址：zqh3882355@163.com；cici12323@tom.com。

由于编者水平有限，书中难免有疏漏和不足之处，恳请广大读者和同人提出宝贵意见，以便再版时进行修正。

编著者

2022 年 7 月

目 录
Contents

Unit 1

Unit 2

Unit 3

Unit 4

Unit 5

Unit 6

Unit 7

Unit 8

Unit 13

Unit 1

Text A

Marketing Management Philosophy

Marketing is defined by the American Marketing Association (AMA) as "the activity, set of institutions, and processes for creating, communicating, delivering, and exchanging offerings that have value for customers, clients, partners, and society at large". The term developed from the original meaning which referred literally to going to market with goods for sale. From a sales process engineering perspective, marketing is "a set of processes that are interconnected and interdependent with other functions" of a business aimed at achieving customer interest and satisfaction.

The process of marketing is that of bringing a product to market in which includes these steps: broad market research, market targeting and market segmentation, determining distribution, pricing and promotion strategies, developing a communications strategy, budgeting, and visioning long-term market development goals. Many parts of the marketing process (e.g., product design, art director, brand management, advertising, copywriting, etc.) involve use of the creative arts.

Therefore, marketing management is usually defined as the analysis, planning, implementation, and control of programs designed to create, build, and maintain beneficial exchanges with target buyers for the purpose of achieving organizational objectives. Since we describe marketing management as carrying out tasks to achieve desired exchanges with target markets, what philosophy or concept should guide these marketing efforts? A marketing concept has been defined as a "philosophy of business management" or "a corporate state of mind" or as "an organizational culture". Although scholars continue to debate the precise nature of specific concepts that inform marketing practice, the most commonly cited concepts are as follows.

1. The production concept

A production concept is often proposed as the first of the so-called philosophies that dominates business thought. Keith dated the production era from the 1860s to the 1930s, but other theorists argue that evidence of the production concept can still be found in some companies or industries. Specifically Kotler and Armstrong note that the production philosophy is one of the oldest philosophies that guides sellers and is still useful in some situations. A firm focusing on a production concept specializes in producing as much as possible of a given product or service in order to achieve economies of scale or economies of scope. A production philosophy may be deployed when a high demand for a product or service exists, coupled with certainty that consumer tastes and preferences remain relatively constant.

The basic proposition of the production concept is that customers will choose products and services that are widely available and are of low cost. By concentrating on producing maximum volumes, such a business aims to maximize profitability by exploiting economies of scale. In a production-oriented business, the needs of customers are secondary compared with the need to increase output. Such an approach is probably most effective when a business operates in very high growth markets or where the potential for economies of scale is significant. It is natural that the companies cannot deliver quality products and suffer from problems arising out of impersonal behavior with the customers. Do note, the production concept is a thing of the past and is used when there is very less competition. At such times, the more you produce, the more will be the consumption of the product. An example in this case is Ford, which manufactures a huge number of automobiles through its manufacturing assembly line which is the first of its kind.

2. The product concept

A firm employing a product concept is mainly concerned with the quality of its own product. A product concept is based on the assumption that, all things being equal, consumers will purchase products of a superior quality. The approach is most effective when the firm has deep insights into customers and their needs and desires derived from research or intuition and understands consumers' quality expectations and reservation prices. For example, Sony Walkman or Apple iPod were innovative products that addressed consumers' unmet needs. Although the product orientation has largely been supplanted by the marketing orientation, firms practicing a product orientation can still be found in haute couture and in arts marketing.

One problem which has been associated with the product concept is that it might also lead to marketing myopia. Thus companies need to take innovations and features seriously and provide only those that the customer needs. The customer needs should be given priority. In the past, several of Microsoft products have been brought under the hammer with people feeling more and more disgruntled with the operating systems because of lack of innovation and new features. Each microsoft operating system appears almost similar with just few tweaks. On the other hand, innovating too soon becomes a problem. Several innovative products are marked as experimental in the market instead of being adopted as a result of which these products have less shelf life and might have to be taken off the market. Thus companies following the product concept need to concentrate on their technology so that they provide with excellent feature-rich and innovative products for optimum customer satisfaction.

3. The selling concept

The selling concept is thought to have begun during the Great Depression and continued well into the 1950s although examples of this concept can still be found today. During World War II, industry geared up for accelerated wartime production. When the war was over, this stimulated industrial machine to turn to producing consumer products. By the mid 1950s supply was starting to outpace demand in many industries. Businesses had to concentrate on ways of selling their products. Numerous sales techniques such as closing, probing, and qualifying were all developed during this period and the sales department had an exalted position in a company's organizational structure.

The selling concept proposes that customers, be individual or organizations, will not buy enough of the organization's products unless they are persuaded to do so through a large-scale selling and promotion effort. So organizations should undertake selling and promotion of their products for marketing success. The consumers typically are inert and they need to be goaded for buying by converting their inert need into a buying motive through persuasion and selling action. This approach is typically practiced with unsought goods—those that consumers do not normally think of buying, like life insurance, vacuum cleaners, fire fighting equipments including fire extinguishers. These industries are seen having a strong network of sales force. This concept is applicable for the firms having overcapacity in which their goal is to sell what they produce than what the customer really wants.

A firm following a selling concept focuses primarily on the selling/promotion of the firm's existing products, rather than determining new or unmet consumer needs or desires. Consequently, this entails simply selling existing products, using promotion and direct sales techniques to attain the highest sales possible. One study found that industrial companies are more likely to hold a sales orientation than consumer goods companies. The approach may also suit scenarios in which a firm holds dead stock.

4. The marketing concept

The marketing concept is perhaps the most common philosophy used in contemporary marketing. It holds that achieving organizational goals depends on integrating marketing activities toward determining and satisfying the needs and wants of target markets more effectively and efficiently than competitors do. Let's take an example of two eternal rivals—Pepsi and Coke Cola. Both of these companies have similar products. However, the value propositions presented by both are different. These companies thrive on the marketing concept. Where Pepsi focuses on youngsters, Coke Cola delivers on a holistic approach. Also the value proposition by Coke Cola has been better over ages as compared with Pepsi, which shows that Coke Cola especially thrives on the marketing concept, i.e., it delivers a better value proposition as compared with its competitor.

Firms adopting a marketing orientation typically engage in extensive market research to gauge consumer desires, use R&D to develop a product attuned to the revealed information, and then utilize promotion techniques to ensure consumers are aware of the product's existence and the benefits it can deliver. Scales designed to measure a firm's overall market orientation have been developed and found to be relatively robust in a variety of contexts.

The marketing concept often has three prime facets, which are:

Customer orientation: A firm in the market economy can survive by producing goods that persons are willing and able to buy. Consequently, ascertaining consumer demand is vital for a firm's future viability and even existence as a going concern.

Organizational orientation: In this sense, a firm's marketing department is often seen as of prime importance within the functional level of an organization. Information from an organization's marketing department would be used to guide the actions of other departments within the firm. As an example, a marketing department could ascertain (via marketing research) that consumers desired a new type of product, or a new usage for an existing product. With this in mind, the marketing department would inform the Research and Development (R & D) department to create a prototype of a product/service based on consumers' new desires. The production department would then start to manufacture the product, while the marketing department would focus on the promotion, distribution, pricing, etc. of the product. Additionally, a firm's finance department would be consulted with respect to securing appropriate funding for the development, production and promotion of the product. Interdepartmental conflicts may occur, should a firm adhere to the marketing orientation.

Mutually beneficial exchange: In a transaction in the market economy, a firm gains revenue, which thus leads to more profits/market share/sales. A consumer, on the other hand, gains the satisfaction of a need/want, utility, reliability and value for money from the purchase of a product or service. As no one has to buy goods from any one supplier in the market economy, firms must entice consumers to buy goods with contemporary marketing ideals.

5. The societal marketing concept

Societal marketing was put forth as a concept by Phillip Kotler, who is often referred to as father of marketing, in the 1970s. However, it is only in the past couple of decades that this form of marketing has matured into a reality, with every company trying to incorporate this marketing style in their products and services.

So what is societal marketing concept? Although every form of marketing aims to boost sales of products and services of a firm, and help a company earn profit, this concept is a bit different in origin. By following marketing ethics incorporated into this form of marketing, firms not only ensure that there is profit in the business, they also take care of the fact that there is a well-being and growth of the society on a whole. Given below are the definition put forth by Kotler and Alan: "The societal marketing concept holds that the organization's task is to determine the needs, wants, and interests of target markets and to deliver the desired satisfactions more effectively and efficiently than competitors, in a way that preserves or enhances the consumer's and the society's well-being."

Therefore, marketers must endeavor to satisfy the needs and wants of their target markets in ways that preserve and enhance the well-being of consumers and society as a whole. It is closely linked with the principles of corporate social responsibility and of sustainable development. As a number of scholars and practitioners have argued, marketers have a greater social responsibility than simply satisfying customers and providing them with superior value. Organizations that adopt a societal marketing perspective typically practice triple bottom line reporting whereby they publish social impact and environmental impact reports alongside financial performance reports. Sustainable marketing or green marketing is an extension of societal marketing.

The societal marketing concept questions whether the pure marketing concept is adequate in an age of environmental problems, resource shortages, rapid population growth, worldwide economic stress, and neglected social services. It calls upon marketers to take social and ethical considerations into their marketing practices. They must balance and judge the usual conflicting criteria of company profits, consumer satisfaction, and society's interests, as illustrated in Figure 1-1:

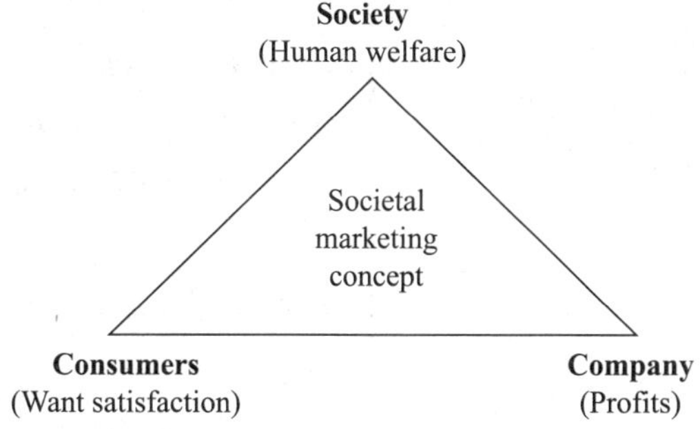

Figure 1-1

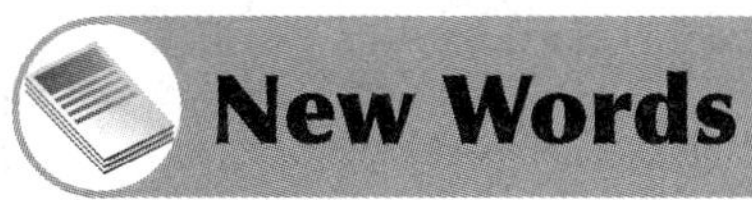

New Words

institution [ˌɪnstɪ'tuːʃn] *n.*（大学、银行等规模大的）机构

offering ['ɔːfərɪŋ] *n.* 出售物；供品

original [ə'rɪdʒənl] *adj.* 最初的；独创的，新颖的；原始的

literally ['lɪtərəli] *adv.* 逐字地，照字面地；确实地，真正地

interconnected [ɪntə(r)kə'nektɪd] *adj.* 互相连接的，互相联系的

distribution [ˌdɪstrɪ'bjuːʃn] *n.* 分布

pricing ['praɪsɪŋ] *n.* 定价
budget ['bʌdʒɪt] *vt.* 把……编入预算 *n.* 预算
vision ['vɪʒn] *vt.* 幻想，想象
involve [ɪn'vɒlv] *vt.* 包含；使参与，牵涉
beneficial [ˌbenɪ'fɪʃl] *adj.* 有利的，有益的
corporate ['kɔːrpərət] *adj.* 法人的；公司的；社团的；全体的
specific [spə'sɪfɪk] *adj.* 具体的；明确的
dominate ['dɒmɪneɪt] *v.* 支配，影响；占有优势
impersonal [ɪm'pɜːrsənl] *adj.* 不受个人感情影响的；没有人情味的
consumption [kən'sʌmpʃn] *n.* 消费；消耗；耗尽；消耗量
manufacture [ˌmænju'fæktʃə] *vt.* 制造，生产
assumption [ə'sʌmpʃn] *n.* 假定，假设；承担
superior [sjuː'pɪəriə] *adj.*（级别、地位）较高的；（在质量等方面）较好的
intuition [ˌɪntju'ɪʃn] *n.* 直觉；直觉力
innovative ['ɪnəvətɪv] *adj.* 创新的；革新的
unmet [ˌʌn'met] *adj.* 未满足的；未相遇的；未应付的
orientation [ˌɔːriən'teɪʃn] *n.* 方向，定位，取向
supplant [sə'plænt] *vt.* 把……排挤掉，取代
myopia [maɪ'əʊpiə] *n.* 短视，缺乏深谋远虑
innovation [ˌɪnə'veɪʃn] *n.* 改革，创新
disgruntled [dɪs'grʌntld] *adj.* 不满的；怏怏，不高兴的
optimum ['ɑːptɪməm] *adj.* 最适宜的 *n.* 最佳效果；最适宜条件
overcapacity [ˌəʊvəkə'pæsəti] *n.* 生产能力过剩
entail [ɪn'teɪl] *vt.* 需要；牵涉
attain [ə'teɪn] *vt.* 达到，获得
scenario [sə'næriəʊ] *n.* 设想，方案，预测；剧情概要
contemporary [kən'tempəreri] *adj.* 当代的，现代的
integrate ['ɪntɪgreɪt] *vt.* 使一体化，使整合
competitor [kəm'petɪtə] *n.* 竞争者，对手
eternal [ɪ'tɜːrnl] *adj.* 永生的，不朽的，永恒的
rival ['raɪvl] *n.* 对手，竞争者
holistic [həʊ'lɪstɪk] *adj.* 整体的；全盘的
extensive [ɪk'stensɪv] *adj.* 广阔的，广大的；范围广泛的
gauge [geɪdʒ] *vt.*（用仪器）测量；确定容量，体积或内容
utilize ['juːtəlaɪz] *vt.* 利用，使用
promotion [prə'məʊʃn] *n.* 促进，增进；提升
robust [rəʊ'bʌst] *adj.* 强健的；稳固的；耐用的
prime [praɪm] *adj.* 最好的；首要的
ascertain [ˌæsər'teɪn] *vt.* 弄清，确定，查明
viability [vaɪə'bɪləti] *n.* 生存能力；可行性
via ['vaɪə] *prep.* 经过，通过；凭借
prototype ['prəʊtətaɪp] *n.* 原型，雏形
appropriate [ə'prəʊprɪət] *adj.* 适当的，合适的，恰当的
conflict ['kɒnflɪkt] *n.* 冲突；矛盾 *vi.* 冲突；抵触；争斗
transaction [træn'zækʃn] *n.* 交易，业务，事务
revenue ['revənuː] *n.* 收益；财政收入
reliability [rɪˌlaɪə'bɪləti] *n.* 可靠，可信赖
entice [ɪn'taɪs] *vt.* 诱惑，引诱；怂恿
incorporate [ɪn'kɔːrpəreɪt] *vt.* 包含；组成公司；使混合
boost [buːst] *vt.* 增加，促进，提高；鼓励
preserve [prɪ'zɜːrv] *vt.* 保护；保持，保存
enhance [ɪn'hæns] *vt.* 加强；提高，增加
extension [ɪk'stenʃn] *n.* 伸展，扩大，延伸；延长

adequate ['ædɪkwət] *adj.* 足够的；适当的

criteria [kraɪ'tɪərɪə] *n.*（批评、判断等的）标准，准则

illustrate ['ɪləstreɪt] *vt.* 说明，表明；阐述

Phrases

marketing philosophy 营销理念

at large 详细地；充分地；总体地

refer to 指的是；参考；涉及

from a... perspective 从……的角度

aim at 以……为目标；针对；(以……)瞄准

market segmentation 市场细分

for the purpose of 为了……起见；借以

carry out 执行；完成

as follows 如下

be proposed as 被提名为，被推荐为

couple with 与……连接在一起

concentrate on 专心于，把思想集中于

arise out of 产生于，起因于

assembly line 流水线；(工厂产品的)装配线

have a deep insight into 有深刻的洞察力

derive from 起源于；源自

reservation price 保留价格，最低销售价格

haute couture 高级女式时装

give priority to 给……以优先权；优先考虑

shelf life（包装食品的）货架期，保存限期

gear up for 为……做准备

turn to 求助于；(使)转向

convert into 把……转变成；转化成

life insurance 寿险；人寿保险

thrive on 靠……茁壮成长

dead stock 滞销品

attune to 使调和；习惯于

in a variety of contexts 在各种情况下

be of prime importance 极其重要

with respect to 关于，(至于)谈到

adhere to 附着，依附；坚持

mutually beneficial 互惠的

societal marketing 社会营销；社会行销

put forth 提出

mature into 成长为……

in origin 起初；起源

marketing ethics 营销伦理；营销道德

on the whole 大体上，基本上，总的来看

endeavor to 努力

sustainable development 可持续发展

Abbreviations

AMA (American Marketing Association) 美国市场营销协会

R&D (Research and Development) 研究与开发

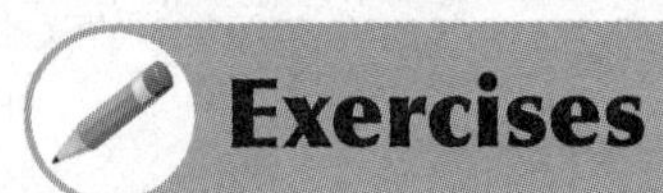

Exercises

EX. 1 Answer the following questions according to Text A.

(1) What is the definition of marketing according to the American Marketing Association?

(2) What is the basic proposition of the production concept?

(3) What is the basic assumption of the product concept?

(4) What problem might the product concept lead to? And what do companies need to do to solve this problem?

(5) What does the selling concept propose?

(6) What does a firm following a selling concept primarily focus on?

(7) Which concept is perhaps the most common philosophy used in contemporary marketing? And what does it hold?

(8) What are the three prime facets of the marketing concept?

(9) With the societal marketing concept, what must those marketers endeavor to do?

(10) What reports should organizations publish if they adopt a societal marketing perspective?

EX. 2 Translate the following phrases from English into Chinese and vice versa.

(1) give priority to ____________________

(2) have a deep insight into ____________________

(3) market segmentation ____________________

(4) marketing ethics ____________________

(5) marketing philosophy ____________________

(6) 可持续发展 ____________________

(7) 经济大萧条 ____________________

(8) 短视，缺乏深谋远虑 ____________________

(9) 生产能力过剩 ____________________

(10) 把……排挤掉，取代 ____________________

EX. 3 Translate the following into Chinese.

The marketing concept is one of the most important marketing philosophies. At its very core are the customer and his or her satisfaction. The marketing concept and philosophy state that the organization should strive to satisfy its customers' wants and needs while meeting the organization's goals. In simple terms, "the customer is king."

The implication of the marketing concept is very important for management. It is not something that the marketing department administers, nor is it the sole domain of the marketing department. Rather, it is adopted by the entire organization. From top management to the lowest levels and across all departments of the organization, it is a philosophy or way of doing business. The customer's needs, wants, and satisfaction should always be foremost in every manager and employee's mind. Wal-Mart's motto of "satisfaction guaranteed" is an example of the marketing concept. Whether the Wal-Mart employee is an accountant or a cashier, the customer is always first.

EX. 4 **Fill in the blanks with the words and phrases given below.**

rectifies	contributes to	reasonable	pace	reliable
at large	responding	fundamental	pulse	standard

Benefits of Marketing Concept

The major benefits of marketing concept are described below.

Benefits to firms: A firm that believes in the marketing concept always feels the (1)________ of the market through continuous marketing audit and marketing research. It is fast in (2)________ to the changes in buyer behavior. It (3)________ any drawback in its product and this proves beneficial to the firm. The firm gives more importance to planning, research and innovation and its decisions are no longer based on hunches but on (4)________ scientific data and the proper interpretation of such data. The profits for the firm become more certain.

Benefits to consumers: The concept on the part of various competing firms to satisfy the consumer puts the later in an enviable position. (5)________ prices, better quality and easy availability at convenient places are some of the benefits that accrue to the consumer as a direct result of marketing concept.

Benefits to society: The practice of marketing concept (6)________ better lifestyle, better (7)________ of living and also results in the development of entrepreneurial talents. All these sets the (8)________ for social and economic development. Thus the marketing concept benefits the organization, the consumer and society (9)________. A proper understanding of this concept is (10)________ to the study of modern marketing.

Text B

The Marketing Mix: 4Ps of Marketing

Although the idea of marketers as mixers of ingredients caught on, marketers could not reach any real consensus about what elements should be included in the mix until the 1960s. The 4Ps, in its modern form, was first proposed in 1960 by E. Jerome McCarthy, who presented them within a managerial approach that covered analysis, consumer behavior, market research, market segmentation, and planning. The "marketing mix" gained widespread acceptance with the publication, in 1960, of E. Jerome McCarthy's text, "Basic Marketing: A Managerial Approach" which outlined the ingredients in the mix as the memorable 4Ps, namely product, price, place, and promotion.

The marketing mix is based upon four controllable variables that a company manages in its effort to satisfy the corporation's objectives as well as the needs and wants of a target market. Once there is understanding of the target market's interests, marketers develop tactics, using the 4Ps, to encourage buyers to purchase product. The successful use of the model is predicated upon the degree to which the target market's needs and wants have been understood, and the extent to which marketers have developed and correctly deployed the tactics. Today, the marketing mix or marketing program is understood to refer to the "set of marketing tools that the firm uses to pursue its marketing objectives in the target market".

1. *Product in the marketing mix*

The product aspects of marketing deal with the specifications of the actual goods or services, and how it relates to the end-user's needs and wants. The product element consists of product design, new product innovation, branding, packaging, and labelling. The scope of a product generally includes supporting elements such as warranties, guarantees, and support. Branding, a key aspect of the product management, refers to the various methods of communicating a brand identity for the product, brand, or company. A product can be divided into three parts. The core product, the actual product, and the augmented product. Before deciding on the product component, there are some questions which you need to ask yourself.

1) What product are you selling?

2) What would be the quality of your product?

3) Which features are different from the market?

4) What is the USP of the product?

5) Will the product be branded as sub brand or completely new?

6) What are the secondary products which can be sold along with the primary product?

Based on these questions, several product decisions have to be made. These product decisions will in turn affect the other variables of the mix. For example,you plan on launching a car which will have the highest quality. Thus the pricing, promotions, and placing would have to be altered accordingly. Thus as long as you don't know your product, you cannot decide any other variable of the marketing mix. However, if the product features are not fitting in the mix, you can alter the product so that it finds a place for itself in the marketing mix.

2. *Pricing in the marketing mix*

This refers to the process of setting a price for a product, including discounts. The price need not be monetary; it can simply be what is exchanged for the product or service, e.g., time, energy, or attention or any sacrifices consumers make in order to acquire a product or service. The price is the cost that a consumer pays for a product—monetary or not. Methods of setting prices are in the domain of pricing science.

Pricing of a product depends on a lot of different variables and hence it is constantly updated. Major consideration in pricing is the costing of the product, the advertising and marketing expenses, any price fluctuations in the market, distribution costs, etc. Many of these factors can change separately. Thus the pricing has to be such that it can bear the brunt of changes for a certain period of time. However, if all these variables change, then the pricing of a product has to be increased and decreased accordingly.

Along with the above factors, there are also other things which have to be taken into consideration when deciding on a pricing strategy. Competition can be the best example. Similarly, pricing also affects the targeting and positioning of a product. Pricing is used for sales promotions in the form of trade discounts. Based on these factors, there are several pricing strategies, one of which is implemented for the marketing mix.

3. *Place (or Distribution) in the marketing mix*

This refers to how the product gets to the customer; the distribution channels and intermediaries such as wholesalers and retailers who enable customers to access products or services in a convenient manner. This third P has also sometimes been called Place, referring to the channel by which a product or service is sold (e.g., online vs. retail), and also referring to how the environment in which the product is sold can affect sales.

Place refers to the distribution channel of a product. If a product is a consumer product, it needs to be available as far and wide as possible. On the other hand, if the product is a premium consumer product, it will be available only in select stores. Similarly, if the product is a business product, you need a team which interacts with businesses and makes the product available to them. Thus, the place where the product is distributed depends on the product and pricing decisions.

Distribution has a huge effect on the profitability of a product. Consider a company which has a national distribution for its product. An increase in petrol rates will in fact bring about drastic changes in the profitability of the company. Thus supply chain and logistics decisions are considered as very important costing decisions of the firm. The firm needs to have a full-proof logistics and supply chain plan for its distribution.

4. *Promotion in the marketing mix*

Promotions in the marketing mix include the complete integrated marketing communications which, in turn, include Above the Line (ATL) and Below the Line (BTL) advertising as well as sales promotions. Promotions are dependent a lot on the product and pricing decision. What is the budget for marketing and advertising? What stage is the product in? If the product is completely new in the market, it needs brand/product awareness promotions, whereas if the product is already existing, then it will need brand recall promotions.

Promotions also decide the segmentation targeting and positioning of the product. The right kind of promotions affect all the other three variables—the product, price, and place. If the promotions are effective, you might have to increase distribution points, you might get to increase the price because of the rising brand equity of the product, and the profitability might support you in launching even more products. However, the budget required for extensive promotions is also high. Promotions are considered as marketing expenses and the same needs to be taken into consideration while deciding the costing of the product.

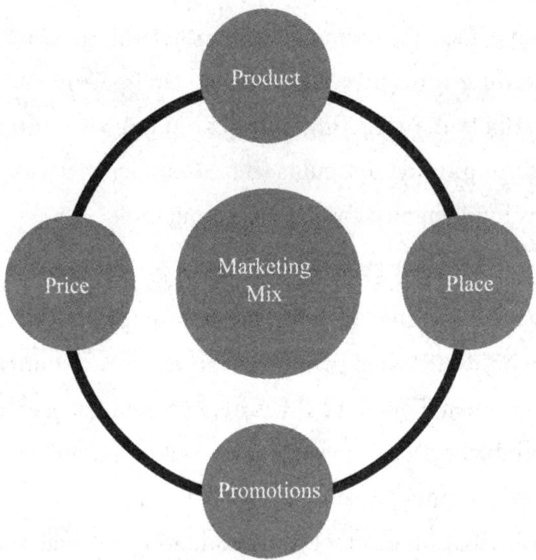

Figure 1-2

As as we see from Figure 1-2, all the four variables of marketing mix are interrelated and affect each other. By increasing the pricing of the product, demand of the product might lessen, and lesser distribution points might be needed. On the other hand, the product Unique Selling Proposition (USP) can be such that maximum concentration is on creating brand awareness, thereby increasing need of better pricing and more promotions. Finally, the overall marketing mix can result in your customer base asking for some improvement in the product, and the same can be launched as the upgraded product.

Marketing mix plays a crucial role while deciding the strategy of an organization. It is the first step even when a marketing plan or a business plan is being made. This is because, the marketing mix decision will also affect segmentation, targeting and positioning decisions. Based on products, segmentation and targeting will be done. Based on the price, positioning can be decided. And these decisions will likely affect the place and promotion decisions. Thus, the marketing mix strategy goes hand in hand with segmentation targeting and positioning.

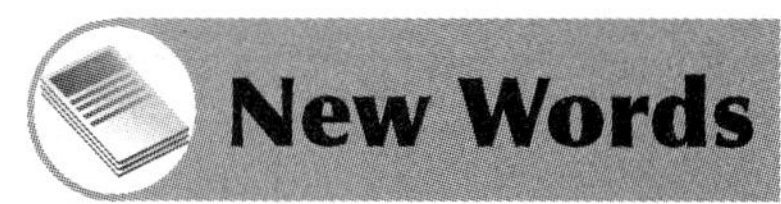

New Words

ingredient [ɪn'griːdiənt] *n.* （构成）要素；（混合物的）组成部分；（烹调的）原料

managerial [ˌmænə'dʒɪriəl] *adj.* 经理的；管理上的

gain [geɪn] *vt.* 获得，赢得；增加

outline ['aʊtlaɪn] *vt.* 概述，略述

memorable ['memərəbl] *adj.* 显著的，难忘的；重大的，著名的

variable ['veriəbl] *n.* 可变因素，变量

tactic ['tæktɪk] *n.* 战术，策略，战略；手段

predicate ['predɪkeɪt] *vt.* 断言，断定；宣布

objective [əb'dʒektɪv] *n.* 目标，任务

aspect ['æspekt] *n.* 方面

specification [ˌspesɪfɪ'keɪʃn] *n.* 规格；说明书；详述

scope [skəʊp] *n.* 范围；眼界，见识

identity [aɪ'dentəti] *n.* 身份；个性

component [kəm'pəʊnənt] *n.* 成分；组成部分，要素

feature ['fiːtʃə] *n.* 特征，特点；容貌，面貌

launch [lɔːntʃ] *vt.* 发射；发动；开展（活动、计划等）；推出（新产品）

alter ['ɔːltə] *vt.* 改变，更改

discount ['dɪskaʊnt] *vt.* 打折扣，减价出售 *n.* 折扣，贴现

acquire [ə'kwaɪə] *vt.* 获得，取得

domain [də'meɪn] *n.* 范围，领域；领土

strategy ['strætədʒi] *n.* 策略，战略

competition [ˌkɑːmpə'tɪʃn] *n.* 竞争，比赛

positioning [pə'zɪʃn] *n.* 定位；配置，布置

intermediary [ˌɪntə'miːdiəri] *n.* 中间阶段；媒介；中间人，调解人

wholesaler ['həʊlseɪlə] *n.* 批发商

retailer ['riːteɪlə] *n.* 零售商

access ['ækses] *n.* 使用权；通路 *vt.* 使用；存取；接近

geographic [dʒi'ɒgrəfik] *adj.* 地理学的，地理的

available [ə'veɪləbl] *adj.* 可获得的；可购得的；有空的

petrol ['petrəl] *n.* 汽油

drastic ['drɑːstɪk] *adj.* 激烈的；极端的

logistics [lə'dʒɪstɪks] *n.* 物流；后勤

diagram ['daɪəgræm] *n.* 图表，示意图，图解

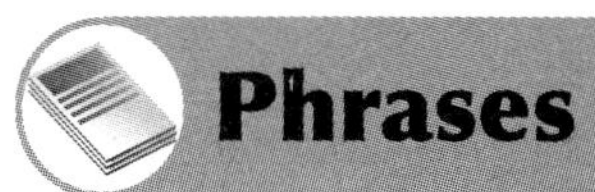

Phrases

catch on 变得流行；投合心意

reach consensus 达成共识

relate to 涉及；与……有关系

consist of 包括，由……组成

brand identity 品牌识别；品牌标识

decide on 就……做出决定

in turn 依次，轮流地；转而

as long as 只要

set a price 定价格

price fluctuation 价格变动，价格波动

make sacrifice 做出牺牲

distribution cost 配送成本

bear the brunt of 首当其冲
take into consideration 考虑到，顾及
sales promotion 促销
in the form of 用……的形式
in a manner 以……的方式
premium consumer product 优质消费品
have an effect on 对……有影响，对……产生效果
petrol rate 汽油价格
supply chain 供应链
as well as 以及，也
brand awareness 品牌认知
brand recall 品牌回忆
brand equity 品牌资产，品牌权益
play a crucial role 起关键作用
go hand in hand with 与……共同行动；与……一致

Abbreviations

USP (Unique Selling Proposition) 独特的销售主张（USP 理论）
ATL (Above The Line) 线上（主要指运用大众媒介影响消费者）
BTL (Below The Line) 线下（主要指与消费者发生直接接触的媒介）

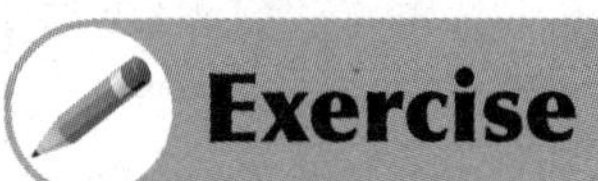

Exercise

EX. Answer the following questions according to Text B.

(1) What are the memorable 4Ps in marketing mix?
(2) What do the product aspects of marketing deal with?
(3) What does the scope of a product generally include?
(4) What does pricing in the marketing mix refer to?
(5) Does the price for a product need to be monetary?
(6) What is the major consideration in pricing a product?
(7) What does place or distribution refer to in the marketing mix?
(8) What factors does the place where the product is distributed depend on?
(9) What do promotions include in the marketing mix?
(10) How do the promotions affect all the other three variables—the product, price, and place?

参考译文（Text A）

市场营销管理哲学

美国市场营销协会将市场营销定义为“为顾客、客户、合作伙伴和整个社会创造、传播、交付和交换有价值的产品的活动、体系和过程”。这个词最初的意思是“带着待售货物去市场”。从销售过程的角度来看，市场营销是企业中“与其他功能相互关联、相互依赖的整套过程”，旨在实现客户的利益和满意度。

市场营销的过程是将产品推向市场的过程，包括以下几个步骤：广泛的市场调查；目标市场选择与市场细分；确定分销、定价和促销策略；制定沟通策略；预算；制定长期的市场发展目标。营销过程中的许多部分（如产品设计、艺术总监、品牌管理、广告、文案等）都涉及创意艺术的运用。

因此，市场营销管理通常被定义为分析、计划、实施和控制那些旨在创建、发展和保持与目标客户进行有益交流的方案，以实现组织目标。既然我们将营销管理描述为执行各项任务，以实现与目标市场的预期交流，那么应该用什么样的理念或哲学来指导这些营销工作呢？营销概念被定义为“企业管理哲学”，或“一种企业精神状态”，或“组织文化”。尽管学者们仍在争论影响营销实践的具体概念的确切性质，但是人们最经常引用的理念如下。

1. 生产理念

生产理念通常被认为是主导商业思想的首要理念。凯斯认为生产时代是从 19 世纪 60 年代到 20 世纪 30 年代，但是其他理论家认为生产观念的证据仍然可以在一些公司或行业中找到。特别是科特勒和阿姆斯特朗指出，生产哲学是“指导销售者的最古老的哲学之一”，并且“在某些情况下仍然有用”。一个信奉生产理念的公司专门生产尽可能多的给定产品或服务，以实现规模经济或范围经济。当人们对某种产品或服务存在高需求时，再加上消费者的品位和偏好保持相对稳定，就可以采用生产哲学。

生产理念的基本主张是顾客会选择可随处获得的低成本产品和服务。这样的企业致力于产量最大化，从而利用规模经济使利润最大化。在以生产为导向的企业中，与增加产量相比，客户的需求是次要的。当一家企业是在高增长市场中运营，或者市场规模经济潜力巨大时，这种方法可能是最有效的。自然地，公司不能提供高质量的产品，并且这种不考虑顾客利益的行为会使公司遇到诸多问题。请注意，生产理念是过去的理念了，适用于竞争非常少的时代。在那样的时代，你生产得越多，消费的产品就越多。福特公司就是这样的例子，它通过第一条生产流水线生产了大量汽车。

2. 产品理念

信奉产品理念的公司主要关心自己产品的质量。产品理念基于这样的假设，即在同等条件下，消费者会购买高质量的产品。当企业通过调查研究或直觉深入了解了消费者及其需求和欲望，并且获悉了消费者的质量期望和能承受的最高价格时，这种方法是最有效的。

例如，索尼随身听或苹果 iPod 都是针对消费者未被满足的需求所设计的创新产品。虽然以产品为导向的理念在很大程度上已经被以营销为导向的理念所取代，但是在高级女式时装定制和艺术产品营销中仍然可以找到以产品为导向的公司。

产品理念也可能会引起营销短视症这一问题。因此，公司需要认真对待创新和特色问题，只提供客户需要的东西，并且应该优先考虑客户的需求。过去，由于缺乏创新和新功能，人们对微软的操作系统越来越不满，微软的几款产品也因此受到抨击。微软的每个操作系统看起来都差不多，只是做了一些微调。另一方面，创新过于频繁也会成为问题。一些创新产品在市场上被称为试验性产品，而不是被采用的产品。因此，这些产品的货架期更短，可能不得不退出市场。因此，遵循产品理念的企业需要专注于自己的技术，为客户提供优质的、功能多样的、创新的产品，以获得最佳的客户满意度。

3. 推销理念

这种销售导向被认为始于大萧条时期，一直持续到 20 世纪 50 年代，尽管这种导向的例子在今天仍然可见。在第二次世界大战期间，工业为加速战时生产做好了充分准备。战争结束后，形势促进了工业机器转向生产消费品。到 50 年代中期，许多行业的产品供应开始超过需求。因此，企业必须专注于销售产品的方式。在此期间，许多销售技巧都得到了发展，如清仓大甩卖、市场探查和斟酌等，而且销售部门在公司的组织结构中地位很高。

推销理念指出，客户，无论是个人还是组织，都不会充分购买某个企业的产品，除非通过大规模的推销和促销活动说服他们。因此，公司应该开展大量的产品促销活动，以实现成功推销。消费者通常不会积极购买，因此销售方需要通过说服和推销行为，将消费者的惰性需求转化为购买动机，从而激励他们购买。这种方法通常适用于冷门商品，即那些消费者通常不会想要购买的商品，如人寿保险、吸尘器、消防设备（包括灭火器）。这些行业被认为拥有强大的销售网络。这一理念适用于产能过剩的企业，它们的目标是销售自己生产的产品，而不是客户真正想要的产品。

遵循推销理念的公司主要关注销售 / 推广公司现有的产品，而不是确定新的或未满足的消费者的需求或愿望。因此，这只需要简单地销售现有的产品，使用促销和直销技术来获得尽可能高的销售额。一项研究发现，工业企业比消费品企业更倾向于以销售为导向。这种方法也适用于公司存有大量滞销品的情况。

4. 市场营销理念

营销理念可能是当代市场营销中最常用的理念。它认为，实现组织目标依赖于整合营销活动，从而比竞争对手更有效地确定和满足目标市场的需求和需要。让我们以两个“宿敌”百事可乐和可口可乐为例，这两家公司都有类似的产品。然而，二者所提出的价值主张是不同的。这些公司靠营销理念而兴旺发达。百事可乐侧重于年轻人，而可口可乐则提供了一种全面整体的方法。此外，多年来可口可乐的价值主张一直比百事可乐更好，这表明可口可乐是靠营销理念而得以蓬勃发展的。与竞争对手相比，它提供了更好的价值主张。

采用营销导向的公司通常会进行广泛的市场调查，以衡量消费者的需求，研发出与公开信息相适应的产品，然后利用促销技术来确保消费者意识到产品的存在及其带来的好处。人们已经研发出用来衡量公司总体市场导向的量表，并且发现能稳健地应用于各种环境中。

营销理念通常有三个主要方面，即：

顾客导向：市场经济中的企业可以通过生产人们愿意并且能够购买的商品生存下来。因此，确定消费者的需求对于企业未来的生存能力甚至企业的持续存在问题都是至关重要的。

组织导向：从这个意义上讲，一家公司的市场营销部门从一个组织的职能层面上来说通常是最重要的。市场营销部收集的信息将用于指导公司内其他部门的行动。例如，市场营销部门可以（通过市场调查）确定消费者想要一种新型产品，或期望现有产品的新用法。基于这一点，市场营销部门会通知研发部门根据消费者的新需求创建一个产品 / 服务的原型。然后生产部门开始生产产品，营销部门则专注于产品的促销、分销、定价等。此外，还应咨询公司的财务部门，以便为该产品的研发、生产和推广争取适量的资金。如果企业坚持以市场为导向，可能会发生部门间的冲突。

互利交换：在市场经济的交易中，企业获得收益，从而获得更多的利润 / 市场份额 / 销售额。另一方面，消费者从购买产品或服务中获得需求或需要、效用、可靠性和物有所值的满足。由于在市场经济中没有人必须从任何一个供应商那里购买商品，企业必须以当代营销理念为导向吸引消费者购买商品。

5. 社会营销理念

社会营销是由被称为“营销之父”的菲利普・科特勒在 20 世纪 70 年代提出的一个理念。然而，直到最近几十年，这种营销形式才逐渐成熟，每家公司都试图将这种营销方式融入他们的产品和服务中。

那么，什么是社会营销理念呢？虽然每一种营销形式都是为了促进企业产品和服务的销售，帮助企业获得利润，但社会营销这一理念的起源有所不同。通过遵循渗透到这种营销理念的营销伦理道德，企业不仅确保了自己的利润，而且还关心整个社会的福祉和发展。下面是科特勒和艾伦给出的定义：

“社会营销理念认为，组织的任务是确定目标市场的需求、愿望和利益，并以一种保持或提高消费者和社会福祉的方式，比竞争对手更有效地提供他们所期望的满意度。”

因此，营销人员必须以保持和提高消费者和整个社会的福祉的方式努力满足目标市场的需求和愿望。它与企业社会责任和可持续发展的原则密切相关。正如许多学者和实践者所主张的那样，营销人员有更大的社会责任，而不仅仅是满足客户并为他们提供更高的价值。采用社会营销视角的组织通常采用三重底线报告，即在发布财务业绩报告的同时，发布社会影响和环境影响报告。可持续营销或环保营销是社会营销的延伸。

社会营销概念质疑纯营销理念在环境问题、资源短缺、人口快速增长、全球经济压力和社会服务被忽视的时代是否恰当。它呼吁营销人员在营销活动中考虑社会和道德因素。他们必须平衡并判断公司利润、消费者满意度和社会利益等通常相互冲突的标准，如图 1-1 所示。

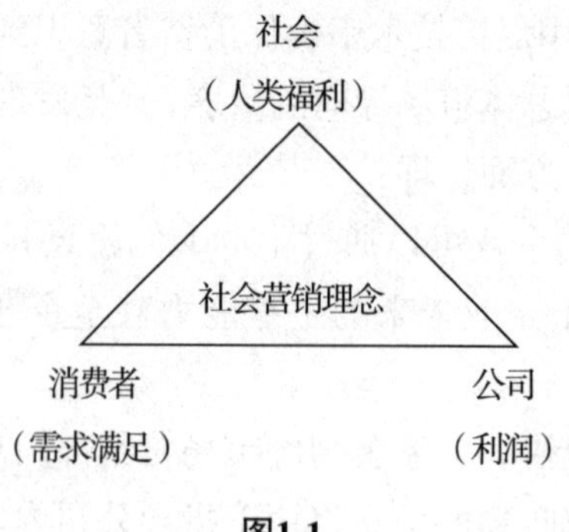

图1-1

Case Wal-Mart Marketing Mix (4Ps) Strategy

Unit 2

Text A

Marketing Environment

The term marketing environment refers to the forces and factors that affect the organization's ability to build and maintain good relationship with its customers. Marketing environment surrounds the organization and impacts the organization too. Marketers have to interact with internal and external people at micro- and macro-level and build internal and external relationships.

1. *Micro-environment*

Company aspect of micro-environment refers to the internal environment of the company. This includes all departments such as management, finance, research and development, purchasing, business operations and accounting. Each of these departments influences marketing decisions. For example, research and development have input as to the features a product can perform and accounting approve the financial side of marketing plans and budget. Marketing managers must watch supply availability and other trends dealing with suppliers to ensure that product will be delivered to customers in the time frame required in order to maintain a strong customer relationship.

Marketing intermediaries refer to resellers, physical distribution firms, marketing services agencies, and financial intermediaries. These are the people who help the company promote, sell, and distribute its products to final buyers. Resellers are those that hold and sell the company's product. They match the distribution to the customers and include places such as Wal-Mart, Target, and Best Buy. Physical distribution firms are places such as warehouses that store and transport the company's product from its origin to its destination. Marketing services agencies are companies that offer services such as conducting marketing research, advertising, and consulting. Financial intermediaries are institutions such as banks, credit companies, and insurance companies.

Another aspect of micro-environment is the customer market. There are different types of customer markets including consumer markets, business markets, government markets, international markets, and reseller markets. The consumer market is made up of individuals who buy goods and services for personal use or use in their household. Business markets include those that buy goods and services for use in producing their own products to sell. This is different from the reseller market which includes businesses that purchase goods to resell for a profit. The government market consists of government agencies that buy goods to produce public services or transfer goods to others who need them. International markets include buyers in other countries and include customers from the previous categories. Competitors are also a factor in the micro-environment and include companies with similar offerings for goods and services. To remain competitive, a company must consider who their biggest competitors are while considering its own size and position in the industry. The company should develop a strategic advantage over their competitors.

The final aspect of the micro-environment is publics, which is any group that has an interest in or effect on the organization's ability to meet its goals. For example, financial publics can hinder a company's ability to obtain funds, affecting the level of credit a company has. Media publics include newspapers and magazines that can publish articles of interest regarding the company and editorials that may influence customers' opinions. Government publics can affect the company by passing legislation and laws that put restrictions on the company's actions. Citizen-action publics include environmental groups and minority groups and can question the actions of a company and put them in the public spotlight. Local publics are neighborhood and community organizations and will also question a company's effect on the local area and the level of responsibility of their actions. The general public can affect the company as any change in their attitude, whether positive or negative, can cause sales to go up or down because the general public is often the company's customer base.

2. *Macro-environment*

The macro-environment refers to all forces that are part of the larger society and affect the micro-environment. It includes concepts such as demography, economy, natural forces, technology, politics, and culture. The purpose of analyzing the macro marketing environment is to understand the environment better and to adapt to the social environment and change through the marketing effort of the enterprise to achieve the goal of the enterprise marketing.

Demography refers to studying human populations in terms of size, density, location, age, gender, race, and occupation. This is a very important factor for marketers to study and helps to divide the population into market segments and target markets. An example of demography is classifying groups of people according to the year they were born. These classifications can be referred to as baby boomers, who are born between 1946 and 1964, generation X, who are born between 1965 and 1976, and generation Y, who are born between 1977 and 1994. Each classification has different characteristics and causes they find important. This can be beneficial to a marketer as they can decide who their product would benefit most and tailor their marketing plan to attract that segment. Demography covers many aspects that are important to marketers including family dynamics, geographic shifts, workforce changes, and levels of diversity in any given area.

Another aspect of the macro-environment is the economic environment. This refers to the purchasing power of potential customers and the ways in which people spend their money. Within this area are two different economies, subsistence and industrialized. Subsistence economies are based more on agriculture and consume their own industrial output. Industrial economies have markets that are diverse and carry many different types of goods. Each is important to the marketer because each has a highly different spending pattern as well as different distribution of wealth.

The natural environment is another important factor of the macro-environment. This includes the natural resources that a company uses as inputs that affect their marketing activities. The concern in this area is the increased pollution, shortages of raw materials and increased governmental intervention. As raw materials become increasingly scarcer, the ability to create a company's product gets much harder. Also, pollution can go as far as negatively affecting a company's reputation if they are known for damaging the environment. The last concern, government intervention can make it increasingly harder for a company to fulfill their goals as requirements get more stringent.

The technological environment is perhaps one of the fastest changing factors in the macro-environment. This includes all developments from antibiotics and surgery to nuclear missiles and chemical weapons to automobiles and credit cards. As these markets develop it can create new markets and new uses for products. It also requires a company to stay ahead of others and update their own technology as it becomes outdated. They must stay informed of trends so they can be part of the next big thing, rather than becoming outdated and suffering the consequences financially. In order to understand the different spending patterns, marketers also need to take into consideration the development of digital technology and its effect on market growth and employment. It is key for a marketer, especially in a digitally-dominated market, to anticipate demand in order to capitalize on potential market growth. Technology has developed to the extent where purchase patterns can be analyzed in order to forecast future demand.

The political environment includes all laws, government agencies, and groups that influence or limit other organizations and individuals within a society. It is important for marketers to be aware of these restrictions as they can be complex. Some products are regulated by both state and federal laws. There are even restrictions for some products as to who the target market may be, for example, cigarettes should not be marketed to younger children. There are also many restrictions on subliminal messages and monopolies. As laws and regulations change often, this is a very important aspect for a marketer to monitor. As laws and regulations change often, they create barriers that can hugely influence the way in which companies can market their business across the digital community in particular.

The final aspect of the macro-environment is the social environment, which consists of institutions and basic values and beliefs of a group of people. The values can also be further categorized into core beliefs, which is passed on from generation to generation and very difficult to change, and secondary beliefs, which tend to be easier to influence. As a marketer, it is important to know the difference between the two and to focus on marketing campaigns to reflect the values of a target audience. With entering into an age where technology has a key role in the forming of social beliefs and values, cultural diversity has developed within the world of digital communities.

When dealing with the marketing environment it is important for a company to become proactive. By doing so, they can create the kind of environment that they will prosper in and can become more efficient by marketing in areas with the greatest customer potential. It is important to place equal emphasis on both the macro- and micro-environment and to react accordingly to changes within them.

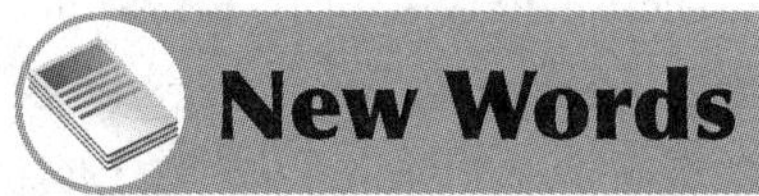

New Words

maintain [meɪn'teɪn] *vt.* 保持；保养；坚持
surround [sə'raʊnd] *vt.* 包围，围绕
impact [ɪm'pækt] *vt.* 影响；碰撞，冲击
internal [ɪn'tɜːnl] *adj.* 内部的；国内的；体内的；内心的
external [ɪk'stɜːnl] *adj.* 外面的，外部的
purchase ['pɜːtʃəs] *v.* 购买，采购
input ['ɪnpʊt] *n.* 输入，投入
approve [ə'pruːv] *vt.* 赞成，同意
accounting [ə'kaʊntɪŋ] *n.* 会计；会计学；记账
financial [faɪ'nænʃl] *adj.* 财务的，财政的；金融的
availability [ə'veɪləbɪləti] *n.* 利用性；可用性；有用；可得到的东西（或人）
trend [trend] *n.* 趋势，倾向
ensure [ɪn'ʃɔː] *vt.* 确保，担保获得；使（某人）获得
frame [freɪm] *n.* 框架；边框
reseller ['riːselə] *n.* 分销商；代理销售商
agency ['eɪdʒənsi] *n.* 机构；代理
promote [prə'məʊt] *vt.* 促进，推进；提升
warehouse ['weəhaʊs] *n.* 仓库，货栈
origin ['ɔːrɪdʒɪn] *n.* 出身；起源，根源
destination [ˌdestɪ'neɪʃn] *n.* 目的地，终点；目的，目标
conduct [kən'dʌkt] *vt.* 引导，带领；传导
consult [kən'sʌlt] *vi.* 咨询；商议，商量
credit ['kredɪt] *n.* 信誉，信用；学分
insurance [ɪn'ʃʊərəns] *n.* 保险
globalization [ˌgləʊbəlaɪ'zeɪʃn] *n.* 全球化，全球性

household ['haʊshəʊld] *n.* 家庭，户；（集合词）全家人

transfer [træns'fɜː] *vt.* 使转移；使调动；转让

previous ['priːviəs] *adj.* 以前的，先前的

category ['kætəgɔːri] *n.* 类型，种类，类别

competitive [kəm'petətɪv] *adj.* 竞争的，比赛的；有竞争力的

strategic [strə'tiːdʒɪk] *adj.* 战略性的，有战略意义的

hinder ['hɪndə] *vt.* 阻碍，妨碍；成为阻碍

obtain [əb'teɪn] *vt.* 获得，得到；达到（目的）

regarding [rɪ'gɑːdɪŋ] *prep.* 关于；就……而论

legislation [ˌledʒɪs'leɪʃn] *n.* 立法，制定法律；法律，法规

spotlight ['spɑːtlaɪt] *n.* 聚光灯；公众注意或突出显著

positive ['pɒzətɪv] *adj.* 积极的；肯定的

negative ['negətɪv] *adj.* 消极的，否定的；否认的

concept ['kɒnsept] *n.* 观念，概念；观点；思想

potential [pə'tenʃl] *adj.* 潜在的，有可能的 *n.* 潜力，潜能

subsistence [səb'sɪstəns] *n.* 存活，生存；生计，维生之道

intervention [ˌɪntə'venʃn] *n.* 介入，干涉，干预

scarce [skeəs] *adj.* 缺乏的，罕见的；

regulation [ˌregju'leɪʃn] *n.* 规则；章程，管理，控制

fulfill [fʊl'fɪl] *vt.* 履行（诺言等）；执行（命令等）

stringent ['strɪndʒənt] *adj.* 严格的；迫切的

surgery ['sɜːrdʒəri] *n.* 外科手术

consequence ['kɒnsɪkwəns] *n.* 结果，成果；后果

digital ['dɪdʒɪtl] *adj.* 数字的，数据的

anticipate [æn'tɪsɪpeɪt] *vt.* 预期；预料，预言

forecast ['fɔːrkaːst] *vt.* 预报，预测；预示

complex [kəm'pleks] *adj.* 复杂的，难懂的；复合的

regulate ['regjuleɪt] *vt.* 调节，调整；控制，管理

Phrases

marketing environment 市场环境

at micro- and macro-level 在微观和宏观层面上

marketing intermediary 营销中介机构

physical distribution firms 实体分销公司；物流企业或公司

financial intermediary 金融中介机构，金融中介

be made up of 由……组成

put restrictions on 限制

minority group 少数群体，少数民族；少数族群

put... in the public spotlight 将……置于公众的聚光灯下

customer base 客户群；顾客基础

adapt to 适应，习惯于

in terms of 根据；就……而言

baby boomer 婴儿潮时期出生的人

tailor to 根据……调整

family dynamics 家庭动态

purchasing power 购买力

industrial output 工业产值（出）

spending pattern 支出形态

raw material 原材料
fulfill one's goal 实现某人的目标
nuclear missile 核导弹
chemical weapon 化学武器
credit card 信用卡
stay ahead of 保持领先地位
stay informed of 随时了解
the big thing 重要的事
rather than 而不是
federal law 联邦法
in particular 尤其，特别
be categorized into 被归类为
core belief 核心信仰，核心信念
pass on 传递
secondary belief 二级信念
cultural diversity 文化多样性
place emphasis on 强调；注重，着重于

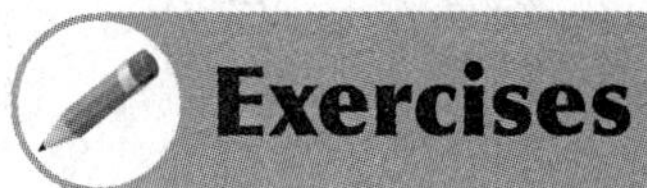

Exercises

EX. 1 Answer the following questions according to Text A.

(1) What does marketing environment refer to?
(2) What do marketing intermediaries refer to?
(3) What are financial intermediaries?
(4) What types of markets do customer markets include?
(5) How are business markets different from reseller markets?
(6) What concepts does the macro-environment of marketing include?
(7) What does demography refer to?
(8) What does the economic environment of the macro-environment refer to?
(9) What is the concern in the natural environment?
(10) What are the two types of beliefs which the values can be further categorized into?

EX. 2 Translate the following phrases from English into Chinese and vice versa.

(1) customer base ________________
(2) marketing environment ________________
(3) stay ahead of ________________
(4) stay informed of ________________
(5) at micro- and macro-level ________________
(6) 由……组成 ________________
(7) 预期；预料，预言 ________________
(8) 竞争的，比赛的 ________________
(9) 咨询；商议，商量 ________________
(10) 全球化，全球性 ________________

EX. 3 **Translate the following into Chinese.**

Marketing environment refers to the forces or variables of the outer and inner environment of a firm that affect the marketing management's ability to build and maintain the successful relationships with the customer. The marketing environment framework consists of macro-environment and micro-environment. Micro-environment variables are close to the firm and include the suppliers, marketing intermediaries, customer markets, competition & publics. Micro-environment also refers to the internal environment of the company and affects not only marketing but also all the departments such as management, finance, research and development, human resources, purchasing, operations and accounting. Macro-environment deals with the demographic, economic, technological, natural, socio-cultural and politico-legal environment of the markets.

Micro- and macro-environments have a significant impact on the success of marketing campaigns, and therefore the factors of these environments should be considered in-depth during the decision making process of a strategic marketer. Considering these factors will improve the success of your organization's marketing campaign and the reputation of the brand in the long term.

EX. 4 **Fill in the blanks with the words and phrase given below.**

controllable	affects	refers to	consists	serve
demography	relationship	representatives	forces	relatively

Marketing Environment

The key elements of marketing environment are internal environment, micro-environment, and macro-environment.

1. *Internal Environment*

Internal factors like men, machine, money, material, etc. on which marketing decision depends (1)________ internal marketing environment. The internal environment (2)________ the forces that are within the organization and (3)________ its ability to serve its customers. It includes marketing managers, sales (4)________, marketing budget, marketing plans, procedures, inventory, logistics, and anything within the organization which affects marketing decisions, and its(5)________ with its customers.

2. *Micro-Environment*

Individuals and organizations that are close to the marketing organization and directly impact its ability to (6)________ its customers, make marketing micro-environment. The micro-environment refers to the (7)________ that are close to the marketing organization and directly impact the customer experience. It includes the organization itself, its suppliers, marketing intermediaries, customers, markets or segments, competitors, and publics. Happenings in micro-environment is

(8)________ controllable for the marketing organization.

3. Macro-Environment

Macro environment refers to all forces that are part of the larger society and affects the micro-environment. It includes (9)________, economy, politics, culture, technology, and natural forces. Macro-environment is less (10)________.

Text B

Environmental Scanning

Environmental scanning can be defined as the study and interpretation of the political, economic, social and technological events and trends which influence a business, an industry or even a total market. The factors which need to be considered for environmental scanning are events, trends, issues, and expectations of the different interest groups. Environmental scanning is one of the essential components of the global environmental analysis. Environmental monitoring, environmental forecasting and environmental assessment complete the global environmental analysis. The global environment refers to the macro-environment which comprises industries, markets, companies, clients, and competitors.

Environmental scanning is an ongoing process and organizations are always refining the way their particular company or business goes through the process. Environmental scanning reinforces productive strategic plans and policies that can be implemented to make the organization get the maximum use of the business environment they are in. Environmental scanning not only helps the business find its strengths in its current environment, it also finds the weakness of competitors, identifies new markets, potential customers and upcoming technological platforms and devices that can be best used to sell or market the product or service. Thus, environmental scanning helps a business improve their decision-making process in times of risk to the external and internal environments the business is in.

1. Process

When scanning the environment, the organization needs to look at all the influences of the company. The scanning process makes the organization aware of what the business environment is about. It allows the organization to adapt to and learn from that environment, allowing itself to easily respond and react to any changes in both the internal and external business environment. Environmental scanning is a useful tool for strategic management as it helps to create and develop the aims and objectives of the company which assists with the production of the company or organization.

When looking at the weaknesses of the organization's placing in the current business environment, a formal environmental scanning is used. A common formal environmental scanning process has five steps. The five steps are fundamental in the achievement of each step and may develop each other in some form.

The first step of the environmental scanning process requires the identification of the needs and the issues that have occurred that caused the organization to decide an environmental scanning is required. Before starting the process there are several factors that need to be considered which include the purpose of the scanning, who will be participating in the processes and the amount of time and the resources that will be allocated for the duration of the scanning process.

The second step of the scanning process is gathering information. All the needs of the organization are translated into required pieces of information that will be useful in the process.

The third step is analyzing all the information that the business has collected. When analyzing the information, organizations are made aware of the trends or issues that they may be influenced by.

Step four of the environmental scanning process is all about the communication of the results obtained in step three. The appropriate decision makers analyze the translated information of the potential effects of the organization. All the information is presented in a simple and concise format.

With all the information obtained from steps three and four, step five is all about making informed decisions. Management creates appropriate steps that will position the organization in the current business environment.

2. PESTEL analysis

There are a number of common approaches on how the external factors can be identified and examined. These factors indirectly affect the organization but cannot be controlled by it. One approach could be the PEST analysis. PEST stands for Political, Economic, Social and Technological. Two more factors, the environmental factor and legal factor, are defined within the PESTEL analysis. The segmentation of the macro-environment according to the six presented factors of the PESTEL analysis is the starting point of the global environmental analysis. The six environmental factors of the PESTEL analysis are the following.

2.1 Political factors

The company or organization needs to consider the political environment when creating business strategies. The entire political environment includes looking at government policies and the risk and instability of current political factors. Political risks can include an unexpected loss of ownership, or changes in labor laws which might increase the cost of the company's workforce. However, business can often anticipate issues by performing a political risk analysis. The political instability can influence the business and the duration of time that business or organization is profitable.

2.2 Economical factors

Economic factors of the business environment are all the variables that impact how consumers spend their money and the power of that purchase. There are multiple factors that exist at any time. An example of an economic factor is the recent recession that influenced people to spend less and save more, which has impacted current consumer spending patterns. The economic development of a country is an important element when scanning the economic environment. Countries are often categorized as either "developing" or "developed". The exchange rate of a country can have an extensive impact on the profitability of a business. Relatively small changes in the exchange rate may be the difference between profit and loss. When promoting and selling a product, it is important for an organization to consider the extra financial information including current rates, taxes, etc. in the economy of the country.

2.3 Socio-cultural factors

Socio-cultural factors look at the demographic characteristics of the current business environment. They look at the values, customs and norms of the factors of which a company or organization is placed. When looking at the socio-cultural factors, it is important to consider the social values of the environment. Organizations look at the cultural characteristics of the society and consider all values and customs that are often associated with the culture while they try to market and sell the product or service, such as values, beliefs, language, religion, education, literacy, time orientation, and lifestyle.

2.4 Technological factors

Technological factors are becoming a lot more important in the modern day business environment. New technology produces new opportunities for companies and organizations to create, sell and promote a product. Technology is rapidly growing and forever changing. Telecommunication technology, for example cellphones and laptops, are increasing the opportunity within an organization to promote and sell a product. The Internet has made information available to the consumer to easily compare current prices of a product or service with the prices of the competitors of the same product or service. The Internet has also created more opportunity to market the product or service via the use of social media.

2.5 Environmental factors

Environmental factors of the PESTEL analysis include natural resources that are affected by the processes of selling and marketing products or services. The two main environmental trends that need to be considered when evaluating the natural environment are the increased pollution and growing shortage of raw materials. Government regulations are creating practices that encourage environmental sustainability. A business might, for example, utilize recyclable and biodegradable packaging, thus making the most of the environmental opportunities to create a sustainable organization in the current natural environment.

2.6 Legal factors

Legal factors include the laws and regulations of a state. The laws and regulations will influence the way in which an organization will market or sell products and services. Legal factors influence trade agreements between different governments and states. The governments that have a well-developed public policy about selling and marketing goods may limit competition and place other obligations on retailers.

3. SWOT Analysis

SWOT analysis, or situation analysis, is a strategic planning technique used to identify the key internal and external factors which are seen as important to achieve an objective. SWOT stands for Strength, Weakness, Opportunity, and Threat. The internal factors considered are the strengths and weaknesses where the opportunities and threats are external factors that are all used and considered to help improve the overall decision-making process in dynamic strategic situations the business is facing.

The strengths are positive characteristics in the internal business environment which can be capitalized on to increase the overall organizations' performancees. The weaknesses are factors of the internal environment which may restrict and interfere with the positive organizational performance. The internal environment factors include finance, production, research, development, and marketing. The opportunities include factors of the external environment that act like stepping stones for the organization to achieve its current strategic goals. The threats include the factors that have an effect and may interrupt the organization from achieving the goals. Threats often come out of the external business environment.

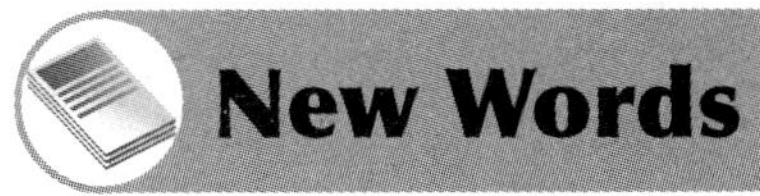

New Words

scan [skæn] *vt.* 扫描；细看，细查

interpretation [ɪnˌtɜːprɪ'teɪʃn] *n.* 理解；解释，说明

expectation [ˌekspek'teɪʃn] *n.* 期望，期待；预期；前程

essential [ɪ'senʃl] *adj.* 必要的，基本的；本质的；精华的

global ['gləʊbl] *adj.* 全球的，全球性的

assessment [ə'sesmənt] *n.* 评估，评价

strength [streŋθ] *n.* 优点，长处；力量

current ['kɜːrənt] *adj.* 现在的，当前的；流行的

identify [aɪ'dentɪfaɪ] *vt.* 确定；识别，认出

upcoming ['ʌpkʌmɪŋ] *adj.* 即将来到的，即将出现的

platform ['plætfɔːm] *n.* 平台；站台；月台；讲台

device [dɪ'vaɪs] *n.* 装置，设备

fundamental [ˌfʌndə'mentl] *adj.* 基础的，基本的；根本的，重要的

achievement [ə'tʃiːvmənt] *n.* 成就，成绩；完成，达到

identification [aɪˌdentɪfɪ'keɪʃn] *n.* 鉴定，识别；身份证明；认同

occur [ə'kɜː] *vi.* 发生；出现

amount [ə'maʊnt] *n.* 量，数量；总额

concise [kən'saɪs] *adj.* 简明的，简洁的；精炼的

instability [ˌɪnstə'bɪləti] *n.* 不稳定，不稳固

ownership ['əʊnəʃɪp] *n.* 所有权；物主身份

perform [pə'fɔ:m] *vt.* 执行，履行

profitable ['prɑ:fɪtəbl] *adj.* 有利可图的，可赚钱的

recession [rɪ'seʃn] *n.* 经济衰退，不景气；后退，撤退

categorize ['kætəgəraɪz] *vt.* 把……归类，把……分门别类

demographic [ˌdemə'græfɪk] *adj.* 人口统计学的；人口统计的

custom ['kʌstəm] *n.* 习惯，惯例

religion [rɪ'lɪdʒən] *n.* 宗教

literacy ['lɪtərəsi] *n.* 读写能力；素养；识字

laptop ['læptɒp] *n.* 便携式计算机

evaluate [ɪ'væljueɪt] *vt.* 评价

recyclable [ˌri:'saɪkləbl] *adj.* 可循环再用的

biodegradable [ˌbaɪəʊdɪ'greɪdəbl] *adj.* 能进行生物降解的

legal ['li:gl] *adj.* 合法的；法定的；法律的

agreement [ə'gri:mənt] *n.* 协定，协议；同意，一致

obligation [ˌɒblɪ'geɪʃn] *n.* 义务，责任；债务

overall ['əʊvərɔ:l] *adj.* 全面的，综合的，总体的；全部的，全体的

performance [pə'fɔ:məns] *n.* 表现；执行；表演

restrict [rɪ'strɪkt] *vt.* 限制，限定；约束，束缚

interrupt [ˌɪntə'rʌpt] *vt.* 打断（别人的话等）；阻止；截断

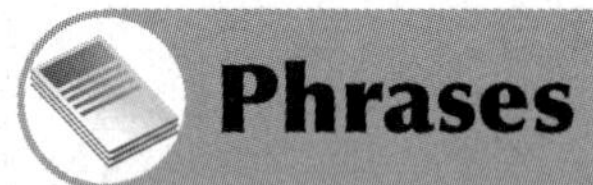

Phrases

environmental scanning 环境侦察；环境扫描

be defined as 被定义为

go through 完成；检查；通过

in times of 在……的时刻，在……的时期

react to 对……作出反应

assist with 在……给予帮助

participate in 参加

be translated into 被翻译成……

starting point 出发点；起始点

labor law 劳动法

exchange rate 汇率，兑换率

have an extensive impact on 对……有广泛影响

social value 社会价值观

time orientation 时间取向

telecommunication technology 电信技术，通信技术

trade agreement 贸易协定；劳资协议，雇佣合同

capitalize on 充分利用……

interfere with 干预；阻挠

stepping stone 垫脚石；跳板

achieve the goal 实现目标

come out of 由……产生，从……出来

PESTEL (Political, Economic, Social, Technological, Environmental, and Legal) PESTEL 分析模型又称大环境分析，其每一个字母代表一个因素：政治因素、经济因素、社会因素、技术因素、环境因素和法律因素。

SWOT (Strengths, Weaknesses, Opportunities, and Threats) SWOT 分析法，即基于内外部竞争环境和竞争条件下的态势分析。

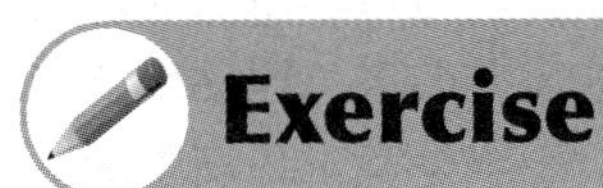

EX. **Answer the following questions according to Text B.**

(1) What is the definition of environmental scanning?

(2) What factors need to be considered before starting the environmental scanning process?

(3) What are the five steps of the scanning process?

(4) What factors are defined within the PESTEL analysis?

(5) What does the entire political environment include?

(6) What are the economic factors of the business environment?

(7) What do the socio-cultural factors look at?

(8) What are the two main environmental trends that need to be considered when evaluating the natural environment?

(9) What is SWOT analysis?

(10) What does SWOT stand for?

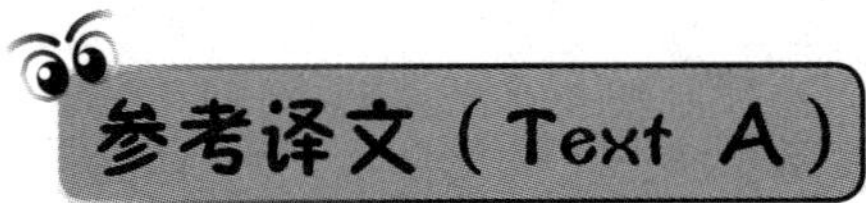

市场营销环境

术语“营销环境”是指影响组织与顾客建立并维持良好关系的各种影响力和因素。营销环境围绕并影响着组织。营销人员必须在微观和宏观层面上与内部和外部人员互动，建立内部和外部关系。

1. 微观环境

从公司方面来说，微观环境指公司的内部环境，包括管理、财务、研发、采购、经营和会计等所有部门。每个部门都会影响营销决策。例如，研发部投入研发产品的功能，会计部批准营销计划和预算的财务相关事宜。市场经理必须密切关注供应商的供货情况和其他趋势，确保产品能在规定的时间内交付给客户，以保持良好的客户关系。

营销中介机构是指经销商、物流公司、营销服务机构和金融中介机构。这些机构的人帮助公司向最终买家推销、销售和分销产品。经销商是那些持有和销售公司产品的人。它们匹配客户的产品配送，包括沃尔玛、塔吉特和百思买这样的大型超市。物流公司是诸如存储产品的仓库以及将产品从产地运输到目的地的场所。营销服务机构是提供诸如营销研究、广告和咨询等服务的公司。金融中介机构是银行、信贷公司和保险公司等机构。

微观环境的另一个方面是客户市场。客户市场有不同的类型，包括消费者市场、商业市场、政府市场、全球化国际市场和经销商市场。消费者市场由购买商品和服务供自己或家庭使用的个人构成；商业市场包括那些购买商品和服务用于生产自己的产品来销售的市场，这与经销市场不同；经销市场包括购买商品以转售获利的商家；政府市场由政府机构组成，它们购买商品是为了提供公共服务，或者将商品转让给其他需要的人；国际市场包括其他国家的买家，也包括先前提及的市场类别中的客户。竞争对手也是微观环境中的一个因素，包括提供类似商品和服务的公司。为了保持竞争力，公司必须在考虑自身规模和行业地位的同时，考虑谁是最大的竞争对手。公司应该发展相对于竞争对手的战略优势。

微观环境的最后一个方面是公众。公众是指对组织实现其目标的能力有利益关系或有影响的任何群体。例如，金融公众会阻碍一家公司获得资金的能力，从而影响该公司的信贷水平。媒体公众包括报纸和杂志，可以发表有关公司利益的文章和社论，可能影响客户的意见。政府公众可以通过立法限制公司的行为从而影响公司。市民团体包括环保组织和少数群体，他们可以质疑一家公司的行为，并将其置于公众的聚光灯下。社区公众是社区和社区组织，他们也会质疑公司对当地产生的影响和公司行为的责任水平。公众可以影响公司，因为只要他们态度发生改变，无论是积极的还是消极的，都可能导致销售上升或下降，因为公众通常是公司的客户群。

2. 宏观环境

宏观环境是指宏观社会中影响微观环境的各种因素，包括诸如人口统计、经济、自然力量、技术、政治和文化等概念。分析宏观营销环境是为了更好地了解环境，并通过营销工作适应社会环境及其变化，以实现企业的营销目标。

人口学是指对人口的规模、密度、位置、年龄、性别、种族和职业等方面进行研究的科学。这对于营销人员来说是一个非常重要的研究因素，有助于将人群进行市场细分和确定目标市场。人口统计学的一个例子是根据人们的出生年份对人群进行分类。这些分类有1946年至1964年出生的婴儿潮一代、1965年至1976年出生的X代人，以及1977年至1994年出生的Y代人。每种分类都有不同的特点以及重要的原因。这对市场营销人员是有益的，因为自己可以决定自己的产品会使哪些人群受益最多，从而调整营销计划，以吸引这一细分市场。人口统计学涵盖了许多对市场营销人员来说很重要的方面，包括家庭动态、地理位置变化、劳动力变化以及任何特定领域的多样性水平。

宏观环境的另一个方面是经济环境。这是指潜在客户的购买力以及人们花钱的方式。这个领域存在着两个不同类型的经济体，即自给自足型和工业化型。自给自足型经济更多地以农业为基础，消耗自己的工业产出。工业化经济的市场是多样化的，消费着许多不同类型的商品。每种市场对营销人员来说都很重要，因为每一种都有着截然不同的消费模式以及不同的财富分配方式。

自然环境是宏观环境中另一个重要因素，包括公司用于投入并影响其营销活动的自然资源。这个方面令人担忧的问题是污染加剧、原材料短缺和政府干预力度加大。随着原材料越来越稀缺，公司生产产品变得越来越难。此外，如果公众知道公司在污染破坏环境，也会对公司的声誉造成极其负面的影响。最后一个令人关注的问题是，政府干预会使公司越来越难实现目标，因为要求越来越严格。

技术环境可能是宏观环境中变化最快的因素之一，包括从抗生素、外科手术到核导弹、化学武器，再到汽车和信用卡等所有发展。随着这些市场的发展，它可以为产品创造新的市场和新的用途。它还要求公司保持领先地位，在技术过时时更新自己的技术。他们必须随时了解趋势，这样才能成为重大事件的“弄潮儿”，而不是任由过时，承受经济上的后果。为了理解不同的消费模式，营销人员还需要考虑数字技术的发展及其对市场增长和就业的影响。对于市场营销人员来说，尤其是在以数字为主导的市场中，预测需求以利用潜在的市场增长至关重要。技术已经发展到可以分析购买模式以预测未来需求的程度。

政治环境包括影响或限制社会中其他组织和个人的所有法律、政府机构和团体。对于营销人员来说，了解这些限制很重要，因为它们可能很复杂。有些产品同时受到州和联邦法律的监管，有些法律甚至限制某些产品的目标市场，如香烟不应该销售给年龄较小的儿童。在潜意识信息和垄断方面也有很多限制。由于法律法规经常变化，这是一个营销人员需要监测的重要方面。由于法律和法规经常变化，其产生的障碍会极大地影响企业营销业务的方式，尤其在数字社区中。

宏观环境的最后一个方面是社会环境。社会环境由社会群体的制度、基本价值观和信仰组成。价值观还可以进一步分为核心信念和次级信念，前者是代代相传的，很难改变，而后者往往更容易受到影响。作为一名营销人员，了解两者之间的区别，并使营销活动集中反映目标受众的价值观是很重要的。随着技术在社会信念和价值观形成中发挥关键作用的时代的到来，文化多样性在数字社区的世界已经得到了长足发展。

在处理营销环境时，公司必须积极主动，这一点是很重要的。这样做，他们可以创造一种能使其蓬勃发展的环境，并可以更有效地在客户潜力最大的领域进行营销活动。因此，必须同时重视宏观和微观环境，并对其中的变化作出相应的反应。

Case SWOT of Coca Cola

Unit 3

Text A

Consumer Behavior

Consumer behavior refers to the processes consumers go through, and reactions they have towards products or services. It is to do with consumption, and the processes consumers go through around purchasing and consuming goods and services. Consumers recognize needs or wants, and go through a process to satisfy these needs. Consumer behavior includes types of products purchased, money spent, frequency of purchases and what influences them to make the purchase decision or not. There is a lot that influences consumer behavior, with contributions from both internal and external factors. Internal factors include attitudes, needs, motives, preferences and perceptual processes, whilst external factors include marketing activities, social and economic factors, and cultural aspects. There are also physical factors that influence consumer behavior, for example if a consumer is hungry, then this physical feeling of hunger will influence him so that he goes and purchases a sandwich to satisfy the hunger.

1. Consumer involvement

Involvement is the perceived importance or personal relevance of an object or event. It is about the degree to which the consumer feels attached to the product or brand, and the loyalty felt towards it. Involvement has both cognitive and affective elements: It plays on both the brain and the emotions. For example, a car owner might say, "I love my old Ambassador (affective) because it never lets me down (cogonitive)." There can be three levels of involvement:

Low level of involvement occurs if attributes are irrelevant to consequences;

Medium level of involvement occurs if the attributes only link to function;

High product involvement will come about if the consumer feels that product attributes are strongly-linked to end goals or values. Although it is the behavior of the decision-maker that determines the level of involvement of a decision, there are three common factors, which increase the likelihood of high involvement. These are the cost of purchase relative to income, the amount of time for which the purchase will be owned, and the extent to which the purchase reflects the self-image.

High-involvement purchases are those products, which figure greatly in the consumer's lifestyle. In other words, they involve decisions which are important to get right, preferable time. Typically, the products with which the consumer is highly involved will also be the ones which the consumer knows most about, and about which he has strong opinions. For example, a technology-savvy IT professional might have very strong views on which PC would give the best performance. Discrepant information (a salesperson's attempt to persuade him to try another brand, for example) is discounted and disparaged, and may even lower the esteem of the source of the information (the IT professional will think the salesperson is stupid, or is trying to unload an inferior brand of computer). On the other hand, a computer novice is less likely to have formed a close involvement with a product and hence is more likely to be prepared to listen to what the salesperson has to say. This means that high-involvement consumers are hard to persuade; they are not easily swayed by advertising or even by persuasive sales pitches. High involvement always has a strong affective component, and this does not necessarily mean a high cost commitment. People also fall in love with cheap products. So involvement does not always equate to price. A high-involvement good is not necessarily a high-priced one, nor is a low-involvement good necessarily a cheap one. Smokers can become very involved with their brand of cigarettes costing very few. Conversely, some people may not get involved deeply with a highly costly five-star hotel.

2. Types of consumer behavior

Wants are unlimited and the resources to satisfy these wants are limited. So the consumers think rationally before buying any product. Buying a toothpaste is totally different from buying a luxury car. The more expensive the good is, the more information is required by the consumer. There are four types of consumer buying behavior on the basis of buyer involvement while purchasing any product.

2.1 Complex buying behavior

Consumers go through complex buying behavior when they are highly involved in a purchase and aware of significant differences among brands. Consumers are highly involved when the product is expensive, bought infrequently, risky and highly self-expressive. Typically the consumer does not know much about the product category and has much to learn. For example, a person buying a personal computer may not know what attribute to look for. Many of the product features like "16K memory", "disc storage", and "screen resolution" carry no meaning to him or her. This buyer will pass through a learning process characterized by first developing beliefs about the product, then attitudes, and then making a thoughtful purchase choice. The marketer of a high-involvement product must understand the information-gathering and evaluation behavior of high-involvement consumers.

The marketer needs to develop strategies that assist the consumer in learning about the attributes of the product class, their relative importance, and the high standing of the company's brand on the more important attributes. The marketer needs to differentiate the brand's features, use mainly print media and long copy to describe the brand's benefits, and motivate store sales personnel and the consumer's acquaintances to influence the final brand choice.

2.2 Dissonance-reducing buying behavior

Sometimes the consumer is highly involved in a purchase but sees little difference in the brands. The high involvement is again based on the fact that the purchase is expensive, infrequent, and risky. In this case, the consumer will shop around to learn what is available but will buy fairly quickly because brand differences are not pronounced. The consumer may respond primarily to a good price or to purchase convenience.

After the purchase, the consumer might experience dissonance that stems from noticing certain disquieting features of the product or hearing favorable things about other brands. The consumer will be alert to information that might justify his decision. The consumer will first act, then acquire new beliefs and end up with a set of attitudes. Here marketing communications should aim to supply beliefs and evaluations that help the consumer feel good about his or her brand choice.

2.3 Habitual buying behavior

Many products are bought under conditions of low-consumer involvement and the absence of significant brand differences. Consider the purchase of salt. Consumers have little involvement in this product category. They go to the store and reach for the brand. If they keep reaching for the same brand, it is out of habit, not strong brand loyalty.

There is good evidence that consumers have low involvement with most low-cost, frequently purchased products. Consumer behavior in these cases does not pass through the normal belief/attitude/behavior sequence. Consumers do not search extensively for information about the brands, evaluate their characteristics, and make a weighty decision on which brand to buy. Instead, they are passive recipients of information as they watch television or see print ads. Ad repetition creates brand familiarity rather than brand conviction. Consumers do not form a strong attitude towards a brand but select it because it is familiar. After purchase, they may not even evaluate the choice because they are not highly involved with the product. So the buying process is brand beliefs formed by passive learning, followed by purchase behavior, which may be followed by evaluation.

Marketers of low-involvement products with few brand differences find it effective to use price and sales promotions to stimulate product trial, since consumers are not highly committed to any brand. In advertising a low-involvement product, a number of things should be observed. The ad copy should stress only a few key points. Visual symbols and imagery are important because they can easily be remembered and associated with the brand.

2.4 Variety-seeking buying behavior

Some buying situations are characterized by low-consumer involvement but significant brand differences. Here consumers are often observed to do a lot of brand switching. An example occurs in purchasing cookies. The consumer has some beliefs, chooses a brand of cookies without much evaluation, and evaluates it during consumption. But the next time, the consumer may reach for another brand out of boredom or a wish for a different taste. Brand switching occurs for the sake of variety rather than dissatisfaction.

The marketing strategy is different for the market leader and the minor brands in this product category. The market leader will try to encourage habitual buying behavior by dominating the shelf space, avoiding out-of-stock conditions, and sponsoring frequent reminder advertising. Challenger firms will encourage variety seeking by offering lower prices, deals, coupons, free samples and advertising that presents reasons for trying something new.

3. Consumer behavior models

Consumer behavior models are essential tools that marketers can use to help understand why consumers buy or do not buy a product. The different types of models are the black box model, the personal variable model, and the comprehensive model, and each model has a specific focus. The black box model concentrates on external stimuli, the personal variable model focuses on internal stimuli within the consumer, and the comprehensive model studies a combination of external and internal stimuli.

Consumer behavior models vary in terms of the complexity of the behavior that is being studied. The primary purpose of studying consumer behavior is for marketers to better understand and therefore better target consumers in their marketing strategies. It is a very complicated science, and marketers can observe and make some correlations between advertising and consumer response, but the main question of what makes a person buy or do not buy a product is too individual and cannot be explained with one or even several behavior models.

3.1 The black box model

The black box model, also called the stimulus-response model, is one of the most simple types of consumer behavior models. The black box can be thought of as the region of the consumer's brain that is responsible for purchasing decisions. Environmental stimuli, such as economics, technology, and culture, combine with marketing stimuli, like the product, price, and promotion, inside the black box, where decisions are made. This model ignores variables within the consumer and focuses on marketing and environmental variables that produce the desired response.

3.2 The personal variable model

The personal variable model is another one of the major types of consumer behavior models. Unlike the black box model, where external stimuli is the main focus, the personal variable model studies what internal factors affect consumer behavior and purchasing decisions. This model specifically ignores external stimuli, such as marketing techniques, and concentrates on internal psychological variables. These variables include lifestyle, motivations, and personality.

It also looks at individual decision-making processes, such as problem recognition, alternative evaluation, as well as post-purchase behavior.

3.3 The comprehensive model

The final major types of consumer behavior models are the comprehensive models. As the name might suggest, this type of model takes into account both environmental and internal stimuli when studying purchasing behavior. This type of model is one of the most complex studies because many variables are in play. It is beneficial because it is the only model that can be used to study how different external stimuli react in different types of personalities and demographics. It is, however, difficult to determine the accuracy of the conclusions drawn from these studies because of the number of variables.

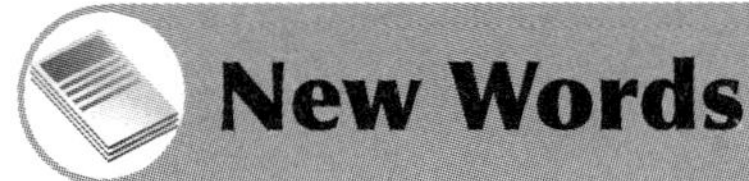

New Words

reaction [ri'ækʃn] *n.* 反应；反作用力

frequency ['friːkwənsi] *n.* 频繁性；频率

contribution [ˌkɑːntrɪ'bjuːʃn] *n.* 贡献；捐赠，捐助

motive ['məʊtɪv] *n.* 动机，原因；主旨

perceptual [pər'septʃuəl] *adj.* 知觉的，有知觉的；感性的

involvement [ɪn'vɒlvmənt] *n.* 参与，加入；牵连

perceive [pər'siːv] *vt.* 察觉，发觉；意识到

relevance ['reləvəns] *n.* 相关性，关联

loyalty ['lɔɪəlti] *n.* 忠心；忠诚，忠实

cognitive ['kɒgnətɪv] *adj.* 认知的，认识的

affective [ə'fektɪv] *adj.* 情感的，表达感情的

attribute [ə'trɪbjuːt] *n.* 属性；（人或物的）特征

medium ['miːdiəm] *adj.* 中等的，中级的

likelihood ['laɪklihʊd] *n.* 可能，可能性

self-image ['self-'ɪmɪdʒ] *n.* 自我形象

savvy ['sævi] *adj.* 有常识的；机智的

discrepant [dɪ'skrepənt] *adj.* 有差异的；相差的；矛盾的

disparage [dɪ'spærɪdʒ] *vt.* 蔑视，贬损

esteem [ɪ'stiːm] *n.* 尊敬，尊重

inferior [ɪn'fɪriə] *adj.* （质量等）低劣的；下级的，下等的

novice ['nɒvɪs] *n.* 初学者，新手

persuasive [pə'sweɪsɪv] *adj.* 有说服力的，令人信服的；劝诱的

commitment [kə'mɪtmənt] *n.* 致力，献身；承担义务；承诺

equate [i'kweɪt] *vt.* 等同，使相等；相当于

conversely ['kɒnvɜːsli] *adv.* 相反地；反过来，反之

rationally ['ræʃnəli] *adv.* 讲道理地，理性地

luxury ['lʌkʃəri] *n.* 奢侈，豪华；奢侈品

infrequently [ɪn'friːkwəntli] *adv.* 稀少地；罕见地

characterize ['kærəktəraɪz] *vt.* 赋予……特色；表示……的典型

differentiate [ˌdɪfə'renʃieɪt] *vt.* 区分，区别，辨别

motivate ['məʊtɪveɪt] *vt.* 刺激，激发；使有动机，促动

acquaintance [ə'kweɪntəns] *n.* 对……有了解；相识的人，熟人

dissonance ['dɪsənəns] *n.* 不一致，不和谐

convenience [kən'viːniəns] *n.* 方便，便利

disquiet [dɪs'kwaɪət] *vt.* 使不安，使烦恼；使不平静

justify ['dʒʌstɪfaɪ] *vt.* 证明……有理；为……辩护，对……做出解释

habitual [hə'bɪtʃuəl] *adj.* 习惯的，惯常的；习以为常的

sequence ['siːkwəns] *n.* 顺序；序列

weighty ['weɪti] *adj.* 重大的，重要的；严重的

dissatisfaction [ˌdɪsˌsætɪs'fækʃn] *n.* 不满，不平；令人不满的事物

minor ['maɪnə] *adj.* 较小的；少数的

sponsor ['spɒnsə] *vt.* 赞助

coupon ['kuːpɒn] *n.* 优惠券

comprehensive [ˌkɒmprɪ'hensɪv] *adj.* 综合的；广泛的；有理解力的

stimuli ['stɪmjʊlaɪ] *n.* 刺激；刺激物，促进因素

combination [ˌkɒmbɪ'neɪʃn] *n.* 结合；结合体，联合体，混合体

complexity [kəm'pleksəti] *n.* 复杂性，错综复杂的状态

primary ['praɪməri] *adj.* 首要的，主要的

complicated ['kɒmplɪkeɪtɪd] *adj.* 复杂难懂的；结构复杂的

consumer behavior 消费者行为

internal factor 内部因素

external factor 外部因素

physical factor 物理因素；身体因素

consumer involvement 顾客参与度；消费者介入程度

feel attached to 对……感到依恋；喜爱，爱慕

be irrelevant to 与……不相干，与……不相关

be relative to 和……有关系

be involved with 参与；与……有关联；涉及

sales pitch 推销员的宣传腔调

not necessarily 未必，不一定

on the basis of 以……为基础；根据，依据

pass through 经过，经历；通过

shop around 货比三家

stem from 来自，起源于；出于

be alert to 对……警惕，对……警觉

end up with 结束，以……告终

marketing communications 营销传播

brand loyalty 品牌忠诚度

make a weighty decision 作出重大决定

brand familiarity 品牌熟悉度

brand conviction 品牌信念

form a strong attitude towards 对……形成强烈的态度

be committed to 献身于，致力于

the ad copy 广告文案

visual symbol 视觉符号

brand switching 品牌转移

for the sake of 为了……；为了……的利益

consumer behavior model 消费者行为模式

black box model 黑箱模型

personal variable model 个人变量模型

marketing strategy 营销策略

stimulus-response model 刺激—反应模式	alternative evaluation 评估备选方案
be thought of as 被认为是	take into account 重视，考虑；顾及
environmental variable 环境变化因素	be in play 起作用；处于运动中
psychological variable 心理变化因素	

Abbreviations

IT (Information Technology) 信息技术
PC (Personal Computer) 个人计算机

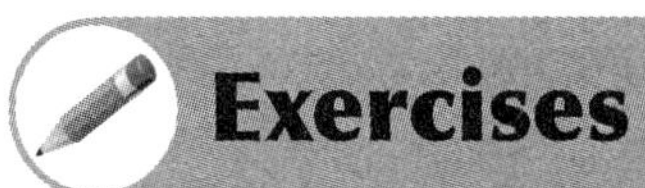

Exercises

EX. 1 Answer the following questions according to Text A.

(1) What does consumer behavior refer to? And what is it to do with?
(2) What are the three levels of customer involvement?
(3) What are the three common factors which increase the likelihood of high customer involvement?
(4) What are the four types of consumer buying behavior on the basis of buyer involvement while purchasing any product?
(5) When are consumers highly involved in a purchase?
(6) What should marketing communications aim to do if the consumer experiences dissonance after a purchase?
(7) What are the different types of consumer behavior models?
(8) What variables does the black box model ignore and focus on?
(9) What variables does the personal variable model ignore and concentrate on?
(10) Why is the comprehensive model one of the most complex studies?

EX. 2 Translate the following phrases from English into Chinese and vice versa.

(1) brand conviction ____________________ ____________________
(2) brand loyalty ____________________ ____________________

(3) consumer behavior model ________________ ________________
(4) consumer involvement ________________ ________________
(5) marketing communications ________________ ________________
(6) 营销策略 ________________ ________________
(7) 个人变量模型 ________________ ________________
(8) 评估备选方案 ________________ ________________
(9) 忠心；忠诚，忠实 ________________ ________________
(10) 习惯的，惯常的 ________________ ________________

EX. 3 Translate the following into Chinese.

The consumer decision making is a complex process which involves all the stages from problem recognition to post-purchase activities. All the consumers have their own needs in their daily lives and these needs make them make different decisions. These decisions can be complex depending on their opinion about a particular products, evaluating and comparing, selecting and purchasing among the different types of products. Therefore, understanding and realizing the core issue of the process of consumer decision making and utilize the theories in practice is becoming a common view point by many companies and people.

Although it seems as if we make some purchases spontaneously, in reality we make these buying decisions only after we have undergone a series of steps: problem recognition, information search, evaluation of alternatives, product purchase, and post-purchase evaluation. These steps are known as the consumer decision-making process. The length of time and the amount of effort consumers devote to a particular purchasing decision depend on the importance of the desired product to the consumer. Purchases with high levels of potential social or economic consequences (perceived risk) are said to be high-involvement purchase decisions. Routine purchases that pose little risk to the consumer are low-involvement decisions. Consumers generally invest more time and effort in buying decisions for high-involvement products than in those for low-involvement products.

EX. 4 Fill in the blanks with the words and phrase given below.

particular	capitalize on	satisfaction	vow	restoring
reject	attempt	imbalance	favors	expectations

Post-purchase Evaluation

Post-purchase evaluation is the last stage of decision making, where the consumer evaluates the quality of the decision he or she made. The buyer feels either (1)________ at the removal of the initial problem that started the decision-making process or dissatisfaction with the purchase. Usually consumers are satisfied if purchases meet their (2)________ .

Sometimes, however, consumers experience post-purchase anxieties called cognitive dissonance. Cognitive dissonance is a(n) (3)________ among a person's knowledge, beliefs, and attitudes. A consumer, for example, may experience dissonance after choosing a(n) (4)________ automobile over several other models when some of the rejected models have desired features that the chosen one does not provide. Dissonance is likely to increase 1) as the dollar values of purchases increase, 2) when the (5)________ alternatives have desirable features that the chosen alternatives do not provide, and 3) when the purchase decision has a major effect on the buyer. In other words, cognitive dissonance is more likely with high-involvement purchases than with those that require low-involvement.

The consumer may (6)________ to reduce dissonance by looking for information to support the chosen alternative or by seeking reassurance from acquaintances who are satisfied purchasers of the product. The individual may also avoid information that (7)________ a rejected alternative. Marketers can help buyers to reduce cognitive dissonance by providing information that supports the chosen alternative. A final way the consumer can deal with dissonance is to change product options, thereby (8)________ the cognitive balance. He or she could decide that one of the rejected alternatives would have been the best choice and (9)________ to purchase that item in the future. Marketers can (10)________ this by using something like "If you're unhappy with them, try us" in their advertising.

Text B

Factors Influencing Consumer Behavior

Consumer behavior is the process involved when individuals select, purchase, use, and dispose of goods, services, ideas, or experiences to satisfy their needs and desires. It is the buying behavior of individuals who will use the products they purchase. In their efforts to understand why and how consumers make buying decisions, marketers borrow extensively from the sciences of psychology and sociology and need to take into account the factors influencing consumer behavior.

1. Internal or psychological factors

The buying behavior of consumers is influenced by a number of internal or psychological factors. The most important ones are motivation and perception.

1.1 Motivation

In the words of William J Stanton, "A motive can be defined as a drive or an urge for which an individual seeks satisfaction. It becomes a buying motive when the individual seeks satisfaction through the purchase of something." A motive is an inner urge (or need) that moves a person to take purchase action to satisfy two kinds of needs: 1) biogenic needs which arise from physiological states of tension such as thirst, hunger; 2) psychogenic needs which arise from psychological states of tension such as needs for recognition, esteem.

So, motivation is the force that activates goal-oriented behavior. Motivation acts as a driving force that impels an individual to take action to satisfy his needs. So it becomes one of the internal factors influencing consumer behavior.

1.2 Perception

Human beings have considerably more than five senses. Apart from the basic five (touch, taste, smell, sight, hearing) there are senses of direction, the sense of balance, a clear knowledge of which way is down, and so forth. Each sense is feeding information to the brain constantly, and the amount of information being collected will seriously overload the system if one takes it all in. The brain, therefore, selects from the environment around the individual and cuts out the extraneous noise. An example of cognitive mapping as applied to perception of product quality might run as follows.

The consumer uses the input selector to select clues and assign values to them. For quality, the clues are typically price, brand name and retailer name. There are strong positive relationships between price and quality in most consumers' perceptions, and brand name and quality; although the retailer name is less significant, it still carries some weight.

For example, many consumers would feel confident that big bazaar would sell higher-quality items than the local corner shop, but might be less able to distinguish between food bazaar and giant hyper store. The information is subjective in that the consumer will base decisions on the selected information. Each of us selects differently from the environment and each of us has differing views. Information about quality will be pigeonholed or categorized: the individual may put Scoda Octavia in the same category as Mercedes Benz or perhaps put Sony in the same slot as Aiwa.

2. Social factors

Human beings are social animals. We need people around to talk to and discuss various issues to reach better solutions and ideas. Social factors influencing consumer buying decision can be classified as below.

2.1 Reference groups

Every individual has some people around who influence him in any way. Reference groups comprise of people that individuals compare themselves with. Every individual knows some people in the society who become his idols in due course of time. Coworkers, family members, relatives, neighbors, friends, seniors at workplace often form reference groups. Reference groups are generally of two types: primary group and secondary group.

Primary group consists of individuals one interacts with on a regular basis. Primary group includes friends, family members, relatives and coworkers. All of them influence the buying decisions of consumers. A married individual would show strong inclination towards buying products which would benefit not only him but also his family members as compared to a bachelor. Family plays an important role in influencing the buying decisions of individuals. A consumer who has a wife and child at home would buy for them rather than spending on himself. An individual entering into marriage would be more interested in buying a house, car, household items, furniture and so on. When an individual gets married and starts a family, most of his buying decisions are taken by the entire family.

Every individual goes through the following stages and shows a different buying need in each stage:

Bachelorhood: Purchases alcohol, beer, bike, mobile handset. (Spends lavishly)

Newly married: Tend to purchase a new house, car, household furnishings. (Spends sensibly)

Family with children: Purchases products to secure his as well as his family's future.

Empty nest (Children getting married)/Retirement/Old age: Medicines, health products, and necessary items.

Secondary groups share indirect relationship with the consumer. These groups are more formal and individuals do not interact with them on a regular basis.

2.2 Roles and status

A person participates in many groups like family, clubs, and organizations. The person's position in each group can be defined in terms of role and status. A role consists of the activities that a person is expected to perform. Each role carries a status. People choose products that communicate their role and status in society.

3. Cultural factors

Cultural factors have a significant effect on an individual's buying decision. Every individual has different sets of habits, beliefs, and principles which he develops from his family status and background. What they see from their childhood becomes their culture. Cultural factors consist of culture, sub-culture, and social class.

3.1 Culture

Culture is the most fundamental determinant of a person's wants and behavior. The growing child acquires a set of values, perception preferences and behavior through his family and other key institutions. Culture influences the pattern of consumption and the pattern of decision-making considerably. Marketers have to explore the cultural forces and have to frame marketing strategies for each category of culture separately to push up the sales of their products or services. But culture is not permanent and changes gradually and such changes are progressively assimilated within society.

Culture is a set of beliefs and values that are shared by most people within a group. The groupings considered under culture are usually relatively large, but at least in theory a culture can be shared by a few people. Culture is passed on from one group member to another, and in particular is usually passed down from one generation to the next; it is learned, and is, therefore, both subjective and arbitrary.

Culture can change over a period of time, although such changes tend to be slow, since culture is deeply built into people's behavior. From a marketing viewpoint, therefore, it is probably much easier to work within a given culture than to try to change it.

3.2 Sub-culture

Each culture consists of smaller sub-cultures that provide more specific identification and socialization for its members. Sub-culture refers to a set of beliefs shared by a subgroup of the main culture, which include nationalities, religions, racial groups, and geographic regions. Many sub-cultures make up important market segments and marketers have to design products and marketing programs tailored to their needs.

Although this subgroup will share most of the beliefs of the main culture, they share among themselves another set of beliefs, which may be at odds with those held by the main group. For example, Indians are normally seen as orthodox, conservative people. Another example is that, the urban educated or upper class exhibits more trace of individualism although Indian culture is mostly collective in nature.

3.3 Social class

Consumer behavior is determined by the social class to which they belong. The classification of socio-economic groups is known as Socio-Economic Classification (SEC). Social class is relatively a permanent and ordered division in a society whose members share similar value, interest and behavior. Social class is not determined by a single factor, but is measured as a combination of various factors, such as income, occupation, education, authority, power, property, ownership, lifestyles, consumption pattern, etc.

There are three different social classes in our society, i.e., upper class, middle class, and lower class. These three social classes differ in their buying behavior. Upper-class consumers want high-class goods to maintain their status in the society. Middle-class consumers purchase carefully and collect information to compare different producers in the same line and lower-class consumers buy on impulse sometimes.

Again there could be education considerations. A rich but not well-educated people will not normally buy a computer. We should consider another factor of social mobility where a person gets up in the social ladder (for example, poor can become middle class and middle class can become rich or the children of uneducated family can attain higher education) or down in the social ladder (for example, rich can become poor or the children of a highly educated family may not continue study).

Therefore, marketing managers are required to study carefully the relationship between social classes and their consumption pattern and take appropriate measures to appeal to the people of those social classes for whom their products are meant.

4. Economic factors

Consumer behavior is influenced largely by economic factors. Economic factors that influence consumer behavior are as follows.

4.1 Personal income

The personal income of a person is a determinant of his buying behavior. The gross personal income of a person consists of disposable income and discretionary income. The disposable personal income refers to the actual income (i.e., money balance) remaining at the disposal of a person after deducting taxes and compulsorily deductible items from the gross income. An increase in the disposable income leads to an increase in the expenditure on various items. A fall in the disposable income, on the other hand, leads to a fall in the expenditure on various items.

The discretionary personal income refers to the balance remaining after meeting basic necessities of life. This income is available for the purchase of shopping goods, durable goods and luxuries. An increase in the discretionary income leads to an increase in the expenditure on shopping goods, luxuries, etc., which improves a person's living standard.

4.2 Family income

Family income refers to the aggregate income of all the members of a family.

Family income influences the buying behavior of the family. The surplus family income, remaining after the expenditure on the basic needs of the family, is made available for buying shopping goods, durables, and luxuries.

4.3 Income expectations

Income expectations are one of the important determinants of the buying behavior of an individual. If he expects any increase in his income, he is tempted to spend more on shopping goods, durables and luxuries. On the other hand, if he expects any fall in his future income, he will curtail his expenditure on comforts and luxuries and restrict his expenditure to bare necessities.

4.4 Savings

Savings also influence the buying behavior of an individual. A change in the amount of savings leads to a change in the expenditure of an individual. If a person decides to save more out of his present income, he will spend less on comforts and luxuries.

4.5 Liquid assets

Liquid assets refer to those assets which can be converted into cash quickly without any loss. Liquid assets include cash in hand, bank balance, marketable securities, etc. If an individual has more liquid assets, he goes in for buying comforts and luxuries. On the other hand, if he has less liquid assets, he cannot spend more on buying comforts and luxuries.

4.6 Consumer credit

Consumer credit refers to the credit facility available to the consumers desirous of purchasing durables and luxuries. It is made available by the sellers, either directly or indirectly through banks and other financial institutions. Hire purchase, installment purchase, direct bank loans, etc., are the ways by which credit is made available to the consumers.

Consumer credit influences consumer behavior. If more consumer credit is available on liberal terms, expenditure on comforts and luxuries increases, as it induces consumers to purchase these goods and raise their living standard.

4.7 Other economic factors

Other economic factors like business cycles, inflation, etc. also influence the consumer behavior.

5. Personal factor

Personal factors also influence consumer behavior. The important personal factors which influence consumer behavior are age, occupation, income, and lifestyle.

Age is one of the important personal factors influencing consumer behavior. People buy different products at their different stages of lifecycle. Their taste, preference, etc., also change.

Occupation or profession of a person influences his buying behavior. The lifestyles and buying considerations and decisions differ widely according to the nature of the occupation. For instance, the buying of a doctor can be easily differentiated from that of a lawyer, teacher, clerk businessman, landlord, etc. So, the marketing managers have to design different marketing strategies to suit the buying motives of different occupational groups.

Income is another factor which can exert influence on shaping the consumption pattern. Income is an important source of purchasing power. So, the buying pattern of people differs with different levels of income.

Lifestyle is a person's pattern or way of living as expressed in his activity, interests, and opinions. It portrays the "whole person" interacting with the environment. Marketing managers have to design different marketing strategies to suit the lifestyles of the consumers.

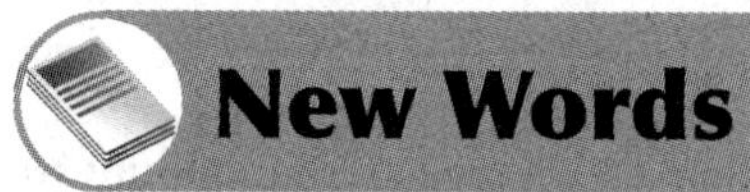

New Words

psychology [saɪ'kɒlədʒi] *n.* 心理学；心理状态，心理特点

sociology [ˌsəʊsi'ɒlədʒi] *n.* 社会学；群体生态学

drive [draɪv] *n.* 驱动力

urge [ɜːrdʒ] *n.* 推动力；刺激，冲动

biogenic [ˌbaɪəʊ'dʒenɪk] *adj.* 源于生物的，生物造成的

physiological [ˌfɪzi'ɒlədʒikl] *adj.* 生理的；生理学的

tension ['tenʃn] *n.* 紧张，不安；紧张气氛

psychogenic [ˌsaɪkəʊ'dʒenɪk] *adj.* 心理的，精神性的

activate ['æktɪveɪt] *vt.* 激活；使活动，起动

goal-oriented [gəʊl-'ɔːrɪəntɪd] *adj.* 面向目标的

impel [ɪm'pel] *vt.* 推动，推进；敦促

considerably [kən'sɪdərəbli] *adv.* 非常；相当地

overload [ˌəʊvə'ləʊd] *vt.* 给……增加负担；超负荷；使超载

extraneous [ɪk'streɪniəs] *adj.* 无关的，不相干的；外来的，外部的

pigeonhole ['pɪdʒɪnhəʊl] *vt.* 把……搁在分类架上；把……隔成小格

slot [slɒt] *n.* 位置；狭槽，水沟

idol ['aɪdl] *n.* 偶像，崇拜物

progressively [prə'gresɪvli] *adv.* 逐步地；前进地；日益增加地

assimilate [ə'sɪməleɪt] *vi.* 同化；吸收

subjective [səb'dʒektɪv] *adj.* 主观的

arbitrary ['ɑːbɪtri] *adj.* 任性的，随心所欲的；主观的，武断的

racial ['reɪʃl] *adj.* 种族的；人种的

orthodox ['ɔːθədɑːks] *adj.* 正统的，规范的；公认的，普遍赞同的

conservative [kən'sɜːvətɪv] *adj.* 保守的

up-market [ʌp-'mɑːkɪt] *adj.* 高档的，高档消费的

individualism [ˌɪndɪ'vɪdʒuəlɪzəm] *n.* 个人主义，利己主义

division [dɪ'vɪʒn] *n.* 分开，分隔；部门

authority [ə'θɔːrəti] *n.* 权威，权力；学术权威

discretionary [dɪ'skreʃənəri] *adj.* 任意的，自由决定的；酌情行事的

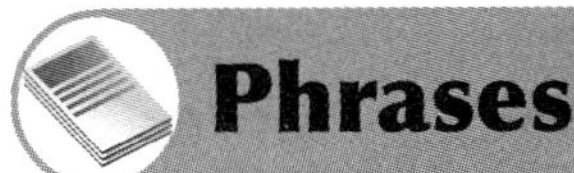

Phrases

dispose of 解决；将（某物）处理掉
take action 采取行动，行动起来
arise from 产生于，起因于
a driving force 驱动力
act as 充当……，担任……；起……的作用
apart from 此外；撇开……来说
cut out 切断；删除；停止
apply to 适用于，运用于
assign to 分配给，指定给
carry weight 有影响力，举足轻重
big bazaar 大型百货商店
hyper store 超级市场
as below 如下
reference group 参照群体
comprise of 包括；由……组成，由……构成
on a regular basis 经常地，有规律地
empty nest 空巢
sub-culture 亚文化
social class 社会阶层
push up 提高，增高
in theory 理论上
from a marketing viewpoint 从市场营销的角度
tailor to one's needs 调整以满足某人的需求
be at odds with 与……有争执；与……不和，相左
belong to 属于；为……之一员
social mobility 社会流动
social ladder 社会阶梯
take appropriate measures 采取适当的措施
appeal to 对……有吸引力；向……投诉；向……呼吁
at the disposal of 由……自由支配；任凭……使用
liquid asset 流动资产
credit facility 银行提供信用；信用透支；融通便利
be desirous of 想要……；渴望……
installment purchase 分期付款购货
living standard 生活水平，生活标准
business cycle 经济同期，商业周期
be differentiated from 区别于……
exert influence on 对……施加影响

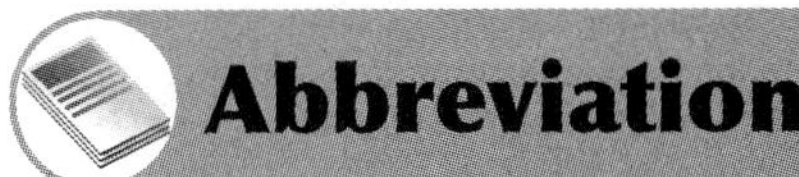

Abbreviation

SEC (Socio-Economic Classification) 社会经济分类

Exercise

EX. Answer the following questions according to Text B.

(1) What is consumer behavior?

(2) What are the most important internal factors which influence the buying behavior of consumers?

(3) In most consumers' perceptions, what are the clues for quality of products?

(4) What are the two types within reference groups?

(5) What factors make up the cultural factors which influence the buying behavior of consumers?

(6) What does sub-culture refer to?

(7) What are the buying behavior of those three social classes like?

(8) What economic factors are mentioned to influence the buying behavior of customers?

(9) What does consumer credit refer to? And how does consumer credit influence consumer behavior?

(10) Why can occupation or profession of a person influence his buying behavior?

参考译文（Text A）

消费者行为

消费者行为是指消费者经历的过程，以及他们对产品或服务的反应。它与消费有关，与消费者购买和消费商品和服务的过程有关。消费者认识到需求，并通过一个过程来满足这些需求。消费者行为包括购买产品的种类、花费的金额、购买的频率以及影响其购买决策的因素。影响消费者行为的因素很多,既有内部因素,也有外部因素。内部因素包括态度、需求、动机、偏好和感知过程，外部因素包括营销活动、社会经济因素和文化方面。也有影响消费者行为的物理因素。例如，如果一个消费者饿了，那么这种饥饿的物理感觉会影响他，这样他就会去买一个三明治来满足饥饿感。

1. 消费者参与度

参与度是一个物体或事件被感知到的重要性或与个人的相关性，它是关于消费者对产品或品牌的依恋程度和忠诚度。参与度包括认知和情感两个方面：它同时作用于大脑和情感。例如,一位车主可能会说,“我爱我的旧大使车（情感）,因为它从不让我失望（认知）。”参与度可以有三个层次：

如果属性与结果无关，就会出现低参与度；

如果属性只和功能有关，则会出现中等参与度；

如果消费者认为产品属性与最终目标或价值紧密相关，就会产生高产品参与度。虽然是决策者的行为决定了对决策的参与程度，但是增加高参与度的可能性有三个常见的因素，即相对于收入的购买成本、购买过程所需的时间，以及购买在多大程度上反映了自我形象。

高参与度购买的东西是指那些在消费者生活方式中占有重要地位的产品。换句话说，它们涉及最好是一开始就做正确的重要决策。通常消费者高度参与的产品也是消费者最了解的产品，并且他对该产品有明确的立场。例如，精通技术的 IT 专业人员可能对性能最好的个人计算机有非常明确的看法。不一致的信息（例如，销售人员试图说服他尝试另一个品牌）会被低估和贬损，甚至可能降低对信息来源的尊重（IT 专业人员会认为销售人员很愚蠢，或者认为销售人员正在试图销售处理劣质品牌的计算机）。另一方面，计算机新手不太可能与产品建立密切的联系，因此他们更愿意倾听销售人员的意见。这意味着高参与度消费者很难被说服，他们不容易被广告甚至是有说服力的销售说辞左右。高参与度总是有很强的情感成分，但这并不一定意味着高成本的投入。人们也会爱上便宜的产品。因此，参与度并不总是等同于价格。高参与度商品不一定是高价商品，低参与度商品也不一定便宜。吸烟的人可能会对价格低廉的品牌香烟非常感兴趣。相反，一些人可能不会对一家昂贵的五星级酒店产生浓厚的兴趣。

2. 消费者行为类型

需求是无限的，然而满足这些需求的资源却是有限的，所以消费者在购买任何产品之前都要理性思考。买牙膏和买豪华车完全不同。商品越贵，消费者需要的信息就越多。基于买方在购买任何产品时的参与程度，可将消费者的购买行为分成四种类型。

2.1 复杂型购买行为

当消费者高度参与购买过程，并意识到品牌间的重大差异时，他们会经历复杂的购买行为。当产品价格昂贵、购买频率低、风险高、自我表现力强时，消费者就会高度参与。通常情况下，消费者对产品类别了解不多，需要学习很多东西。例如，一个购买个人计算机的人可能不知道要寻找什么属性，该产品的许多功能，如“16K 内存”“光盘存储”“屏幕分辨率”，对他来说毫无意义。这位购买者就将经历一个学习过程，首先培养对产品的信念，然后是态度，最后再做出深思熟虑的购买选择。高参与度产品的营销人员必须懂得收集信息，并对高参与度消费者的行为进行评估。

市场营销人员需要制定策略，帮助买方了解产品类别的属性、相对重要性，以及公司品牌在更重要属性上的高知名度。营销人员需要区分品牌特征，使用平面媒体和大量的信息描述品牌优势，并激励商店销售人员和购买者认识的人来影响最终的品牌选择。

2.2 和谐型购买行为

有时，消费者高度参与了购买过程，但却没有看出品牌之间的差别。高参与度再次基于这样一个事实，即购买的物品是昂贵的，购买频率低且有风险。在这种情况下，购买者会货比三家，了解有哪些可购产品。但他们会很快购买，因为品牌差异并不明显。买方可能主要是对价格是否合理、购买是否方便作出反应。

购买后，消费者可能会因为注意到产品的某些令人不安的特性或听到其他品牌的优点而感到不值得。消费者将密切注意那些可能证明其决定合理的信息。他们会先采取行动，然后获得新的信念，最终形成各种态度。这时，营销传播旨在提供信念和评价，帮助消费者对自己的品牌选择感觉良好。

2.3 习惯型购买行为

许多产品是在消费者参与度低、品牌差异不明显的情况下购买的。以买盐为例：消费者几乎不熟悉这类产品，他们会去商店购买某个品牌的盐。如果他们一直买同一个品牌的盐，那是出于习惯，而不是因为很强的品牌忠诚度。

有充分的证据表明，消费者对大多数低成本、经常购买的产品的参与度很低。在这些情况下，消费者的行为不会以正常的“信念—态度—行为”序列呈现。消费者不会广泛地搜索有关品牌的信息，评估它们的特性，并对购买哪个品牌做出重大决定。相反，当他们看电视或平面广告时，他们是信息的被动接受者。重复播放的广告创造的是品牌熟悉度，而不是品牌信念。消费者对一个品牌没有形成强烈的态度，只是因为熟悉了而选择它。购买后，他们甚至可能不会评估，因为他们对产品的参与度不高。所以购买过程首先是通过被动学习形成品牌信念，然后发生购买行为，最后可能是评价购买行为。

很少有品牌差异的低参与度产品的营销人员发现，利用价格和促销来刺激产品试用是有效的，因为买方并没有高度忠实于某个品牌。广告在宣传低参与度产品时应注意：广告文案应该只强调关键点，视觉符号和图像很重要，因为它们容易让人记住并与品牌有关联。

2.4 求变型购买行为

有些购买的特点是消费者参与度低，但品牌差异显著。在这种情况下，经常可以看到消费者做大量的品牌转移，购买饼干就是一个例子。消费者有一定的信念，并在没有太多评价的情况下选择某个品牌的饼干，且在消费过程中对其进行评价。但是下一次，消费者可能会因为厌倦或者希望有不同的口味而选择另一个品牌。品牌转移是因为寻求变化而不是因为不满意。

在这类产品中，市场大品牌和小品牌的营销策略是不同的。大品牌将通过控制货架空间、避免缺货以及赞助频繁的提示性广告等方式来鼓励习惯性的购买行为。具有挑战能力的公司将通过降低价格、提供优惠券、免费样品、发布新事物的广告来鼓励顾客的求变行为。

3. 消费者行为模型

消费者行为模型是营销人员用来理解消费者购买或不购买某种产品的基本工具，包括黑盒模型、个人变量模型和综合模型，每个模型都有特定的关注点。黑盒模型关注外部刺激，个人变量模型关注消费者内部刺激，综合模型研究外部刺激和内部刺激的结合。

消费者行为模型因所研究行为的复杂性而异。对于营销人员来说，研究消费者行为的主要目的是更好地了解消费者，从而在营销策略中有效地锁定消费者市场。这是一门非常复杂的科学，营销者可以密切观察广告和消费者反应之间的关系，并将两者关联起来。但让人们购买或不购买一个产品这个主要问题过于个人化，无法用一种甚至几种行为模型来解释。

3.1 黑盒模型

黑盒模型，又称刺激—反应模型，是消费者行为模型中最简单的一种。黑盒可以被认为是消费者大脑中负责做出购买决策的区域。环境刺激，如经济、技术和文化，与营销刺激，如产品、价格和促销，在做出决策的黑盒中结合起来。该模型忽略了消费者内部的变量，将重点放在产生期望反应的市场和环境变量上。

3.2 个人变量模型

个人变量模型是消费者行为模型的另一种主要类型。与以外部刺激为主要焦点的黑盒模型不同，个人变量模型研究的是影响消费者行为和购买决策的内部因素。这个模型忽略了外部刺激，比如营销技巧，而专注于内部的心理变量。这些变量包括生活方式、动机和个性。它还关注个人决策过程，如问题识别、替代性评估以及购后行为。

3.3 综合模型

消费者行为模型的最后一种主要类型是综合模型。顾名思义，这种模型在研究购买行为的同时考虑了环境和内部刺激因素。这类模型是最复杂的研究之一，因为有许多变量在起作用。该模型的益处在于它是唯一可以用来研究不同的外部刺激在不同类型的人格和人口统计中如何反应的模型。然而，由于变量的数量较大，很难确定这些研究结论的准确性。

Case How Does Food Company Phillsbury Arouse Consuming Passions in China?

Unit 4

Text A

The Consumer Decision-Making Process

The consumer decision making is a complex process which involves all the stages from problem recognition to post-purchase activities. All the consumers have their own needs in their daily lives and these needs make them make different decisions. These decisions can be complex depending on the consumers' opinion about a particular product, evaluating and comparing, selecting and purchasing among the different types of product. Therefore, understanding and realizing the core issue of the process of the consumer decision making and utilize the theories in practice is becoming a common view point by many companies and people.

Five Stage Model initially proposed by Cox et al. (1983) is considered to be one of the most common models of consumer decision-making process and it involves five various stages. These stages are problem/need recognition, information search, evaluation of alternatives, purchase decision, post-purchase evaluation. This simple model clearly illustrates and explains how the consumers make a purchasing decision.

1. *Problem/Need recognition*

Problem/Need recognition is the first stage of the model. Recognition of a problem arises in the situation where an individual realizes the difference between the actual state of affairs and desired state of affairs. The recognition of a problem or need depends on different situations and circumstances such as personal or professional and this recognition results in creation of a purchasing idea. For instance, consumers may recognize the need to buy a laptop when there is need to carry it and use it in different places, which is convenient compared to a desktop computer.

Need recognition at various levels often occurs during the process of encountering with the product at various circumstances. In other words, an individual might not be aware of the need for a specific product until he encounters with the product as a result of engaging in "window-shopping", media advertisements, or in a range of other circumstances. The human need has no limit. Therefore, the problem recognition is a repetitive in nature. According to Maslow theory, human being is always dissatisfied, when an individual's one need is satisfied, another one will come out and this trend continues repetitively. A consumer buying process example at this phase could be a college freshman, Sarah, who has a computer that is starting to run slowly. She is getting ready to start the semester and needs a computer that will efficiently help her with her assignments.

2. Information search

The next stage of the model is information search. Once the need is recognized, the consumer is likely to search more product-related information before directly making a purchase decision. However, different individuals are involved in search process differently depending on their knowledge about the product, their previous experience or purchases or on some external information such as feedback from others.

Information searching process itself can be divided into two parts: the internal search and external search. In the internal search, consumers compare the alternatives from their own experiences and memories, depending on their own past experiences and knowledge. For example, searching for fast food can be an example for internal search because customers often use their knowledge and tastes to choose the right product they need rather than asking someone for an advice. On the other hand, external search ends to be for bigger purchases such as home appliances or gadgets. For instance, consumers who wish to buy new furniture or a mobile phone tend to ask friends' opinion and advice or search in the magazines and media before making a purchasing decision.

Customer example: Sarah, the college student, may start seeking information to help resolve her immediate problem, which is speeding up her computer. Depending on what she finds, she may also begin searching for options for purchasing a new computer.

3. Evaluation of alternatives

After gathering enough information, the consumer gets into comparing and evaluating that information in order to make the right choice. In this stage the consumer analyzes all the information obtained through the search and considers various alternative products and services, comparing them according to the needs and wants. Moreover, other various aspects of the product such as size, quality, brand, and price are considered at this stage. Therefore, this stage is considered to be an important stage during the whole consumer decision-making process. The process of evaluation of alternatives can sometimes be difficult, time consuming and full of pressure for a consumer. This is because it is quite hard to find an ideal product or service that satisfies the needs of the customer as there are numerous factors that hinder the consumer purchasing decision-making process. For instance, when it comes to online hotel reservation or furniture purchasing evaluation process, it can be quite complex. Several factors and aspects need to be considered before making a purchasing decision. Factors such as age, culture, taste, and budget have all impact on the evaluation process by the consumer. For example, when purchasing a furniture, the young people consider the factors such as convenience and price whereas the old people are likely to consider the quality and design. Marketers attempt to influence the outcome of this step in three ways. First, they try to educate consumers about attributes they view as important in evaluating a particular class of products. Usually they will emphasize the dimensions in which their product excels. Second, they identify which evaluative criteria are important to an individual and attempt to show why a specific brand fulfills those criteria. Last, they try to induce a customer to expand the evoked set to include the product being marketed.

Customer example: In this phase, Sarah might be making a comparison list of multiple computers. The list may include prices, features, and reviews.

4. *Purchase decision*

Once the information search and evaluation process is over, the consumer makes the purchasing decision and this stage is considered to be the most important stage throughout the whole process. In this stage, the consumer makes decision to make a final purchase as he or she has already reviewed all the alternatives and came to a final decision point. Purchases can further be classified into three different types: planned purchase, partially purchase, and impulse purchase. There are a number of factors that can affect the purchasing process. For example, the desired product may not be available at the stock. In this case, the purchase process is delayed and consumer may consider buying the product through online stores rather than visiting traditional physical stores. Department store sales assistants also play in integral role in terms of impacting consumer purchase decision in a positive way from a business point of view and this impact must not be done in a pushy manner, in which case it can prove to be counter-productive.

Customer Example: Now that the college student, Sarah, has decided to buy, she is likely eager to make the purchase and get her computer. She may, therefore, be more likely to buy the computer if she gets free and expedited shipping.

5. *Post-purchase evaluation*

The final stage in the consumer decision-making process is post-purchase evaluation stage. Many companies tend to ignore this stage as this takes place after the transaction has been done. However, this stage is critical to retain customers. In short, customers compare products with their expectations and are either satisfied or dissatisfied. This can then greatly affect the decision process for a similar purchase from the same company in the future, mainly at the information search stage and evaluation of alternatives stage. If customers are satisfied, this results in brand loyalty, and the information search and evaluation of alternative stages are often fast-tracked or skipped completely. As a result, brand loyalty is the ultimate aim of many companies.

On the basis of either being satisfied or dissatisfied, a customer will spread either positive or negative feedback about the product. The opinions of peers, friends, and family regarding the purchases made is specified as one of the most important factors affecting the outcome of post-purchase evaluation, whose opinions regarding product evaluations tend to impact customer's level of satisfaction regardless of their level of objectivity. Also, cognitive dissonance (consumer confusion in marketing terms) is common at this stage; customers often go through the feelings of post-purchase psychological tension or anxiety. Questions include: "Have I made the right decision?", "Is it a good choice?", etc. Therefore, at this stage, companies should carefully create positive post-purchase communication to engage the customers.

Customer example: When Sarah makes it to this phase of her buying decision process, she is using the computer and discovering what she likes and doesn't like. Reading resources that show her how to better utilize the computer could make her like it more.

New Words

stage [steɪdʒ] *n.* 阶段；舞台

recognition [ˌrekəg'nɪʃn] *n.* 认识，识别；承认，认可

common ['kɒmən] *adj.* 普通的；共同的，共有的

initially [ɪ'nɪʃəli] *adv.* 最初，起初

propose [prə'pəuz] *vt.* 提议，建议

actual ['æktʃuəl] *adj.* 实际的，真实的

circumstance ['sɜːkəmstəns] *n.* 环境，境遇，条件，状况

professional [prə'feʃənl] *adj.* 专业的，职业的

creation [kri'eɪʃn] *n.* 制造，创造；创造物，产物

convenient [kən'viːniənt] *adj.* 方便的

encounter [ɪn'kauntə] *vi.* 碰见，尤指不期而遇

repetitive [rɪ'petətɪv] *adj.* 重复的

dissatisfied [dɪs'sætɪsfaɪd] *adj.* 感到不满的，不满意的

phase [feɪz] *n.* 阶段；方面，侧面

assignment [ə'saɪnmənt] *n.* 任务，工作

feedback ['fiːdbæk] *n.* 反馈

appliance [ə'plaɪəns] *n.* 家用电器；器具，器械，装置

gadget ['gædʒɪt] *n.* 玩意，小配件，小装置

furniture ['fɜːnɪtʃə] *n.* 家具

resolve [rɪ'zɒlv] *vt.* 解决；决心，决定

immediate [ɪ'miːdiət] *adj.* 立即的；直接的，最接近的

option ['ɒpʃn] *n.* 选项；选择权；选择

analyze ['ænəlaɪz] *vt.* 分析

reservation [ˌrezə'veɪʃn] *n.* 预订，预约；保留

outcome ['aʊtkʌm] *n.* 结果；成果

emphasize ['emfəsaɪz] *vt.* 强调，着重

dimension [daɪ'menʃn] *n.* 尺寸；维度；范围

excel [ɪk'sel] *vt.* 优于，擅长

evaluative [ɪvælju'eɪtɪv] *adj.* 可估价的

induce [ɪn'djuːs] *vt.* 引起；归纳；引诱

expand [ɪk'spænd] *vt.* 扩张，使……变大

evoke [ɪ'vəʊk] *vt.* 唤起，产生，引起

comparison [kəm'pærɪsn] *n.* 比较，对照

multiple ['mʌltɪpl] *adj.* 多重的，多个的

review [rɪ'vjuː] *vt.* 回顾；评论；复习

impulse ['ɪmpʌls] *n.* 冲动，搏动	retain [rɪ'teɪn] *vt.* 保持；留在心中，记住
integral ['ɪntɪgrəl] *adj.* 完整的；构成整体所必需的	skip [skɪp] *vt.* 跳过；略过；遗漏
counter-productive [ˌkaʊntə-prə'dʌktɪv] *adj.* 产生相反结果的，事与愿违的	ultimate ['ʌltɪmət] *adj.* 极限的；最后的；终极的
expedite ['ekspədaɪt] *vt.* 加速，加快	objectivity [əb'dʒektɪvəti] *n.* 客观性，客观现实

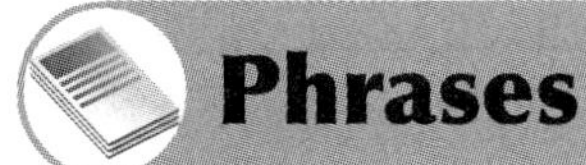

Phrases

depend on 依赖，依靠；取决于；随……而定
arise in 产生于
result in 引起，导致
encounter with 与……不期而遇，碰见
as a result of 因为……，由于……的结果
a rang of 一系列
in nature 实际上；性质上，本质上
according to 根据，按照
come out 出现；出版
be divided into 划分为，被分成
tend to 倾向，易于
speed up（使）加速，增速
when it comes to 当涉及，当谈到
attempt to 尝试或企图……
be classified into 分（类）为……
partially planned purchase 部分计划性购买
impulse purchase 冲动消费，冲动购物
at the stock 库存的；现货的
physical store 实体店
sales assistant 销售助理
in a positive way 以积极的态度；以正面的方式
from a business point of view 从商业的角度而言
in a pushy manner 以咄咄逼人的方式
now that 既然；由于，因为
be eager to 盼望，渴望
regardless of 不管，不顾

Exercises

EX. 1 Answer the following questions according to Text A.

(1) What is the consumer decision making?
(2) What stages does Five Stage Model of consumer decision-making process involve?
(3) In what situation does recognition of a problem arise?
(4) Why is human being always dissatisfied according to Maslow theory?
(5) What parts can information searching process itself be divided into?

(6) Why is searching for fast food an example for internal search?
(7) Why can the process of evaluation of alternatives be sometimes difficult for a consumer?
(8) What types can purchases be further classified into in the stage of purchasing decision?
(9) Which stage is critical to retain customers?
(10) Whose opinions might be one of the most important factors affecting the outcome of post-purchase evaluation?

EX. 2 **Translate the following phrases from English into Chinese and vice versa.**

(1) at the stock ____________________
(2) depend on ____________________
(3) from a business point of view ____________________
(4) impulse purchase ____________________
(5) partially planned purchase ____________________
(6) 耗费时间的 ____________________
(7) 划分为，被分成 ____________________
(8) 强调，着重 ____________________
(9) 多重的，多个的 ____________________
(10) 反馈 ____________________

EX. 3 **Translate the following into Chinese.**

In an early study of the buyer decision process literature, Frank Nicosia identified three types of buyer decision-making models. They are the univariate model (He called it the “simple scheme”.) in which only one behavioral determinant was allowed in a stimulus-response type of relationship; the multi-variate model (He called it a “reduced form scheme”.) in which numerous independent variables were assumed to determine buyer behavior; and finally the “system of equations” model (He called it a “structural scheme” or “process scheme”.) in which numerous functional relations (either univariate or multi-variate) interact in a complex system of equations. He concluded that only this third type of model is capable of expressing the complexity of buyer decision processes. Nicosia builds a comprehensive model involving five modules. The encoding module includes determinants like “attributes of the brand” “environmental factors” “consumer’s attributes” “attributes of the organization”, and “attributes of the message”. Other modules in the system include consumer decoding, search and evaluation, decision, and consumption.

EX. 4 **Fill in the blanks with the words and phrase given below.**

diminishing	substitute	utility	measure	assumptions
available	maximize	capable of	allocate	marginal

Economic Man Model

In economic man model, consumers follow the principle of maximum utility based on the law of diminishing marginal utility. Economic man model is based on the following effects.

Price effect: The lower the price of the product is, the more the quantity purchase will be.

Substitution effect: The lower the price of the (1)________ product is, the lower the utility of the original product purchase will be.

Income effect: When more income is earned, or more money is (2)________, quantity purchased will be more.

The economic theory of buyer's decisionmaking was based on the following (3)________.

As consumer resources are limited, he would (4)________ the available money which will maximize the satisfaction of his needs and wants.

Consumers have complete knowledge about the (5)________ of each product and service, i.e., they are (6)________ completing the accurate satisfaction that each item is likely to produce.

As more units of the same item are purchased, the (7)________ utility or satisfaction provided by the next unit of the item will keep on decreasing, according to the law of (8)________ marginal utility.

Price is used as a(n) (9)________ of sacrifice in obtaining the goods or services. The overall objective of the buyer is to (10)________ his satisfaction out of the act of purchase.

Text B

Types of Decision-Making Process and DMU

1. Types of decision-making process

Decision making is an art and a science which has been studied over generations. The secret of marketing lies in learning what the customer wants and how to influence the customers decision-making process so that he buys our product above competition.

Behind a simple decision making process, there are many thought processes which influence the decision making. A buyer may take an emotional, spur of the moment decision, or he may take a well thought out and researched decision. Based on his observation, different processes can be defined for decision making.

Decision making mainly depends on the involvement of the customer. There are high-involvement products and there are low-involvement products. Similarly, there are consumer products and industrial products. Involvement in industrial products will generally be higher as compared to commercial products because the amount of investment in industrial products is also huge. Thus based on the above arguments, there are mainly three types of decision-making processes which can be defined.

1.1 Extensive decision-making process

This type of decision-making process is used when the product is a very high-involvement product, possible a high-investment product as well. Typical examples include buying a house for a consumer, or buying a new manufacturing plant in case of industries. In both cases, there are multiple people involved, and the decision making is extensive as the customer wants to get maximum benefits. There are also risks involved in such endeavours, hence extensive decision making is done.

1.2 Limited decision-making process

Buying a television or buying a car will be a limited decision-making process. When you are buying such white goods, the investment is nominal and not very high. At the same time, you have some experience with the product as you regularly watch television and you regularly sit in cars. Thus, you do not spend as much time on buying these products. Nowadays, the limited decision-making process is further helped with the presence of online media, where people know a lot about the product while sitting at home. The speed of the limited decision making is dependent on the customer's experience and his knowledge about the product as well as the amount of time he has to make the decision.

1.3 Routine decision-making process

Routine decision making happens in day to day life like buying a soap or shampoo. In this case, the customer is more likely to stick to a single brand for a long time. He is unlikely to switch to different brands because he wants to invest minimum time in routine decision making. There are a lot of things which influence the routine decision-making process, like regular advertising by FMCG companies. This is because the routine things are brought over and over again. And once the company gets such a customer, they are likely to reap long-term profits from the same customer.

Thus, the above three are the different type of decision-making processes. Depending on the type of customer and the amount of investment in the product, the decision-making process may vary from time to time.

2. DMU

A decision-making unit (DMU), also called buying center, brings together "all those members of an organization who become involved in the buying process for a particular product or service".

The concept of a DMU was developed in 1967 by Robinson, Farris, and Wind. A DMU consists of all the people of an organization, who are involved in the buying decision. The decision to purchase involves those with purchasing and financial expertise; those with technical expertise and of course the top-management. The concept of a DMU formulates the understanding of purchasing decisionmaking in complex environments. Some of the key factors influencing DMU's activities include:

- Buy class (e.g., straight rebuy, new task or modified rebuy);
- Product type [e.g., materials, components, plant and equipment and MRO (maintenance,

repair and operation)];

• Importance of the purchase.

2.1 Members of the DMU

The decision-making unit is a collection or team of individuals who participate in a buyer decision process. Generally, DMU relates to business or organizational buying decisions rather than to those of a family for example. There are a number of key players in this process namely the initiators, the gatekeepers, the buyers, the deciders, the users, and the influencers. Let's consider these individually prior to applying the decision-making unit to an example of organizational buying.

Influencers are those who may have a persuasive role in relation to the deciders. They may be specialists who make recommendations based upon experience and their knowledge of products and services. Examples are consultants employed by businesses to help deciders make a final decision, or another example might be lawyers employed to offer legal advice. There are also informal influencers such as family and friends, and people that you meet at trade associations or informal gatherings. The relationship among the key players will be different for every organization and in every purchase situation. Individuals may be influencers as well as initiators, and therefore, none of these categories is mutually exclusive, that is, stand alone, since there is much crossover and blurring around the edges of roles.

Initiators are the players who recognize that there is a need to be satisfied or a problem to be solved. This might come from a drive for efficiency due to the fact that some equipment will need replacing. There could be many reasons which stimulate the initiation.

Gatekeepers are individuals who press the stop/go button in the process. Often gatekeepers will be proactive in searching for information and delivering recommendations for those decision-makers further up the line. On other occasions, gatekeepers can be seen stalling the flow of the decision-making process.

Buyers are the professional function within an organization generally responsible for purchasing. They are given a brief with a series of criteria against which to judge potential products or services and their suppliers. They tend to be responsible for sourcing and negotiation.

Deciders in a large organization certainly are responsible for making the final deal or decision. Their role carries the responsibility of placing the final order. They might be senior managers or agents acting on behalf of an organization in the market. The deciders will review information provided from lower down the buyer decision process from the buyers, gatekeepers, and the original initiators.

Users are those who put the service or product into operation once the deal has been clinched. Their opinions will be important especially if they are using manufacturing equipment, flying aircraft, using software to improve customer satisfaction, and so on. Users will be heavily involved in the post-purchase evaluation phase of the buyer decision-making process.

In some cases the DMU is an informal ad hoc group, but in other cases, it is a formally sanctioned group with specific mandates, criteria, and procedures. The formation of the buying centers or decision-making unit (DMU) is considered as an important process and therefore depends on several factors like: the size of the company and skills of the personalities and staff members, the type of product/service that is needed, the type of the organization, the different buying process stages (BPS), the duration of the relationships between the buyer (the organization) and sellers or suppliers, and the technologies that are used in the production.

2.2 Types of buying decisions

There are four main buying decisions that can be distinguished in the area of organizational buyers.

Straight rebuy: This is a routine, low involvement purchase. Minimal information is needed and consideration of alternatives is not needed. This type of purchase is handled by the purchase department and is usually purchased from a list of approved suppliers. Examples of straight rebuy are repeat purchases of office supplies, and small components.

Modified rebuy: This type of purchase is similar to a straight rebuy with more information and people involved. The buyer may want to reconsider suppliers, prices, terms, or modify product specifications.

New-task buying: New-task buying is deemed the most complex buying situation because it is a first-time purchase of a major product. Several people are involved in the decision because there can be high amounts of money and risk. Much information is gathered and evaluations of alternatives are explored. It is also complex as the decision makers have little experience with the product before the purchase can be made. The buying center has the challenge of finding out all the organization's needs and communicating the product's ability of meeting the needs.

Systems buying: This type of buying is purchasing a packaged solution to a problem from a single supplier. This originates from governments buying packages, such as a major communications system. Instead of buying separate components, buyers look for suppliers who supply the components and assemble the package for them.

2.3 Decision-making process

When the DMU wants to purchase a certain product or service, the following steps are taken inside the buying center or the DMU.

• Need or problem recognition: The recognition can start for two reasons. The first reason can be to solve a specific problem of the company. The other reason can be to improve a company's current operations/performance or to pursue new market opportunities.

• Determining product specification: The specification includes the peculiarities which the product/service that is going to be purchased must contain.

• Supplier and product search: This process contains the search for suppliers that can meet a company's product or service needs. First a supplier that matches with the specifications of the company has to be found. The second condition is that the supplier can satisfy the organizations financial and supply requirements.

• Evaluation of proposals and selection of suppliers: The different possible suppliers will be evaluated by the different departments of the company.

• Selection of order routine: This stadium starts after the selection of the supplier. It mainly consists of negotiating and agreeing with the supplier about certain details.

• Performance feedback and evaluation: Performance and quality of the purchased goods will be evaluated.

In this process of making decisions different roles can be given to certain members of the center of the unit depending on the importance of the part of the organization.

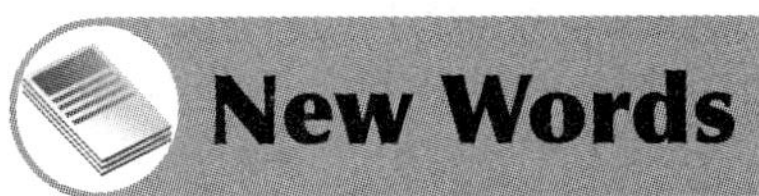

New Words

spur [spɜː] *n.* 激励因素

commercial [kə'mɜːʃl] *adj.* 商业的，贸易的

typical ['tɪpɪkl] *adj.* 典型的；特有的，特别的；代表性的

endeavor [ɪn'devə] *n.* 尽力，努力；力图

nominal ['nɒmɪnl] *adj.* 微不足道的；票面上的；名义上的

presence ['prezns] *n.* 出席，到场；存在

routine [ruː'tiːn] *n.* 常规，例行程序

shampoo [ʃæm'puː] *n.* 洗发香波，洗发剂

minimum ['mɪnɪməm] *n.* 最低限度；最小量

reap [riːp] *vt.* 收获，获得

modify ['mɒdɪfaɪ] *vt.* 修改，更改；修饰

initiator [ɪ'nɪʃieɪtə] *n.* 创始者，首倡者，发起人

specialist ['speʃəlɪst] *n.* 专家，行家

consultant [kən'sʌltənt] *n.* 顾问，咨询者

employ [ɪm'plɔɪ] *vt.* 雇用；使用，利用

mutually ['mjuːtʃuəli] *adv.* 互相地

exclusively [ɪk'skluːsɪvli] *adv.* 专门地，特定地；专有地，排外地

crossover ['krɒsəʊvə] *n.* 交叉，交叠；跨界

blurring ['blɜːrɪŋ] *n.* 模糊

sourcing ['sɔːsɪŋ] *n.* 采购

negotiation [nɪˌgəʊʃi'eɪʃn] *n.* 协商，谈判

clinch [klɪntʃ] *vt.* 解决（争端、交易），达成（协议）

sanction ['sæŋkʃn] *n.* 制裁，处罚；约束力；批准，认可

mandate ['mændeɪt] *vi.* 强制执行；委托办理

minimal ['mɪnɪməl] *adj.* 最小的，极少的

handle ['hændl] *vt.* 处理，对待；操作

deem [diːm] *vt.* 认为，视为；主张，断定

major ['meɪdʒə] *adj.* 主要的，重要的

pursue [pə'sjuː] *vt.* 追求；追捕

peculiarity [pɪˌkjuːli'ærəti] *n.* 特性，特质

contain [kən'teɪn] *vt.* 容纳，包含；抑制，克制

proposal [prə'pəʊzl] *n.* 建议，提议；求婚

stadium ['steɪdiəm] *n.* 体育场，运动场

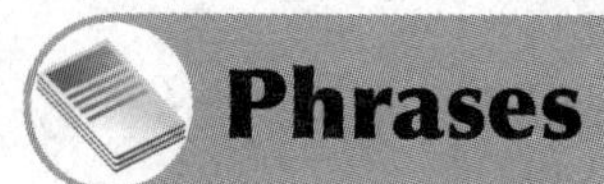

Phrases

lie in 在于；位于
manufacturing plant 制造厂，生产厂
in case of 万一，如果发生；防备
white goods 白色家电
online media 在线媒体，网络媒体
stick to 坚持；遵守
switch to 切换到，转到，转变成
in relation to 与……有关
make recommendations 提出建议
trade association 贸易协会
informal gathering 非正式聚会
place an order 定购（货物），预订
carry the responsibility 承担责任
on behalf of 为了……的利益；代表……
ad hoc group 特设小组
be similar to 与……相似，类似于
originate from 起源；来自……，源于……
match with 使……与……相配

Abbreviations

DMU (Decision-Making Unit) 决策单元
FMCG (Fast Moving Consumer Goods) 快速消费品
MRO (Maintenance, Repair, and Operation) 非生产原料性质的工业用品
BPS (Buying Process Stage) 购买过程阶段

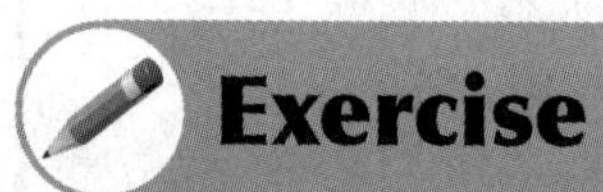

Exercise

EX. Answer the following questions according to Text B.

(1) What does the secret of marketing lie in?
(2) What are the three main types of decision-making processes?
(3) When is extensive decision-making process used?
(4) What does the speed of the limited decision making depend on?
(5) Whom does the decision to purchase involve?
(6) Who are the key players in the buyer's decision-making process?
(7) Who are initiators?
(8) What are the main four types of buying decisions?

(9) Why is new-task buying deemed the most complex buying situation?

(10) What steps are taken inside the buying center when the DMU wants to purchase a certain product or service?

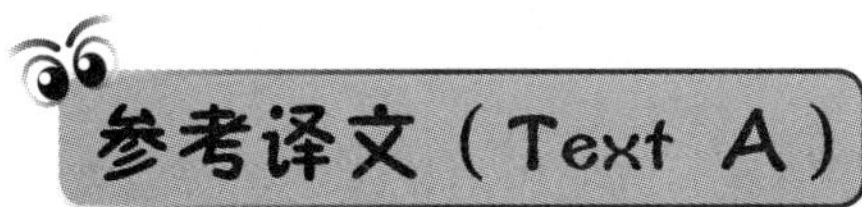

参考译文（Text A）

消费者决策过程

消费者决策是一个复杂的过程，涉及从问题识别到购买后活动的各个阶段。所有的消费者在日常生活中都有自己的需求，这些需求让他们做出不同的决策。这些决策可能是复杂的，取决于消费者对特定产品的看法，对不同类型产品的评估和比较、选择和购买。因此，理解和认识消费者决策过程的核心问题，并在实践中运用这些理论，已经成为许多企业和人们的共识。

Cox 等（1983）最初提出的五阶段模型被认为是消费者决策过程中最常见的模型之一，它涉及五个不同的阶段。这些阶段是问题 / 需求识别、信息搜索、选择评估、购买决策和购买后评价。这一简单的模型清楚地说明和解释了消费者是如何做出购买决定的。

1. 问题 / 需求识别

问题 / 需求识别是模型的第一阶段。当一个人意识到实际状态和期望状态之间的差异时，就会产生对问题的认识。对问题或需求的认识取决于不同的情境和情况，如个人的或专业的情况，且这种认识导致消费者产生购买想法。例如，在需要携带比台式电脑更方便的笔记本电脑，并在不同的地方使用它时，消费者可能会意识到购买笔记本电脑的需求。

在不同情况下接触具体产品的过程中，往往会出现不同层次的需求识别。换句话说，直到在“橱窗购物”、媒体广告或一系列其他情况下接触到该产品的时候，他或她才可能意识到对某一特定产品的需求是无限的。因此，问题识别在本质上具有重复性。根据马斯洛理论，人总是不满足的，当一个人的一种需求得到满足时，另一种需求就会出现，这种趋势会不断重复。大学新生莎拉可能是消费者购买过程这一阶段的例子。她的电脑出现了运行缓慢的情况。她就要开学了，需要一台新的电脑，能帮助她有效完成作业。

2. 信息搜索

该模型的下一个阶段是信息搜索。一旦需求得到确认，消费者很可能会在直接做出购买决定之前搜索更多与产品相关的信息。然而，不同的人在搜索过程中所涉及的内容是不同的，这取决于他们对产品的了解程度、以往的经验或购买情况，或一些外部信息，如来自他人的反馈。

信息搜索过程本身可以分为两部分：内部搜索和外部搜索。在内部搜索中，消费者根据自己过去的经验和知识，从自己的经验和记忆中比较各种可选产品。例如，搜索快餐可能就是内部搜索的一个例子，因为客户经常根据自己的了解和口味来选择他们需要的适当产品，而不是向别人寻求建议。另一方面，外部搜索是为了购买诸如家用电器或家具等较大产品而进行的。例如，想要购买新家具或手机的消费者往往会先征求朋友的意见和建议，或在杂志和媒体上搜索相关信息，然后再做出购买决定。

客户案例：大学生莎拉可能会开始寻找信息，以帮助解决当前的问题，即加快电脑运行速度的问题。根据找到的信息，她可能还会开始搜索购买新电脑的各种选择。

3. 选择评估

在收集足够的信息之后，消费者开始比较和评估这些信息，以便做出正确的选择。在这个阶段，消费者分析通过搜索获得的所有信息，考虑各种备选产品和服务，并根据需求和需要进行比较。此外，这个阶段还考虑了产品的其他各个方面，如尺寸、质量、品牌和价格。因此，这一阶段被认为是整个消费者决策过程中的重要阶段。对消费者来说，评估备选产品的过程有时是困难的、耗时的和充满压力的。这是因为很难找到理想的产品或服务来满足客户的需求，因为有很多因素阻碍消费者的购买决策过程。例如，当涉及在线酒店预订或家具购买评估过程时，这个过程可能非常复杂。在做出购买决定之前，消费者需要考虑几个方面的因素。年龄、文化、品位、预算等都会影响消费者的评估过程。例如，在购买家具时，年轻人考虑的是便利和价格，而老年人可能考虑的是质量和设计。营销人员试图通过三种方式来影响选择评估的结果。首先，他们试图让消费者了解他们认为在评估某一类产品时需要考虑的重要属性，通常他们会强调自己产品的优势；其次，他们确定出哪些评价标准对个人来说是重要的，并试图说明某个特定的品牌满足这些标准的原因；最后，他们试图引导顾客扩大备考组，使其包括正在推销的产品。

客户案例：在这个阶段，莎拉可能正在制作有关多台电脑的比较列表。列表可能包括价格、特性和评论。

4. 购买决策

一旦信息搜索和评估过程结束，消费者就会做出购买决策，所以这个阶段被认为是整个过程中最重要的阶段。在这个阶段，消费者做出最后的购买决定，因为他或她已经审查了所有的备选产品，并到了最后的决定时刻。购买可以进一步分为三种不同的类型：计划性购买、部分计划性购买和冲动性购买。许多因素可以影响购买过程。例如，想要的产品可能在库存中没有现货。在这种情况下，购买过程被延迟，消费者可能会考虑网购，而不是去传统的实体店购买。商场销售助理也发挥着不可或缺的作用。他们从商业的角度主动积极地影响着消费者的购买决策。他们不能以咄咄逼人的方式来影响消费者，否则，可能会适得其反。

客户案例：既然大学生莎拉已经决定买了，并且她可能很想买一台电脑。因此，如果她能享受免费且快捷的送货服务，她便很有可能购买这台电脑。

5. 购买后评价

消费者决策过程的最后阶段是购后评价阶段。许多公司往往会忽略这个阶段，因为这个阶段发生在交易完成之后。然而，这个阶段对于留住客户是至关重要的。简而言之，顾客将产品与他们的期望进行比较，要么满意，要么不满意。这就会在很大程度上影响未来从同一家公司购买类似商品的决策过程，其影响主要是在信息搜索和选择评估阶段。如果顾客满意，就会产生品牌忠诚度，信息搜索和选择评估阶段往往会很快完成或完全略过。因此，品牌忠诚度是许多公司的终极目标。

根据满意或不满意的情况，顾客会传播关于产品的正面或负面反馈。同伴、朋友、家人对所购物品的意见被指定为影响购后评价结果的最重要因素之一，其对产品评价的意见无论客观性如何，往往都会影响顾客的满意程度。同时，认知失调（市场营销术语中的消费者混淆）在这个阶段也很常见；顾客往往会感到购后心理紧张或焦虑，问题包括“我做了正确的决定吗？”“这是一个好的选择吗？”等。因此，在这个阶段，企业应该谨慎创设积极的购后沟通活动来留住顾客。

客户案例：当莎拉进入购买决策过程的购后评价阶段时，她正在使用电脑，并发现对于这台电脑，她有喜欢或不喜欢的地方。这时，阅读一些告诉她如何更好地使用这台电脑的资料可以使她更喜欢它。

Case P&G’s Simplifying Solutions to the Proliferation of Consumer Choice

Unit 5

Text A

STP Model of Marketing

STP model of marketing is a three-step approach to building a targeted marketing plan. S stands for segmenting, T for targeting, and P for positioning. The STP method is a strategic concept in the discipline and application of marketing. The STP strategy shows the connections between the marketplace and the methods a company selects to contend in the marketplace. The objective of the STP method is to help the company in its creation and execution of an advantageous marketing mix by learning precisely which benefits the product provides and which customers desire those benefits.

Going through this process allows a business owner and marketing consultants or employees to formulate a marketing strategy that ties company, brand and product benefits to specific customer market segments. STP model of marketing consists of the three main activities: segmenting, targeting, and positioning.

1. Segmenting

Segmenting comprises identifying the market to be segmented; identification, selection, and application of bases to be used in that segmentation, and development of profiles. Segmenting a market has widely been debated over the years as researchers have argued over what variables to consider when dividing the market. Approaches through social, economic, and individual factors, such as brand loyalty, have been considered along with the more widely recognized geographic, physiographic, demographic and behavioral variables. Segmenting a market, therefore, is a process of organizing the market into groups that a business can gain a competitive advantage in. They must, however, avoid over-fragmenting the market as the diversity can make it difficult to profitably serve the smaller markets. The characteristics marketers are looking for are measurability, accessibility, sustainability, and actionability.

Measurability—The understanding of size, purchasing characteristics and value needs of a particular segment.

Accessibility—The ability to communicate with the segment in an effective manner.

Sustainability—The segment is profitable enough to differentiate itself from other segments in the market and maintains the value the business offers.

Actionability—The capability of an organization to create a competitive advantage with its offering in the specific segment of the market.

Depending on company philosophy, resources, product type or market characteristics, a businesses may develop an undifferentiated approach or differentiated approach. In an undifferentiated approach, the marketer ignores segmentation and develops a product that meets the needs of the largest number of buyers. In a differentiated approach the firm targets one or more market segments, and develops separate offers for each segment.

In consumer marketing, it is difficult to find examples of undifferentiated approaches. Even goods such as salt and sugar, which were once treated as commodities, are now highly differentiated. Consumers can purchase a variety of salt products—cooking salt, table salt, sea-salt, rock salt, kosher salt, mineral salt, herbal or vegetable salts, iodized salt, salt substitutes and many more. Sugar also comes in many different types—cane sugar, beet sugar, raw sugar, white refined sugar, brown sugar, caster sugar, sugar lumps, icing sugar (also known as milled sugar), sugar syrup, invert sugar and a plethora of sugar substitutes including smart sugar which is essentially a blend of pure sugar and a sugar substitute. Each of these product types is designed to meet the needs of specific market segments. Invert sugar and sugar syrups, for example, are marketed to food manufacturers where they are used in the production of conserves, chocolate and baked goods. Sugars marketed to consumers appeal to different usage segments. Refined sugar is primarily for use on the table, while caster sugar and icing sugar are primarily designed for use in home-baked goods.

2. Targeting

Targeting is the process of identifying the most attractive segments from the segmentation stage, usually the ones most profitable for the business. It is a follow-on process from segmentation, and is the process of actually determining the select markets and planning the advertising media used to make the segment appealing. Targeting is a changing environment. Traditional targeting practices of advertising through print and other media sources have made way for a social media presence, leading a much more "web-connected" focus. Behavioral targeting is a product of this change, and focuses on the optimization of online advertising and data collection to send a message to potential segments. This process is based around the collection of "cookies", small pieces of information collected by a consumer's browser and sold to businesses to identify potential segments to appeal to. For example, someone consistently accessing photography based searches is likely to have advertisements for camera sales appear, due to the cookie information they deliver showing an interest in this area.

While targeting a market, there are three different market coverage choices to consider—undifferentiated, differentiated, and niche marketing. Choosing which targeting choice to pursue depends on the product or service being offered. Undifferentiated marketing is the best option to focus on the market as a whole and to promote products that have a wide target segment, while differentiated and niche marketing are more specialized and focus on smaller, more selective segments.

Target market is a group of customers within a business' serviceable available market that the business has decided to aim its marketing efforts towards. Target markets consist of consumers who exhibit similar characteristics (such as age, location, income, and lifestyle) and are considered most likely to buy a business' product or service. Primary target markets are those market segments to which marketing efforts are primarily directed, while secondary markets are smaller or less vital to a product's success. It is important for a business to identify and select a target market so it can direct its marketing efforts to that group of customers and better satisfy their needs and wants. This enables the business to use its marketing resources more efficiently, resulting in more cost and time efficient marketing efforts. It allows for better understanding of customers and therefore enables the creation of promotional materials that are more relevant to customer needs. Also, targeting makes it possible to collect more precise data about customer needs and behaviors and then analyze that information over time in order to refine market strategies effectively.

3. Positioning

Positioning is the final stage in the STP process and focuses on how the customer ultimately views your product or service in comparison to your competitors and is important in gaining a competitive advantage in the market. Therefore, customer perceptions have a huge impact on the brands positioning in the market. There are three types of positioning that are key in positioning the brand to a competitive advantage. They are functional positioning, symbolic positioning, and experiential positioning. Functional positioning is focused on the aspects of the products or services that can fulfill consumers' needs or desires. Symbolic positioning is based on the characteristics of the brand that fulfill customers' self-esteem. Experiential positioning is based on the characteristics of the brands that stimulate the sensory or emotional connection with the customers. A combination of the three is key to positioning the brand at a competitive advantage to its immediate competition. Overall, positioning should provide better value than competitors and communicate this differentiation in an effective way to the consumer.

3.1 Positioning statement

Both theorists and practitioners argue that the positioning statement should be written in a format that includes an identification of the target market, the market need, the product name and category, the key benefit delivered and the basis of the product's differentiation from any competing alternatives. A basic template for writing positioning statements is as follows: "For target customer who state of the need or opportunity, the product name is a product category that statement of key benefit—that is, compelling reason to buy. Unlike primary competitive alternative, our product state primary differentiation."

3.2 Process

To be successful in a particular market, a product must occupy an "explicit, distinct and proper place in the minds of all potential and existing consumers". It has to also be relative to other rival products with which the brand competes.

3.2.1 Approaches

A number of different approaches to positioning have been cited as follows:

Approaches	Examples
Positioning against a competitor	Hungry Jack's tastes better (with implication: better than the market leader, McDonald's)
Positioning within a category	Within the prestige car category, Volvo is the safe alternative
Positioning according to product benefit	Toothpaste with whitening or Tartar control (or both)
Positioning according to product attribute	Dove is one-quarter moisturiser
Positioning for usage occasion	Cadbury Roses Chocolates—for gift giving or saying "Thank-you"
Positioning along price lines	a luxury brand or premium brand, an economy brand
Positioning for a user	Johnson and Johnson range of baby products (No Tears Shampoo)
Positioning by cultural symbols	Australia's Easter Bilby (as a culturally appropriate alternative to the Easter Bunny)

3.2.2 Perceptual maps

To identify suitable positions that a company or brand might occupy in a given market, analysts often turn to techniques such as perceptual mapping. Perceptual maps are a diagrammatic representation of consumers' mental representations of the relative place various brands occupy within a category. Traditionally perceptual mapping selects two variables that are relevant to consumers (often, but not necessarily, price and quality) and then asks a sample of the market to explain where they would place various brands in terms of the two variables. Results are averaged across all respondents, and results are plotted on a graph to indicate how the average member of the population views the brand that make up a category and how each of the brands relates to other brands within the same category.

3.3 Positioning

Positioning is the process of identifying concepts for each target segment, selecting the best and communicating it. Positioning strategies help shape a consumers preferences which is a major source in guiding them towards a particular brand. It is essential to assess and analyse the consumers behavior and psyche of how they will or already do perceive the offered brand by recalling the company's communications with them such as advertising or any marketing campaigns. The right positioning strategy at the right time is what can help a brand build the right image of itself in the mind of consumers. It is possible for a business to influence and likely change the positioning of the brand by manipulating various factors that will affect a consumer's attitude with the brand or company. A research on persons' attitudes suggests that a brand's position in a prospective consumer's mind is likely to be determined by the "combined total of a number of product characteristics such as the price, quality, durability, reliability, color, and flavor". The consumer places important weights on each of these product characteristics and it can be possible by using things such as promotional efforts to realign the weights of price, quality, durability, reliability, color and flavor of which can then help adjust the position of a brand in the mind of the prospective consumer.

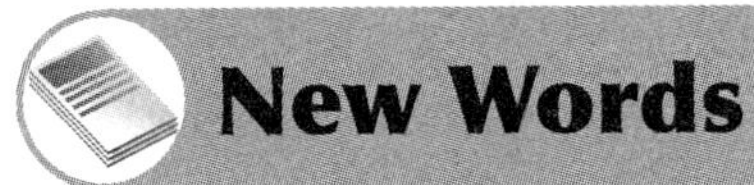

New Words

approach [ə'prəʊtʃ] *n.* 方法，途径；接近

discipline ['dɪsəplɪn] *n.* 学科；符合行为准则的行为（或举止）

application [ˌæplɪ'keɪʃn] *n.* 应用，运用

connection [kə'nekʃn] *n.* 联系

contend [kən'tend] *vi.* 争夺，竞争

execution [ˌeksɪ'kjuːʃn] *n.* 实行，执行；依法处决

advantageous [ˌædvən'teɪdʒəs] *adj.* 有利的

precisely [prɪ'saɪsli] *adv.* 精确地，恰好地

formulate ['fɔːmjuleɪt] *vt.* 构想出，规划，制订；用公式表示

comprise [kəm'praɪz] *vt.* 包含，包括；由……组成，由……构成

profile ['prəʊfaɪl] *n.* 形象；简介；概述；侧面；轮廓

physiographic [ˌfɪzɪəʊ'græfɪk] *adj.* 地文学的，地形学的

measurability [meʒərə'bɪləti] *n.* 测量性；可量性，可测性

accessibility [ək'sesəbləti] *n.* 可达性；易接近，可到达

sustainability [sə'steɪnəbləti] *n.* 持续性，能维持性

undifferentiated [ˌʌndɪfə'renʃieɪtɪd] *adj.* 无差别的，一致的；未分化的

commodity [kə'mɒdəti] *n.* 商品，日用品；有价值的物品

kosher ['kəʊʃə] *adj.* 符合犹太教教规的，合适的

mineral ['mɪnərəl] *adj.* 矿物的，似矿物的

herbal ['ɜːbl] *adj.* 药草的；草本的

iodize ['aɪədaɪz] *vt.* 用碘处理；使含有碘

substitute ['sʌbstɪtjuːt] *n.* 替代物，代替者；替补

beet [biːt] *n.* 甜菜；甜菜根

milled [mɪld] *adj.* 碾碎的，碾磨过的

invert [ɪn'vɜːt] *adj.* 转化的

conserve [kən'sɜːv] *n.* 果酱，蜜饯

appealing [ə'piːlɪŋ] *adj.* 吸引人的，令人心动的

optimization [ˌɒptɪmaɪ'zeɪʃən] *n.* 最佳化，最优化

browser ['braʊzə] *n.* 浏览程序，浏览器

consistently [kən'sɪstəntli] *adv.* 一致地，始终如一地，一贯地

niche [niːʃ] *n.* （特定产品或服务的）用户群

exhibit [ɪg'zɪbɪt] *vt.* 陈列，展览，展示

vital ['vaɪtl] *adj.* 至关重要的

promotional [prə'məʊʃənl] *adj.* 促销的；增进的

refine [rɪ'faɪn] *vt.* 提炼；改善

ultimately ['ʌltɪmətli] *adv.* 最后，最终

view [vjuː] *vt.* 看，看待

perception [pəˈsepʃn] *n.* 知觉；观念；觉察（力）；看法，见解

symbolic [sɪmˈbɒlɪk] *adj.* 象征的，象征性的

experimental [ɪkˌsperɪˈmentl] *adj.* 实验的，根据实验的；试验性的

self-esteem [ˌself-ɪˈstiːm] *n.* 自尊

practitioner [prækˈtɪʃənə] *n.* 从业者，实践者

explicit [ɪkˈsplɪsɪt] *adj.* 明确的，清晰的

distinct [dɪˈstɪŋkt] *adj.* 清晰的，清楚的；明显的；卓越的

proper [ˈprɒpə] *adj.* 适当的，相当的，正当的

existing [ɪgˈzɪstɪŋ] *adj.* 现存的，目前的

occasion [əˈkeɪʒn] *n.* 场合；机会，时机

implication [ˌɪmplɪˈkeɪʃn] *n.* 含义，含意；暗示

prestige [preˈstiːʒ] *n.* 声誉；威信，威望

diagrammatic [ˈdaɪəgræmætɪk] *adj.* 图表的；概略的

representation [ˌreprɪzenˈteɪʃn] *n.* 表现，表征；陈述

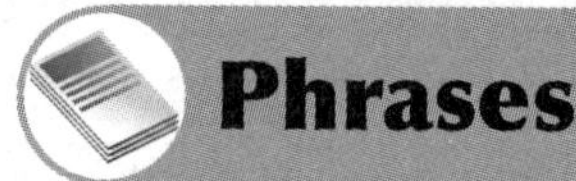

Phrases

stand for 代表

argue over 就……争论

gain a competitive advantage 获得竞争优势

differentiate from 不同于，与……有区别

a variety of 多种多样的

come in different types 有不同的类型

a plethora of 过多的，繁多的

make way for 为……让路；为……腾出地方

online advertising 在线广告，网络广告

data collection 数据收集，数据汇集

due to 由于，因为

niche marketing 缝隙营销，利基行销；利基市场

as a whole 整体来看

be directed to 指向，针对

allow for 允许有；考虑到

fulfill one's self-esteem 实现某人的自尊

in an effective way 以有效的方式

positioning statement 定位陈述，定位说明

compete with 与……竞争

usage occasion 使用场合

premium brand 高档品牌，优质品牌

perceptual mapping 知觉图，认知图表

mental representation 心理表征

make up 构成；弥补

place weight on 重视，侧重于

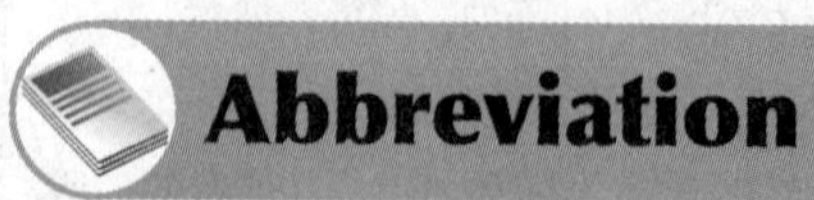

Abbreviation

STP (Segmentation, Targeting, Positioning) 营销战略的三要素，即市场细分目标市场和市场定位

Exercises

EX. 1 Answer the following questions according to Text A.

(1) What is the objective of the STP method?
(2) What does segmenting market comprise?
(3) What are the characteristics of segmenting market the marketers are looking for?
(4) What is targeting?
(5) What are the three different market coverage choices to consider while targeting a market? And what is the difference among them?
(6) Is functional positioning the key to positioning the brand at a competitive advantage to its immediate competition?
(7) What is a basic template for writing positioning statements?
(8) List at least three approaches to positioning a product.
(9) Why do analysts often turn to perceptual mapping?
(10) According to a research on people's attitudes, what characteristics of a product are likely to determine a brand's position in a prospective consumer's mind?

EX. 2 Translate the following phrases from English into Chinese and vice versa.

(1) appeal to ____________
(2) data collection ____________
(3) gain a competitive advantage ____________
(4) in an effective way ____________
(5) niche marketing ____________
(6) 高档品牌；优质品牌 ____________
(7) 在线广告，网络广告 ____________
(8) 商品，日用品 ____________
(9) 最佳化，最优化 ____________
(10) 促销的；增进的 ____________

EX. 3 Translate the following into Chinese.

Market segmentation divides the market into four main sub categories—demographic, geographic, psychographic and behavioral segmentation. After doing market segmentation, the subdivision market will be much more specific and it is relatively easy to understand consumer demand, and enterprises can determine their own service objects according to their business ideology, principles and production technology and marketing power. At the same time, in the segments of the market, the information is easy to understand and feedback. Once the consumer demand changes, enterprises can rapidly change marketing strategy, formulating corresponding countermeasures, in order to adapt to the change of market demand and improve the flexibility and competitiveness of enterprises. Through market segmentation, the enterprise will be able to notice every subdivision market's purchasing potential, satisfying degree, competition and comparative analysis, and to better meet market needs. Meanwhile, the manpower, material resources and funds of any enterprise are limited. Through market segments, after selecting the suitable target market, enterprises can focus more on human, financial, and material resources, to fight for the advantages of local market, and then to occupy their own target market. Segmenting the market allows marketers to better understand the group they are aiming their message at, which is more efficient than aiming at a broad group of people.

EX. 4 Fill in the blanks with the words given below.

recession	commercial	shift	sufficient	involves
competitors	upscale	predict	flourished	lack

Repositioning a Company

In volatile markets, it can be necessary-even urgent-to reposition an entire company, rather than just a product line or brand. When Goldman Sachs and Morgan Stanley suddenly shifted from investment to (1)________ banks, for example, the expectations of investors, employees, clients and regulators all needed to (2)________, and each company needed to influence how these perceptions changed. Doing so involves repositioning the entire firm.

This is especially true of small and medium-sized firms, many of which often (3)________ strong brands for individual product lines. In a prolonged (4)________ , business approaches that were effective during healthy economies often become ineffective and it becomes necessary to change a firm's positioning.(5)________ restaurants, for example, which previously (6)________ on expense account dinners and corporate events, may for the first time need to stress value as a sale tool.

Repositioning a company (7)________ more than a marketing challenge. It involves making hard decisions about how a market is shifting and how a firm's (8)________ will react. Often these decisions must be made without the benefit of (9)________ information, simply because the definition of "volatility" is that change becomes difficult or impossible to (10)________.

Text B

Market Segmentation

Market segmentation is the process of dividing a broad consumer or business market, normally consisting of existing and potential customers, into sub-groups of consumers (known as segments) based on some type of shared characteristics. In dividing or segmenting markets, researchers typically look for common characteristics such as shared needs, common interests, similar lifestyles or even similar demographic profiles. The overall aim of segmentation is to identify high yield segments—that is, those segments that are likely to be the most profitable or that have growth potential-so that these can be selected for special attention (i.e., become target markets).

The rationale for market segmentation is that in order to achieve competitive advantage and superior performance, firms should: (1)identify segments of industry demand, (2)target specific segments of demand, and (3)develop specific "marketing mixes" for each targeted market segment. From an economic perspective, segmentation is built on the assumption that heterogeneity in demand allows for demand to be disaggregated into segments with distinct demand functions.

1. Bases for segmenting consumer markets

A major step in the segmentation process is the selection of a suitable base. In this step, marketers are looking for a means of achieving internal homogeneity (similarity within the segments), and external heterogeneity (differences between segments). In other words, they are searching for a process that minimizes differences between members of a segment and maximizes differences between each segment. In addition, the segmentation approach must yield segments that are meaningful for the specific marketing problem or situation. For example, a person's hair colour may be a relevant base for a shampoo manufacturer, but it would not be relevant for a seller of financial services. Selecting the right base requires a good deal of thought and a basic understanding of the market to be segmented.

In reality, marketers can segment the market using any base or variable provided that it is identifiable, substantial, responsive, actionable, and stable.

Identifiability refers to the extent to which managers can identify or recognize distinct groups within the marketplace.

Substantiality refers to the extent to which a segment or group of customers represents a sufficient size to be profitable. This could mean sufficiently large in number of people or in purchasing power.

Accessibility refers to the extent to which marketers can reach the targeted segments with promotional or distribution efforts.

Responsiveness refers to the extent to which consumers in a defined segment will respond to marketing offers targeted at them.

Actionable segments are said to be actionable when they provide guidance for marketing decisions.

For example, although dress size is not a standard base for segmenting a market, some fashion houses have successfully segmented the market using women's dress size as a variable. However, the most common bases for segmenting consumer markets include geographics, demographics, psychographics, and behavior. Marketers normally select a single base for the segmentation analysis, although, some bases can be combined into a single segmentation with care. For example, geographics and demographics are often combined, but other bases are rarely combined. Given that psychographics includes demographic variables such as age, gender, and income as well as attitudinal and behavioral variables, it makes little logical sense to combine psychographics with demographics or other bases. Any attempt to use combined bases needs careful consideration and a logical foundation.

2. Major types of market segmentation

There are four major different types of market segmentation and all of them vary in their implementation in the real world. Let us discuss each of them in detail.

2.1 Demographic segmentation

Segmentation according to demography is based on consumer-demographic variables such as age, income, family size, socio-economic status, etc. Demographic segmentation assumes that consumers with similar demographic profiles will exhibit similar purchasing patterns, motivations, interests and lifestyles and that these characteristics will translate into similar product/brand preferences. In practice, demographic segmentation can potentially employ any variable that is used by the nation's census collectors. Typical demographic variables and their descriptors are as follows:

Age: e.g., Under 5, 5–8, 9–12, 13–17, 18–24, 25–29; 30–39, 40–49, 50–59, 60+.

Gender: male, female.

Occupation: professional, self-employed, semi-professional, clerical/admin, sales, trades, mining, primary producer, student, home duties, unemployed, retired.

Socio-economic: A, B, C, D, E, or I, II, III, IV or V (normally divided into quintiles).

Marital status: single, married, divorced, widowed.

Family life-stage: young single, young married with no children, young family with children under 5 years, older married with children, older married with no children living at home, older living alone.

Family size/number of dependants: 0, 1–2, 3–4, 5+.

Income: under $10,000, 10,000–20,000, 20,001–30,000, 30,001–40,000, 40,001–50,000, etc.

Educational attainment: primary school, some secondary, completed secondary, some university degree, post graduate or higher degree.

Home ownership: renting, own home with mortgage, home owned outright.

Ethnicity: Asian, African, Aboriginal, Polynesian, Melanesian, Latin-American, African-American; American Indian, etc.

2.2 Behavioral segmentation

Behavioral segmentation divides consumers into groups according to their observed behaviors. Many marketers believe that behavioral variables are superior to demographics and geographics for building market segments and some analysts have suggested that behavioral segmentation is killing off demographics. Typical behavioral variables and their descriptors include:

Purchase/Usage occasion: e.g., regular occasion, special occasion, festive occasion, gift-giving.

Benefit-sought: e.g., economy, quality, service level, convenience, access.

User status: e.g., first-time user, regular user, non-user.

Usage rate/Purchase frequency: e.g., light user, heavy user, moderate user.

Loyalty status: e.g., loyal, switcher, non-loyal, lapsed.

Buyer readiness: e.g., unaware, aware, intention to buy.

Attitude to product or service: e.g., enthusiast, indifferent, hostile, price conscious, quality conscious.

Adopter status: e.g., early adopter, late adopter, laggard.

This type of market segmentation is in boom especially in the smartphone market. For example, Blackberry was launched for users who were business people, Samsung was launched for users who like android and like various applications for a free price, and Apple was launched for the premium customers who want to be a part of a unique and popular niche.

Another example of behavioral segmentation is marketing during festivals. Say on Christmas, the buying patterns will be completely different as compared to buying patterns on normal days. Thus, the usage segmentation is also a type of behavioral segmentation.

2.3 Psychographic segmentation

Psychographic segmentation, which is sometimes called psychometric or lifestyle segmentation, is measured by studying the activities, interests, and opinions (AIOs) of customers. It considers how people spend their leisure, and which external influences they are most responsive to and influenced by. Psychographics is a very widely used basis for segmentation, because it enables marketers to identify tightly defined market segments and better understand consumer motivations for product or brand choice.

While many of these proprietary psychographic segmentation analyses are well-known, the majority of studies based on psychographics are custom designed. That is, the segments are developed for individual products at a specific time. One common thread among psychographic segmentation studies is that they use quirky names to describe the segments.

Application of psychographic segmentation can be seen all across nowadays. For example, Zara markets itself on the basis of lifestyle, where customers who want the latest and differential clothing can visit the Zara stores. Similarly Arrow markets itself to the premium office lifestyle where probably your bosses and super bosses shop for the sharp clothing. Thus, this type of segmentation is mainly based on lifestyle or AIO.

2.4 Geographic segmentation

Geographic segmentation divides markets according to geographic criteria. In practice, markets can be segmented as broadly as continents and as narrowly as neighborhoods or postal codes. Typical geographic variables include:

Country: e.g., Brazil, Canada, China, France, Germany, India, Italy, Japan, UK, US.

Region: e.g., north, northwest, midwest, south, central.

Population density: e.g., central business district (CBD), urban, suburban, rural, regional.

City or town size: e.g., under 1,000, 1,000–5,000, 5,000–10,000... 1,000,000–3,000,000 and over 3,000,000.

Climatic zone: e.g., Mediterranean, temperate, sub-tropical, tropical, polar.

Geodemographic segmentation combines demographic data with geographic data to create richer, more detailed profiles. Geo-cluster approaches are a consumer classification system designed for market segmentation and consumer profiling purposes. They classify residential regions or postcodes on the basis of census and lifestyle characteristics obtained from a wide range of sources. This allows the segmentation of a population into smaller groups defined by individual characteristics such as demographic, socio-economic or other shared socio-demographic characteristics.

A number of proprietary geo-demographic packages are available for commercial use. Geographic segmentation is widely used in direct marketing campaigns to identify areas which are potential candidates for personal selling, letter-box distribution or direct mail. Geo-cluster segmentation is widely used by governments and public sector departments such as urban planning, health authorities, police, criminal justice departments, telecommunications and public utility organizations such as water boards.

Thus, the above are the four main types of market segmentation. Usage based market segmentation, benefit segmentation, price based market segmentation, all these different types of segmentation are a derivative of the above 4 types only.

3. Steps in market segmentation

Segmentation refers to the process of creating small segments within a broad market to select the right target market for various brands. Market segmentation helps the marketers to devise and implement relevant strategies to promote their products among the target market.

A market segment consists of individuals who have similar choices, interests and preferences. They generally think on the same lines and are inclined towards similar products. Once the organizations decide on their target market, they can easily formulate strategies and plans to make their brands popular amongst the consumers. Those steps in market segmentation can be illustrated as follows.

Step 1　Determine the need of the segment

What are the needs of the customers and how can you group customers based on their needs? You have to think of this in terms of consumption by customers or what would each of your customer like to have.

For example, in a region, there are many normal restaurants but there is no Italian restaurant or there is no fast food chain. So, you came to know the need of consumers in that specific region.

Step 2　Identify the segment

Once you know the need of the customers, you need to identify that “who” will be the customers to choose your product over other offerings. Quite simply, you have to decide which type of segmentation you are going to use in this case. Is it going to be geographic, demographic, psychographic or what? The first step gives you a mass of crowd, and in the second step, you have to differentiate the people from within that crowd.

Taking the same above example of Italian restaurant. The target will be children, youngsters, and middle aged people. Italian food is generally not preferred by old age people who prefer food which can be easily chewed.

Step 3　Evaluate the attractiveness of segment

Now, we approach the targeting phase in the steps of market segmentation. Out of the various segments you have identified via demography, geography or psychography, you have to choose which is the most attractive segment for you. This is a tough question to answer.

If you are using psychographic segmentation, then you need to target the psychology of consumers which takes time. So you will not be able to expand faster. But if your product is basic, then you can use demographic segmentation as the base, and expand much faster in surrounding regions. So this step involves deciding on all the different types of segmentation that you can use.

Taking the above example of an Italian restaurant, the restaurant owner realizes that he has more middle aged people and youngsters in his vicinity. So it is better to market his store on weekends and malls where this target group is likely to go. The middle aged people can bring children and elders as per their convenience. So the first target is the middle aged group, and the second target is youngsters. He is using a combination of demographic and geographic segmentation to target middle aged people in his region.

Step 4　Is the segment giving profit?

So, now you have different types of segmentation being analyzed for their attractiveness. Which segment do you think will give you the maximum crowd has been decided in the third step. But which of those segments is most profitable is a decision to be taken in the fourth step. This is also one more targeting step in the process of segmentation.

The Italian restaurant owner above decides that he is getting fantastic profitability from the middle aged group, but he is getting poor profitability from youngsters. Youngsters like fast food and they like socializing. So they order very less, and spend a lot of time at the table, thereby reducing the profitability. So what does the owner do? How does he change this mindset when one of the segments he has identified is less profitable? Let's find out in the fifth step.

Step 5　Position for the segment

Once you have identified the most profitable segments via the steps of market segmentation, you need to position your product in the mind of the consumers. The basic concept is that the firm needs to place a value on its products.

If the firm wants a customer to buy their product, what is the value being provided to the customer, and in his mindset, where does the customer place the brand after purchasing the product? What was the value of the product to the customer and how valuable does he think the brand is? That is the work of positioning. And to complete the process of segmentation, you need to position your product in the mind of your segments.

In the above case we saw that the Italian restaurant owner was finding youngsters unprofitable. So what does he do? How does he target that segment as well? Simple. He starts a fast food chain right next to the Italian restaurant. What happens is, although the area has other fast food restaurants, his restaurant is the only one which offers good Italian cuisine and a good fast food restaurant next door itself. So both, the middle aged target group and the youngsters can enjoy. He has converted the profit earned from the middle aged group into more profit, and has achieved top of the mind positioning for all people in his region.

Step 6 Expand the segment

All segments need to be scalable. So, if you have found a segment, that segment should be such that the business is able to expand with the type of segmentation chosen. If the segment is very niche, then the business will run out of its course in due time. Hence the expansion of the segment is the second last step of market segmentation.

In the above example, the Italian restaurant owner has the best process in his hand—an Italian restaurant combined with a fast food chain. He was using both demographic and geographic segmentation. Now he starts looking at other geographic segments in other regions where he can establish the same concept and expand his business. Naturally, with more expansion he will earn more profits.

Step 7 Incorporate the segmentation into your marketing strategy

Once you have found a segment which is profitable and expandable, you need to incorporate that segment in your marketing strategy. How do you think McDonalds or KFC became such big chains of fast food? They had a very clear process of segmentation because of which it became easier to find regions to target.

With the steps of market segmentation, your segments become clear and then you can adapt other variables of marketing strategy as per the segment being targeted. You can modify the products, keep the optimum price, enhance the distribution and the place and finally promote clearly and crisply to your target audience. Business becomes simpler due to the process of market segmentation.

New Words

rationale [ˌræʃə'næl] *n.* 基本原理，基础理论；理论的说明

heterogeneity [ˌhetərə'dʒiːniːəti] *n.* 异质性，不均匀性，不纯一性

disaggregate [dɪs'ægrɪgeɪt] *vt.* 解开；使崩溃

homogeneity [ˌhɒmədʒə'niːəti] *n.* 同种，同质；均匀性

substantial [səb'stænʃl] *adj.* 大量的；结实的，牢固的；重大的

responsive [rɪ'spɒnsɪv] *adj.* 应答的，响应的

actionable ['ækʃənəbl] *adj.* 可行的；可起诉的，可控告的

identifiability [aɪ'dentɪfaɪə'bɪləti] *n.* 可辨识性，可辨认性，可识别性

substantiality [səbˌstænʃɪæləti] *n.* 实在性，实质性；实体
responsiveness [rɪ'spɒnsɪvnəs] *n.* 响应性，反应性
psychographic [ˌsaɪkəʊ'græfɪk] *n.* 心理描绘图
attitudinal [ˌætɪ'tuːdɪnl] *adj.* 态度的，根据（或表示）个人态度的
foundation [faʊn'deɪʃn] *n.* 基础；地基
census ['sensəs] *n.* 人口普查，统计
descriptor [dɪ'skrɪptə] *n.* 描述信息，描述符号
self-employed [ˌself-ɪm'plɔɪd] *adj.* 个体经营的
semi-professional ['semɪ-prə'feʃənl] *adj.* 半职业性的
clerical ['klerɪkl] *adj.* 文书的；办事员的
quintile ['kwɪntaɪl] *adj.* 五分之一的
widowed ['wɪdəʊd] *adj.* 寡居的；鳏居的
dependant [dɪ'pendənt] *n.* 受赡养者；家眷；侍从；食客
mortgage ['mɔːgɪdʒ] *n.* 抵押
festive ['festɪv] *adj.* 喜庆的，欢乐的，节日的
moderate ['mɒdərɪt] *adj.* 温和的；适度的，有节制的
lapse [læps] *n.* 小错，疏忽；行为失检，失足
hostile ['hɒstl] *adj.* 怀有敌意的，敌对的
laggard ['lægəd] *n.* 落后者
psychometric [ˌsaɪkə'metrɪk] *adj.* 心理测量的，心理测量学的
proprietary [prə'praɪətri] *adj.* （商品）专卖的；专有的，专利的
quirky [kwɜːki] *adj.* 狡诈的；离奇的，古怪的
rural ['rʊərəl] *adj.* 乡下的，农村的
justice ['dʒʌstɪs] *n.* 正义，公正
derivative [dɪ'rɪvətɪv] *adj.* 派生的，衍生的
devise [dɪ'vaɪz] *vt.* 设计，发明；策划，想出
inclined [ɪn'klaɪnd] *adj.* 倾向的；倾斜的
vicinity [və'sɪnəti] *n.* 附近地区，附近，邻近
mindset ['maɪndset] *n.* 观念模式，思维倾向，心态
cuisine [kwɪ'ziːn] *n.* 烹饪；菜肴
scalable ['skeɪləbl] *adj.* 可测量的
crisply [krɪspli] *adj.* 易碎地；干脆地，斩钉截铁地

Phrases

target market 目标市场
from an economical perspective 从经济的角度
build on 基于，以……为基础；依赖
in addition 另外，除此之外
a good deal of 大量的，许多的
in reality 实际上，事实上
provided that 倘若；以…… 为条件
given that 假定，已知，考虑到
make sense 有意义，有道理
socio-economic status 社会经济状况
martial status 婚姻状况
educational attainment 受教育程度
be superior to 优越于
kill off 消灭；杀光
loyalty status 忠诚程度
in boom 在繁荣时期

be responsive to 对……有应答
at a specific time 在特定的时间
postal code 邮递区号
population density 人口密度
residential region 居住区
criminal justice department 刑事司法部
public utility organization 公共事业组织
fast food chain 快餐连锁店
a mass of 大量的
as per 按照，根据

Abbreviations

AIO (Activities, Interests and Opinions) 消费者的行为、兴趣和观点
CBD (Central Business District) 中央商务区

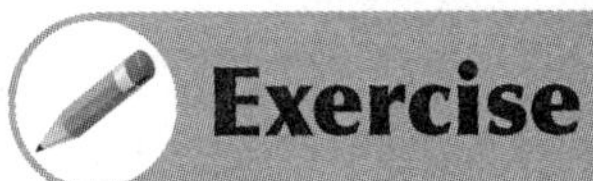

Exercise

EX. Answer the following questions according to Text B.

(1) What is the definition of market segmentation?
(2) What are the most common bases for segmenting consumer markets?
(3) What are the assumptions of demographic segmentation?
(4) According to many marketers, what variables are superior, behavioral variables or demographics?
(5) Can you list at least five typical behavioral variables?
(6) How can psychographic segmentation measured? And what does psychographic segmentation consider?
(7) By whom is geo-cluster segmentation widely used?
(8) What individuals does a market segment consist of?
(9) What do marketers need to do if they have identified the most profitable segments?
(10) What is the second last step of market segmentation?

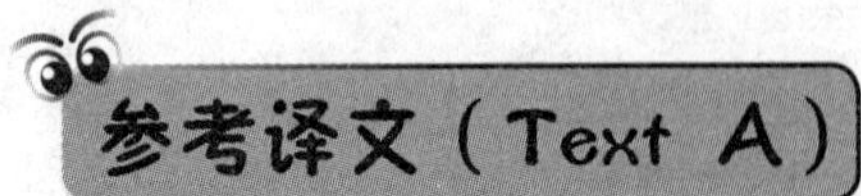

参考译文（Text A）

STP 营销模型

STP 营销模型是建立目标营销计划的三步法。S 代表市场细分，T 代表目标市场，P

代表市场定位。STP 方法是市场营销学及其应用中的一个战略性概念。STP 策略显示了市场和公司选择在该市场中竞争的方法之间的联系。STP 方法的目标是帮助公司创建和实施有效的营销组合，其方式是准确了解产品提供的好处，以及哪些客户希望获得这些好处。

通过这个过程，企业所有者和营销顾问或员工可以制定一种营销策略，将公司、品牌和产品的利益与特定的客户细分市场联系起来。STP 营销模型包括三个主要活动：市场细分、目标定位和市场定位。

1. 市场细分

市场细分包括确定要细分的市场；识别、选择和应用该细分市场中所用的基本依据并形成简介信息。多年来，由于研究人员就市场细分时应考虑哪些变量已经展开了争论，市场细分问题一直备受争议。研究人员已经考虑了将社会、经济和个人因素（如品牌忠诚度）与已被广泛认可的地理、地形、人口和行为变量结合起来的方法。因此，细分市场是将市场组织成企业能够获得竞争优势的群体的过程。然而，它们必须避免过度细分市场，因为多样性可能使企业难以为较小的市场提供有利可图的服务。营销人员寻求的细分市场特征是可测量性、便利性、可持续性和可操作性。

可测量性——了解特定细分市场的规模、购买特点和价值需求。

便利性——能够与细分市场进行有效的沟通。

可持续性——细分市场的盈利能力足以使其区别于市场上的其他细分市场，并保持企业提供的价值。

可操作性——组织能够在特定的市场领域通过提供产品或服务创造竞争优势。

根据公司的理念、资源、产品类型或市场特征，企业可以使用无差异化或差异化方法。采用无差异化方法时，市场营销者忽略市场细分，而开发出满足最多购买者需求的产品。采用差异化方法时，公司以一个或多个细分市场为目标，并为每个细分市场开发各自的产品或用务。

在消费者营销中，很难找到无差异方法的应用实例。甚至像盐和糖这样曾经被视为商品的货物，现在也高度分化了。消费者可以购买各种各样的盐产品——烹调盐、食盐、海盐、岩盐、粗盐、矿物盐、草本盐或蔬菜盐、碘盐、盐替代品，等等。糖也有许多不同的类型——蔗糖、甜菜糖、粗糖、白精制糖、红糖、细白砂糖、糖块、冰糖（也称为研磨糖）、糖浆、转化糖以及大量的糖替代品，包括本质上由纯糖和糖的替代品混合而成的人工合成糖。每种产品类型都是为满足特定细分市场的需求而设计的。例如，转化糖和糖浆被销售给食品制造商，用于生产蜜饯、巧克力和烘焙食品。不同的使用群体喜欢用不同的糖，精制糖主要用于餐桌上，而细白砂糖和冰糖主要用于家庭烘焙食品。

2. 目标定位

目标市场的选定是在市场细分阶段中识别最有吸引力细分市场的过程。对企业来说，它们通常是能带来最大利润的细分市场。它是市场细分的后续过程，实际上是确定选定市场和规划广告媒体以吸引细分市场的过程。目标市场是一个不断变化的环境。传统的平面广告和其他媒体广告的市场定位方式已经被社交媒体所取代，成为“网络连接”的焦点。行为定向就是这种变化的产物，其重点是优化在线广告和数据收集，向潜在的细分市场发送信息。这一过程是基于“甜饼”网络跟踪器（记录上网用户信息的软件）所收集的信息，即消费者浏览器收集的一小部分信息，然后出售给企业，以识别潜在的、需要吸引的细分市场。例如，持续访问基于摄影的搜索网站的人很可能会碰到相机销售广告，因为他们提供的“甜饼”信息显示出他们对该领域感兴趣。

在选定一个市场时，有三种不同的市场范围选择需要考虑——无分化、分化和利基营销。选择哪种目标市场取决于所提供的产品或服务。无分化营销是侧重于将市场作为一个整体进行营销，推销其目标细分市场范围广的产品的最佳选择，而分化和利基营销则更加专业化，侧重于更小、更有选择性的细分市场。

目标市场是企业可以为其提供服务的市场中的消费者群体，也是企业营销工作的目标。目标市场由具有相似特征（如年龄、地点、收入和生活方式）的消费者组成，被认为最有可能购买企业的产品或服务的群体。主要目标市场是那些营销努力主要针对的细分市场，而次要市场对产品成功而言不太重要或重要性较小。对于企业来说，确定和选择一个目标市场是很重要的，这样它就可以将其营销努力导向这群客户，更好地满足他们的需求。企业也能够更有效地利用其营销资源，从而使营销工作具有更高的成本和时间效率。它有助于更好地了解客户，因此能够创建与客户需求更相关的推广材料。此外，定向目标市场使收集有关客户需求和行为的更精确的数据成为可能，然后随着时间的推移分析这些信息，从而有效地改进市场策略。

3. 市场定位

市场定位是 STP 过程的最后一个阶段。市场定位关注的是客户最终如何将你的产品或服务与竞争对手进行比较，这对于企业在市场中获得竞争优势非常重要。因此，顾客感知对品牌在市场中的定位有着巨大的影响。有三种类型的定位是将品牌定位为竞争优势的关键。它们是功能定位、象征性定位和体验式定位。功能定位关注的是能够满足消费者需求或欲望的产品或服务的各个方面；象征性定位以满足消费者自尊的品牌特征为基础；体验式定位是建立在刺激顾客的感官或情感联系的品牌特征的基础上的。这三者的结合是品牌在当前竞争中处于竞争优势的关键。总的来说，市场定位应该提供比竞争对手更好的价值，并以有效的方式向消费者传达这种差异化。

3.1　定位声明

理论家和实践者都认为，定位声明的格式应该包括目标市场的识别、市场需求、产品名称和类别、提供的关键性好处以及产品与其他同类竞争产品的区别之处。撰写定位声明的基本模板如下:“对于（陈述需求或机会）的（目标消费者）来说,（产品名称）是一个（陈述关键性好处，即陈述令人信服的购买理由）的（产品类别）。和（主要竞争对手）不同，我们的产品（陈述主要差异）。”

3.2　过程

要想在某一特定市场取得成功，产品必须“在所有潜在的和现有的消费者心目中占据明确、独特和适当的位置”。它还必须相对于与该品牌相竞争的其他竞争产品。

3.2.1　方法

以下列举了一些不同的定位方法：

方法	例子
竞争定位	汉堡王的口味更好（暗示：比麦当劳的口味更好）
类别内定位	在高端汽车类别中，沃尔沃是安全的选择
产品效益定位	美白或防牙垢牙膏（或两者兼容）

续表

方法	例子
产品属性定位	多芬是四分之一保湿霜
使用场合定位	吉百利玫瑰巧克力——用于送礼或说“谢谢”
价格定位	奢侈品牌或高端品牌，经济品牌
用户定位	强生婴幼儿系列产品（无泪洗发水）
文化符号定位	澳大利亚的复活节兔耳袋狸（作为复活节兔子的文化替代品）

3.2.2 知觉图

为了确定一家公司或一个品牌在特定市场中可能占据的合适位置，分析师通常会求助于知觉图等技术。知觉图是消费者对某一产品类别中各品牌所占相对位置的心理表征的图示。传统的知觉图选择两个与消费者相关的变量（通常，但并不全是价格和质量），然后要求市场样本用这两个变量解释他们会将各种品牌置于何处。调查结果是以所有受访者的平均值来计算的，并被绘制在图表上，以表明普通消费者是如何看待同一产品类别中的各个品牌的，以及每个品牌如何与同类别中的其他品牌相关联的。

3.3 定位

定位是确定各个目标市场的概念、选择最佳概念并对概念进行传播的过程。定位策略有助于塑造消费者偏好，这是引导他们选择特定品牌的主要来源。通过回顾公司对消费者进行的推广活动，如广告或任何营销活动，评估和分析消费者的行为和心理，了解他们如何看待所提供的品牌，这一点极其重要。在正确的时间，采用恰当的定位策略可有助于品牌在消费者心目中树立良好的自我形象。通过操控那些影响消费者品牌或公司态度的各种因素，企业有可能影响和改变品牌的定位。一项关于人们态度的研究表明，品牌在未来消费者心目中的地位很可能是由“产品的综合特征，如价格、质量、耐用性、可靠性、颜色和味道”等决定的。消费者对产品的每一个特征非常重视。因此，企业可以通过诸如促销活动之类的方式重新调整价格、质量、耐用性、可靠性、颜色和味道的权重，从而帮助调整品牌在未来消费者心目中的定位。

Case STP Marketing Model of KFC

Unit 6

Text A

Product Classification

One can say a product is a good service, or idea consisting of a bundle of tangible and intangible attributes that satisfies consumers and is received in exchange for money or some other unit of value.

How an organization views a product depends upon its perspective. The organizations that are production-oriented look at a product basically as a manifestation of resources used to produce it. The organizations that are marketing oriented view a product from the target consumer's perspective as a bundle of benefits, which are functional as well as emotional. Therefore, a product is a bundle of physical, chemical and / or intangible attributes that have the potential to satisfy present and potential customer wants. In addition to the physical Good itself, other elements include the warranty, installation, after-sales service accessories and package.

1. *Three levels of a product*

Consumers often think that a product is simply the physical item that he or she buys. In order to actively explore the nature of a product further, let's consider it as three different products – the core product, the actual product, and finally the augmented product. This concept is known as the Three Levels of a Product, which actually comes in play when you are finalizing a product for your business or when you want to analyze a product. Just like any business, a product has its hierarchy too. A product can be divided into three levels which are a series of different features and benefits which helps in its segmentation, targeting, and positioning. Thus the three levels of a product are the ones which help to define the product in a better manner. These three levels can be illustrated as follows (Figure 6-1):

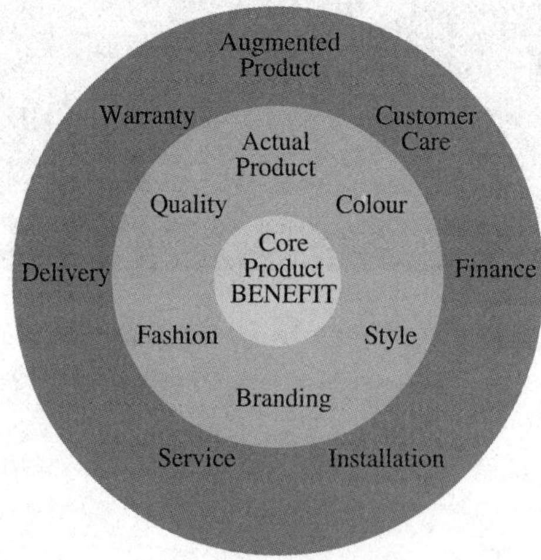

Figure 6-1

1.1 Core product

The core product is not the tangible physical product. You can not touch it. That's because the core product is the benefit of the product that makes it valuable to you. Suppose you are planning on launching your own car manufacturing unit. What would be your core product? Would it be the car itself? no. The core product would be convenience to your customers. Your customers can also travel by bus or taxi. But they prefer cars because of convenience as well several times because of status symbol. Thus the core product in case of Tata cars will be convenience and value for money whereas in case of BMW it will be status symbol.

1.2 Actual product

The actual product is the tangible, physical product. You can get some use out of it. The actual product is the one which is manufactured after a decision has been taken on what your core product is going to be. Thus, from the above example, if your core product is a status symbol, your actual product will be a very high quality product with high pricing. On the other hand, if the product is a convenience product, the production would be on the basis of value for money. Actual products are quantifiable in nature and have properties like color, branding, quality, etc.

1.3 Augmented product

The augmented product is the non-physical part of the product. It usually consists of lots of added value, for which you may or may not pay a premium. So when you buy a car, part of the augmented product would be the warranty, the customer service support offered by the car's manufacturer and any after-sales service. The augmented product is an important way to tailor the core or actual product to the needs of an individual customer. The features of augmented products can be converted into benefits for individuals.

These three levels of a product play a vital part in product management and are also important while deciding the marketing mix of a company. This is mainly because, if there is an augmented product attached to the actual product, then the promotions, placing, and pricing of these augmented products need to be decided. Thus product decisions are generally the primary decisions of the marketing mix.

2. Various classification systems

A product can be classified as tangible or intangible. A tangible product is a physical object that can be perceived by touch such as a building, vehicle, gadget, or clothing. An intangible product is a product that can only be perceived indirectly such as an insurance policy. Services can be broadly classified under intangible products which can be durable or non-durable.

By use—In its online product catalog, retailer Sears Roebuck divide its products into "departments", then present products to potential shoppers according to function or brand. Each product has a Sears item-number and a manufacturer's model-number. Sears uses the departments and product groupings with the intention of helping customers browse products by function or brand within a traditional department-store structure.

By association—A product line is "a group of products that are closely related, either because they function in a similar manner, are sold to the same customer groups, are marketed through the same types of outlets, or fall within given price ranges". Many businesses offer a range of product lines which may be unique to a single organization or may be common across the business's industry. The US Census used to compile revenue figures for the finance and insurance industry by various product lines such as "accident, health and medical insurance premiums" and "income from secured consumer loans". Within the insurance industry, product lines are indicated by the type of risk coverage, such as auto insurance, commercial insurance, and life insurance.

National and international product classifications—Various classification systems for products have been developed for economic statistical purposes. The NAFTA signatories are working on a system that classifies products called NAPCS as a companion to North American Industry Classification System (NAICS). The European Union uses a "Classification of Products by Activity" among other product classifications. The United Nations also classifies products for international economic activity reporting.

The Aspinwall Classification System classifies and rates products based on five variables:

Replacement rate (How frequently is the product repurchased?)

Gross margin (How much profit is obtained from each product?)

Buyer goal adjustment (How flexible are the buyers' purchasing habits with regard to this product?)

Duration of product satisfaction (How long will the product produce benefits for the user?)

Duration of buyer search behavior (How long will consumers shop for the product?)

3. Product classification—types of products

There are three fundamental types of product classification which are durable and non-durable products and pure services. Durable products are those products which are used for longer period of time, such as freezers, cars, mobilephones, shoes, and TV, etc. Non durable products are those products which we need to use quickly as these products expired after some specific period of time, such as all the vegetables, fruits, and juices, etc. Pure services include those benefits that are intangible or inseparable in nature and are offered for sale to customers. Ownership of nothing is transferred because these products are experiential in nature. Accountant, Doctors, Lawyer, and Teaching, etc. are the best examples that indicate the term pure services.

These all products are purchased by either industrial buyer or final consumer. The consumer products are purchased by final consumers for personal consumption. The industrial products are purchased by the organizations for their usage in the processing operations and administration. Moreover, the industrial products are used mostly, which includes consumables like raw materials or paper clips that can be transformed into finished products.

4. *Different forms of products*

These types of products or product classification are as below in two different forms.

4.1 Consumer products

Those products that are purchased by final consumers for personal consumption are called consumer products. The way of purchasing these products provides the basis for the marketer to further classify these products. The following is an important classification of these consumer products on the basis of the manner of purchase and manner of marketing.

Convenience products—Those consumer products that are purchased immediately and frequently with little efforts and comparison are called convenience products. Examples of convenience products include candy, newspaper, soap, fast food, etc. The convenience products are placed at the front locations of the stores in abundance quantity so that they are easily available to the customers. The price of these products is kept lower.

Shopping products—This type of product is purchased less frequently and careful comparison is made by the customer on the price, quality, sustainability, and style. In case of purchase of shopping products, increased time and effort are made by the customers in collection of information and comparison making. Some of examples of shopping products are clothing, furniture, major appliances, used cars, hotels and motel services, etc. These products are distributed in fewer outlets by the marketer along with the strong sales support services that assist customers in their comparison making.

Specialty products—Specialty products are those consumer products that have brand identification or unique characteristics and an important group of customers are happy to purchase these products. Some examples of specialty products include specific brand and kinds of cars, photographic equipment with high price, designer clothes, the services of legal or medical specialist and so on. The customers of such products can make enough effort with them for reaching relevant dealers. However, they do not compare the specialty products normally.

Unsought products—Those consumer products that are either not known to the customers or they are known, but customers do not usually consider them to purchase. The important innovations are usually included in the category of unsought products because the customers get the awareness through advertisement. The examples of unsought products involve life insurance, etc. A lot of personal selling, advertising, and marketing efforts are required for unsought products.

4.2 Industrial products

Those products that are purchased for further processing or for use in operating a business are called industrial products. So the main difference between industrial and consumer product is based on the purpose of purchase of the product. For example, if a lawn mower product is purchased for use around the house, then this lawn mower is categorized in the consumer product. But if the same lawn mower is purchased for use in landscaping business, then this is categorized as an industrial product. Industrial products are classifies into three product types according to the extent to which they are involved and their value in the production process.

Material and parts—Raw materials, natural products, and manufactured materials are included in the category of material and parts. Farm products and natural products are included in raw material part like cotton, wheat, vegetables, fruits, fish, crude petroleum, iron, etc. Component materials and component parts are included in the manufactured area like yarn, wires, cement, iron, tires, small motors, etc. Manufactured material and parts are mostly sold to the industrial users directly. Major marketing factors employed in this category are price and service. The advertising and branding are not so much important. Also the demand of the industrial products is derived demand, which is derived from the consumer demand.

Capital items—Those industrial products that assist the production and operation of customer are called capital items like installations and accessory equipments. Building and fixed equipments are included in the installations. Office equipment and portable factory equipment are included in the accessory equipment. Accessory equipments have much shorter lifetime and they are only helpful in the process of production.

Supplies and services—Supplies contain repair and maintenance items and operating supplies like nails, paint, lubricants, pencil, paper, coal, etc. The supplies are regarded as the industrial convenience products because they are purchased with little effort and time. Business advisory services and repair and maintenance services are included in business services category. These services are given under some contract.

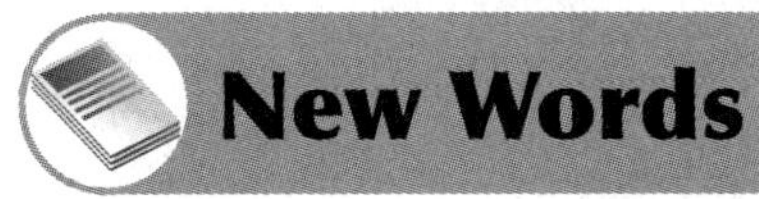

New Words

classification [ˌklæsɪfɪ'keɪʃn] *n.* 分类，分级；类别

perspective [pə'spektɪv] *n.* 观点，看法，视角

manifestation [ˌmænɪfe'steɪʃn] *n.* 表示，显示

warranty ['wɒrənti] *n.* 保证，担保；（商品）保用单；保修期

installation [ˌɪnstə'leɪʃn] *n.* 安装；装置

accessory [ək'sesəri] *n.* 附件，配件；（衣服的）配饰

augment [ɔːg'ment] *vt.* 增强，加强；增加

finalize ['faɪnəlaɪz] *vt.* 完成，使结束

hierarchy ['haɪərɑːki] *n.* 层次，等级制度

quantifiable ['kwɒntɪfaɪəbl] *adj.* 可以计量的

property ['prɒpəti] *n.* 特性，属性；财产，地产
premium ['priːmiəm] *n.* 保险费；附加费；优惠，折扣 *adj.* 优质的；高昂的
browse [braʊz] *vt.* 浏览
outlet ['aʊtlet] *n.* 批发商店；出口，出路
compile [kəm'paɪl] *vt.* 汇编，编辑；编译，编制
coverage ['kʌvərɪdʒ] *n.* 保险项目；范围，规模
signatory ['sɪgnətɔːri] *n.* 签字人，签约国
rate [reɪt] *vt.* 定级；估价
gross [grəʊs] *adj.* 总的；粗的
margin ['mɑːdʒɪn] *n.* 利润；边缘，范围
expire [ɪk'spaɪə] *vi.* 期满；文件、协议等（因到期而）失效
inseperable [ɪn'sepərəbl] *adj.* 不可分割的
experiential [ɪkˌspɪri'enʃl] *adj.* 经验的，经验上的，根据经验的
administration [ədˌmɪnɪ'streɪʃn] *n.* 管理，实行；（政府）行政机关
consumable [kən'sjuːməbl] *n.* 消费品
transform [træns'fɔːm] *vt.* 变换，改变；改观
motel [məʊ'tel] *n.* 汽车旅馆
specialty ['speʃəlti] *n.* 专业，专长；特产；特性
photographic [ˌfəʊtə'græfɪk] *adj.* 摄影的，摄影用的；逼真的
dealer ['diːlə] *n.* 经销商，商人
donation [dəʊ'neɪʃn] *n.* 捐款，捐赠，赠送
landscape ['lændskeɪp] *vt.* 对……做景观美化，给……做园林美化
yarn [jɑːn] *n.* 纱；线
cement [sɪ'ment] *n.* 水泥；胶合剂
capital ['kæpɪtl] *n.* 资本；首都；资源；大写字母
portable ['pɔːtəbl] *adj.* 轻便的，手提的
supply [sə'plaɪ] *n.* 供应，补给；日用（必需）品
maintenance ['meɪntənəns] *n.* 维护，维修；维持
nail [neɪl] *n.* 钉子；指甲，趾甲
lubricant ['luːbrɪkənt] *n.* 润滑剂，润滑油
contract ['kɒntrækt] *n.* 合同，契约，协议

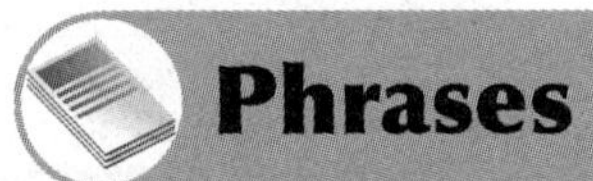

Phrases

a bundle of 一捆，一束
in exchange for 交换
core product 核心产品
actual product 有形产品
augmented product 附加产品，延伸产品
in play 起作用；活动中
status symbol 社会地位或身份象征
after-sales service 售后服务
be attached to 附属于；喜爱，爱慕
insurance policy 保险单
with the intention of 抱有……目的，打算
fall within 应列入……范围内
medical insurance premium 医疗保险费
commercial insurance 商业保险
replacement rate 替换率
gross margin 毛利率

paper clip 纸夹；回形针	brand identification 品牌（号）识别
be transformed into 被转变为……	designer clothes 名牌服装，品牌服装
finished product 成品	lawn mower 割草机，剪草机
business advisory service 商务咨询服务	crude petroleum 原油
convenience product 日用品	accessory equipment 辅助设备，附属设备
in abundance 充足，大量，丰富	under contract 受契约的约束

Abbreviations

NAFTA (*North American Free Trade Agreement*)《北美自由贸易协议》
NAPCS (North American Product Classification System) 北美产品分类系统
NAICS (North American Industry Classification System) 北美产业分类系统

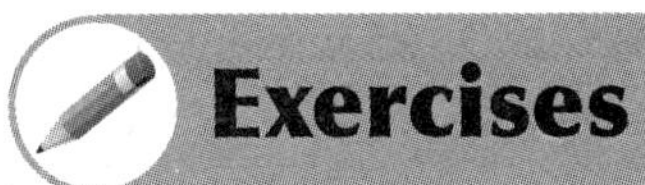

Exercises

EX. 1 Answer the following questions according toText A.

(1) What is the definition of product?
(2) What are the three levels of a product?
(3) What is the core product? Is it tangible?
(4) In case of BMW, what is the core product and the actual product?
(5) What would be part of the augmented product when you buy a car?
(6) How does the Aspinwall Classification System classify and rate products?
(7) What are the three fundamental types of product classification?
(8) On the basis of the manner of purchase and manner of marketing, how are consumer products classified?
(9) What are industrial products? List the three product classifications of industrial products.
(10) Why are the industrial supplies regarded as the industrial convenience products?

EX. 2 Translate the following phrases from English into Chinese and vice versa.

(1) business advisory service ________________
(2) gross margin ________________

(3) replacement rate ________________ ________________

(4) status symbol ________________ ________________

(5) commercial insurance ________________ ________________

(6) 日用品 ________________ ________________

(7) 售后服务 ________________ ________________

(8) 消费品 ________________ ________________

(9) 合同，契约，协议 ________________ ________________

(10) 利润；边缘，范围 ________________ ________________

EX. 3 **Translate the following into Chinese.**

Product management is an organizational lifecycle function within a company dealing with the planning, forecasting, and production, or marketing of a product or products at all stages of the product life cycle. The role may consist of product development and product marketing, which are different (yet complementary) efforts, with the objective of maximizing sales revenues, market share, and profit margins. Product management also involves elimination decisions. Product elimination begins with the identification of elimination candidates, proceeds with the consideration of remedial actions, continues with a projection of the impact on the business as a whole if a candidate product is eventually eliminated, and concludes with the implementation stage, where management determines the elimination strategy for an item. The role of product management spans many activities from strategic to tactical and varies based on the organizational structure of the company. To maximize the impact and benefits to an organization, product management must be an independent function separate on its own.

EX. 4 **Fill in the blanks with the words and phrase given below.**

causing	quarterly	establish	evaluated	distinguish
competitive	overall	balance	various	let alone

Product Planning

The product plan helps resolve issues related to the markets, the types of products and the opportunities that the company will invest in and the resources required to support product development. More specifically, the product plan is used to:

• Define a(n) (1)________ strategy for products to guide selection of development projects;

• Define target markets, customers, (2)________ strengths, and a competition strategy (e.g., competing head-on or finding a market niche);

• Position planned products relative to competitive products and identify what will differentiate or (3)________ these products from the competition;

• Rationalize these competing development projects and (4)________ priorities for development projects;

• Provide a high-level schedule of (5)________ development projects;

• Estimate development resources and (6)________ project resource requirements with a budget in the overall business plan.

Few companies have a formal product planning process, (7)________ a rigorous process. While a product plan is generally prepared on an annual basis, it should be reviewed and updated at least (8)________, if not monthly. Market conditions will change, new product opportunities will be identified, and new product technology will emerge, all (9)________ a potential impact to the product plan. These opportunities need to be (10)________ and the product plan changed if needed.

Text B

Product Decision

Product decision is a critical starting point in the development of any new product. In the development and marketing of products and services, product decisions need to be made. These decisions apply to any kind of product and service and set the base for all other decisions. But which fundamental product decisions need to be made? Product decisions required can be sorted into five categories or stages.

1. Product attributes—stage one of product decisions

Product decisions start by deciding on product attributes. This, in turn, means that the development of a product starts by defining the benefits it will offer to consumers. These benefits are communicated as well as delivered by the product attributes. Thus, in stage one of the product decisions, the product attributes, such as quality, features, style and design, will be defined.

1.1 Product quality

One element of the product attributes is the quality of the product. Although quality can be defined in many ways, we can define it as the characteristics of a product or service that determine its ability to satisfy the customer needs. Therefore, the quality is one of the most important product decisions. It has a direct impact on the product's or service's performance. It is directly linked to customer value and satisfaction. So, we could say: Quality is when the customer is satisfied and will come back, while the product does not (come back).

Total Quality Management (TQM) is an approach that deals with quality in every part of the organization. All parts of the company are involved in the constant improvement of the quality of products, services, and business processes.

To be more specific, defining the product's quality involves two levels or dimensions. These are Quality Level and Quality Consistency.

Firstly, we need to choose a quality level which will support the product's positioning. At this level, the quality can be understood as performance quality: the ability of the product to perform its functions. To give an example, a Mercedes-Benz car provides a higher performance quality than a Dacia Logan: it has a smoother ride, offers more luxury, comfort, lasts longer, etc. The quality level should be chosen so as to meet the target market needs and the quality levels of competing products.

The second level is the Quality Consistency. Here, the product quality means conformance quality. Thus, we refer to freedom from defects and the consistency in delivering the targeted quality level (level of performance). At this level, the Dacia Logan can have as much quality as the Mercedes. Although it does not perform at the same level as the Mercedes (Quality Level), it can deliver the quality that customers pay for and expect (Quality Consistency).

1.2 Product features

Another product attribute that is highly important for the individual product decisions is that of the product features. Obviously, we can offer a product with varying features: a low-level model, without any extras, or a high-level model, with a lot of features. In fact, product features can be seen as a competitive tool for differentiation. By features, we can differentiate our product from competitors' products.

However, just adding features is not the right way to enhance customer value. A remote control does not provide additional value to a customer if it has 250 buttons and vibrates while playing music. The company always has to assess each feature's value to customers first. Do customers really need that feature? Also, the feature's value has to be contrasted to its cost to the company. Only features that add substantial value worth more than the marginal costs should be added.

1.3 Product style and design

Individual product decisions also include the product style and design. Clearly, we can add customer value by means of a distinctive product style and design. While style describes the appearance of the product, design goes deeper. Good design does not only contribute to the product's look, but also to its usefulness. In order to find the right product design, marketers should investigate how customers will use and benefit from the product.

2. *Branding—stage two of product decisions*

Branding is one of the most crucial product decisions. Today, people do not buy a product—they buy a brand. A brand is a name, term, sign, symbol, design or a combination of these elements that identifies the products or services of one seller and differentiates them from those of competitors. Take Coca Cola as an example. If you buy a bottle of coke, you do not only buy the pure beverage, you buy the brand. You buy it because you know and value the worldwide-known brand. For clothing, brands are even more important. Many people do not buy a sweatshirt because of its features-they buy it because there is a label on it showing the brand. They become part of the brand, showing that they have this brand, that they can afford this brand and so on. Thus, a brand is much more than only the product, it is the whole identity around the offerings of a seller.

Therefore, branding adds significant value to a product. In short, a brand is so crucial because customers can attach meanings to brands and develop brand relationships. Branding also help consumers identify products that might benefit them. The brand says something about the product's quality and consistency. And you probably know yourself that buyers who always buy the same brand know that they will get the same benefits, features and quality each time. To go even further, the brand is the basis on which a whole story can be built about the product's special qualities. The product gets an identity with which consumers can identify each time they buy a product of that brand.

Today, branding has become so strong that hardly anything goes unbranded. Even homogenous products such as gasoline or salt are packaged in branded containers or sold as a brand. Likewise, even fruits and vegetables are branded: on many apples, bananas and other fruits and vegetables you find the brand, such as Chiquita Bananas or Pink Lady Apples.

3. Packaging—stage three of product decisions

Going on with the product decisions, we land at packaging. Packaging refers to activities of designing and producing the wrapper or container for a product. The packaging of a product is a more important decision than you would expect it to be. Traditionally, the primary function of a package was to hold and protect the product. However, packaging is nowadays an important marketing tool, too. This is a result of increased competition and offer of products. Packaging must now perform many tasks, which include attracting attention, describing the product, and even making the sale.

To illustrate the importance of packaging, we will look at the highly competitive environment in supermarkets. A normal shopper passes by some 300 items per minute. Therefore, the package may be the seller's best and last chance to influence the buyer. It has become, in fact, a significant promotional tool.

In addition, poorly designed packages can harm a lot. For instance, hard-to-open packages such as DVD cases with sticky labels or sealed plastic clamshell containers do not contribute to the buyer's satisfaction. Indeed, customer frustration is often the result.

Finally, in making packaging decisions, companies should also have environmental considerations. "Green" packaging, meaning the use of environmentally responsible packaging materials, becomes more and more important and adds value to many products.

4. Labelling—stage four of product decisions

Labels perform several functions and are therefore one of the important product decisions. The most straight-forward function is to identify the product or brand. But the label can also describe several things about the product: who made it, where and when was it made, the contents, how it is to be used, etc. Finally, the label can promote a brand. It supports the brand's positioning and may help to connect with customers. By a brand logo, the label can add personality to a brand and contribute to the brand identity.

However, a label should only show and state what is true and what the customer can rely upon. Misleading or deceptive labels must be seen as unfair competition. If labels mislead customers, fail to describe important ingredients or even fail to mention required safety warnings, legal consequences are likely to follow.

Labelling has also been affected recently by unit pricing (the price per unit of standard measure must be stated), open dating (the expected shelf life of the product must be mentioned) and nutritional labelling (the nutritional values in the product must be shown). These elements are required by law.

5. Product support services—stage five of product decisions

Product decisions also include product support services. Usually, the company's offer includes some form of customer service, of product support services. This can be a minor part of the product or a major part of the total offering. Product support services contribute to the augmented product, as defined by the three levels of product. Without doubt, support services do also belong to the significant product decisions because they contribute to the customer's overall brand experience. The key is to keep customers happy after the sale in order to build lasting relationships.

Besides these product decisions, many other choices need to be made. However, these five product decisions build the base for the product development and marketing. If product decisions are made carefully in accordance with consumer needs and wants, the product can become a success.

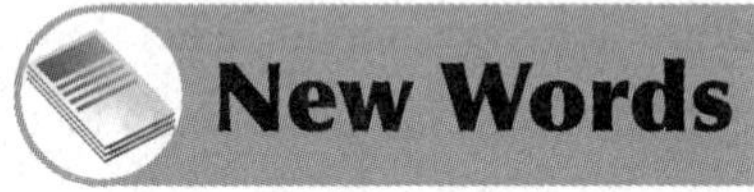

critical ['krɪtɪkl] *adj.* 关键的，极重要的；批评的，爱挑剔的

sort [sɔːt] *vt.* 分类；整顿，整理

consistency [kən'sɪstənsi] *n.* 连贯，前后一致；符合

conformance [kən'fɔːməns] *n.* 顺应，一致

extras ['ekstrəz] *n.* 杂费；附加设备，额外设备

vibrate ['vaɪbreɪt] *vt.*（使）振动/颤动

contrast ['kɒntrɑːst] *vt.* 使对照，使对比；和……形成对照

marginal ['mɑːdʒɪnl] *adj.* 边的，边缘的；旁注的；临界的

investigate [ɪn'vestɪgeɪt] *vt.* 调查

significant [sɪg'nɪfɪkənt] *adj.* 重要的，有意义的

unbranded ['ʌn'brændɪd] *adj.* 未打上烙印的；无物主（姓名或标记）的

homogenous [hə'mɒdʒiːniəs] *adj.* 同质的，纯系的

container [kən'teɪnə] *n.* 容器；箱

likewise ['laɪkwaɪz] *adv.* 同样地；也，而且

wrapper ['ræpə] *n.* 包装纸；封套，封皮

sticky ['stɪki] *adj.* 黏性的

clamshell ['klæmʃel] *n.* 蚌壳；蛤壳式物品

seal [siːl] *vt.* 密封；盖章
frustration [frʌ'streɪʃn] *n.* 挫折，挫败；失意
label ['leɪbl] *vt.* 贴标签于；把……称为
misleading [ˌmɪs'liːdɪŋ] *adj.* 误导性的；骗人的，引入歧途的
nutritional [nju'trɪʃənl] *adj.* 营养的，滋养的

Phrases

product decision 产品决策
apply to 适用于，运用于
be sorted into 归类；分成
product attribute 产品属性
be linked to 与……连接；与……有关联
deal with 应付；对待
to be specific 具体地说
quality consistency 质量稳定性
remote control 遥控，远程控制
contrast to 和……相对照，与……形成对比
by means of 用，依靠；借助于
contribute to 有助于，促成
in short 简而言之，总之
attach... to（使）贴 / 系 / 粘在……上
unit pricing 单位定价
without doubt 毫无疑问地
in accordance with 与……一致，依照

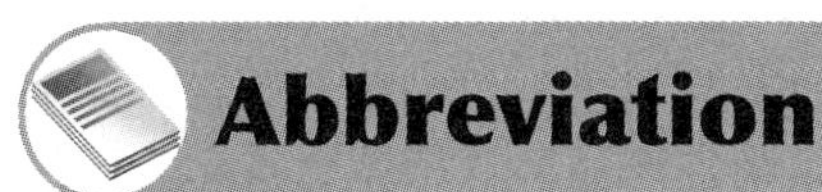

Abbreviation

TQM (Total Quality Management) 全面质量管理

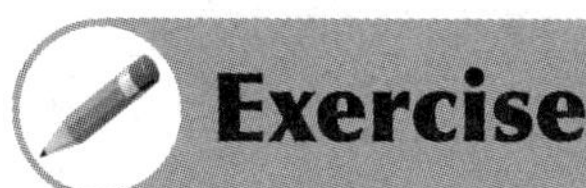

Exercise

EX. Answer the following questions according to Text B.

(1) What is a critical starting point in the development of any new product?
(2) What are the two levels or dimensions involved in defining the product's quality?
(3) When it comes to the Quality Consistency, what does it refer to?
(4) What features should be added to the product?
(5) What should marketers do in order to find the right product design?

(6) What is a brand?

(7) How is the function of packaging nowadays different from the primary function of a package traditionally?

(8) What can the label describe about the product?

(9) How can the label add personality to a brand and contribute to the brand identity?

(10) In what situations are legal consequences likely to follow when it comes to labels?

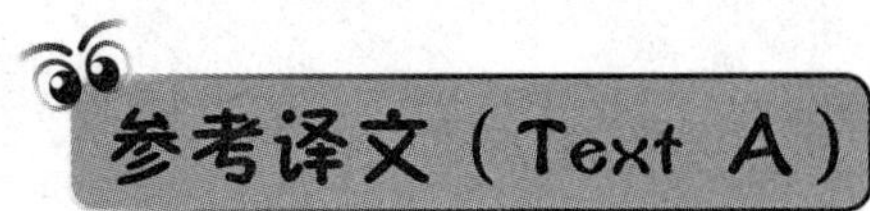

产品分类

我们可以说，产品是一种好的服务，或者是一种由一系列有形和无形的属性组成的理念，这些属性满足消费者的需求，并以金钱或其他价值单位来交换。

组织如何看待产品取决于它的视角。面向生产的组织基本上把产品看作是用于生产产品的资源的一种表现形式；面向市场的组织从目标消费者的角度来看待产品，把它看作是一系列的利益，这些利益既有功能性，也有情感性。因此，产品是一系列物理、化学和/或无形属性，具有满足当前和潜在客户需求的潜力。除实物本身外，其他要素还包括保修、安装、售后配套服务和包装。

1. 产品的三个层次

消费者通常认为产品只是他们购买的实物。为了进一步积极探索产品的本质，我们把它看作三种不同的产品——核心产品、有形产品，最后是附加产品。这个概念被称为产品的三层次理论。当你为企业最终确定一个产品或者当你想分析一个产品的时候，这三个层次就会发挥作用。与任何企业一样，产品也有其层次结构。一个产品可以分为三个层次，它们有不同的特点和好处，有助于市场细分，定向目标市场和定位。因此，产品的三个层次可以更好地定义产品。这三个层次为：

1.1 核心产品

核心产品不是有形的实物产品，你无法触摸它。这是因为核心产品是对你有价值的产品。假设你正在计划推出自己的汽车制造产品。你的核心是什么？是汽车本身吗？不。核心产品是为你的客户制造方便。你的顾客也可以乘公共汽车或出租车，但他们更喜欢汽车，因为方便，也因为汽车是地位的象征。因此，塔塔汽车的核心是方便和物有所值，而宝马的核心是地位的象征。

1.2 有形产品

有形产品是有形的实物产品。你可以从中得到一些有用的东西。有形产品是在你决定了核心产品是什么之后生产出来的。因此，如果产品核心是地位象征，那么你的有形产品将是一个高质量、高价格的产品。如果是一种提供方便的产品，那么产品的基础就是物有所值。有形产品在本质上是可以量化的，具有颜色、品牌、质量等属性。

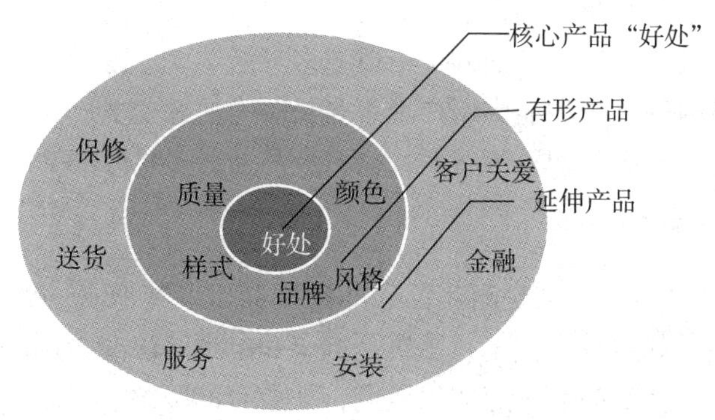

图6-1

1.3 附加产品

附加产品是产品的非实体部分。它通常由许多附加价值组成，可以为其支付或不支付附加费。当你买车的时候，部分附加品是保修、由汽车制造商提供的服务支持和所有的售后服务。附加产品是一种调整核心或有形产品，以满足客户个人需求的重要方式。附加产品的特性可以转化为针对个人的好处。

产品的这三个层次在产品管理中起着至关重要的作用，在决定一个公司的营销组合时也很重要。这主要是因为，有形产品如果有了附加产品，那么也需要对这些附加产品的促销、投放和定价做出决定。因此，产品决策通常是营销组合的主要决策。

2. 不同的分类系统

产品可以分为有形产品和无形产品。有形产品是一种可以通过触摸感知的物体，如建筑物、车辆、小工具或衣服。无形产品是一种只能被间接感知的产品，如保险单。服务可大致分为耐用品和非耐用品两大类，为无形产品。

根据用途——在在线产品目录中，零售商西尔斯·罗巴克公司将其产品分了“货品区”，根据功能或品牌向潜在购物者展示产品。每个产品都有一个西尔斯商品编号和一个制造商的型号。西尔斯使用货品区给产品分组，旨在帮助客户在传统的百货商店中按功能或品牌浏览产品。

根据关联——产品线指的是“一组紧密相关的产品，这些产品要么功能相似，要么是卖给相同的客户群，要么通过相同类型的销售点进行营销，要么都在给定的价格范围内”。许多企业提供一系列的产品线，这些产品线可能是单个组织独有的，也可能是整个行业的通用产品。美国人口普查局过去曾根据诸如“意外、健康和医疗保险费”以及“有担保消费贷款收入”等不同类型的产品线编制金融和保险业的收入数据。在保险行业，产品线是由承保险种来表示的，如车险、商业险、人寿险等。

国家和国际产品分类——为了经济统计的目的，各种产品分类系统得以开发。北美自由贸易协定的签署国正在研究一种被称为 NAPCS 的产品分类系统，将其作为北美工业分类系统（NAICS）的配套产品。欧盟在使用其他产品分类的同时，使用“按活动分类产品”的系统。联合国为了国际经济活动报告也对产品进行了分类。

Aspinwall 分类系统根据五个变量对产品进行分类和评级：

更换率（产品多久重购一次？）

毛利率（每件产品的利润是多少？）

买方目标调整（买方对该产品的购买习惯有多灵活？）

产品满意的持续时间（产品能为用户带来多长时间的好处？）

购买者搜索行为的持续时间（消费者购买该产品需要多长时间？）

3. 产品分类——产品的类型

产品有三种基本类型，分别是耐用品、非耐用品以及纯服务。耐用品是那些能在较长时间内使用的产品，如冰箱、汽车、手机、鞋子和电视等。非耐用品是那些我们需要尽快使用的产品，因为这些产品有一定的保质期，如所有的蔬菜、水果和果汁等。纯服务包括那些在本质上无形或不可分割的给客户的好处，没有发生任何产品的所有权转移，因为这些产品本质上是体验性的，会计、医生、律师和教师等都是诠释“纯服务”一词的最好例子。

所有这些产品都由工业买家或最终消费者购买。消费品是最终消费者为个人消费而购买的。工业产品由企业采购，用于加工经营和管理。此外，工业产品使用最多，包括原材料或回形针等可转化为成品的消耗品。

4. 不同形式的产品

这些产品类型或产品分类的两种不同形式为：

4.1　消费品

最终消费者为个人消费而购买的产品称为消费品。这些产品的购买方式为营销者进一步分类产品提供了依据。以下是根据购买方式和营销方式对这些消费品进行的重要分类。

日用品——那些不费精力、不用作比较就能迅速、频繁地买到的消费品，我们称之为日用品，包括如糖果、报纸、肥皂、快餐等。便利品被大批量地放置在商店的前面，以便顾客很容易买到。这些产品价格较低。

选购品——这类产品购买频率较低，顾客会仔细比较价格、质量、可持续性和风格。在购买选购品时，顾客会花费更多的时间和精力收集信息和作比较。例如服装、家具、大型家电、二手车、酒店和汽车旅馆服务等都是选购品。市场营销人员在较少的经销点对这些产品进行分销，并提供强大的销售支持服务，帮助客户进行比较。

特殊产品——特殊产品是指具有品牌识别或独特特征的消费品，一批重要客户群乐于购买的此类产品。特殊产品的一些例子包括特定品牌和种类的汽车、昂贵的摄影设备、品牌服装、法律或医学专家的服务，等等。这些产品的客户能够花费足够的精力，找到产品的相关经销商。然而，通常情况下，他们不会对特殊产品进行对比。

非需求品——那些消费者未知或已知的，但通常不会考虑购买的消费品。因为消费者是通过广告来了解该类产品的，所以非需求品中包含重大的创新。非需求品包括人寿保险等。营销非需求品需要大量的个人销售活动、广告和营销。

4.2　工业产品

为进一步加工或经营企业而购买的产品称为工业产品。工业产品和消费品的主要区别在于购买产品的目的。例如，如果购买割草机是为了在房屋周围使用，那么这台割草机就属于消费品；但如果购买同一台割草机是用于园林绿化业务，则该割草机被归类为工业产品。根据参与生产过程的程度和价值大小角度，工业产品可划分为三大类。

材料和部件——原材料、天然产品和制造材料属于材料和部件的范畴。原材料部分包括农产品和天然产品，如棉花、小麦、蔬菜、水果、鱼、原油、铁等。组成材料和零部件包含在生产区域中的有纱、电线、水泥、铁、轮胎、小型汽车等。制造材料和部件大多数直接卖给工业用户。这类产品的主要营销要素是价格和服务，广告和品牌并不是那么重要。工业产品需求也是源自消费者需求的派生需求。

资本项目——那些辅助客户生产经营的工业产品称为资本项目，如装置和附属设备。装置包括建造中的固定设备。附属设备包括办公设备和便携式工厂设备。附属设备的使用寿命较短，仅用于协助生产。

供应品和服务——供应品包含维修保养品和生产供应品，如钉子、油漆、润滑油、铅笔、纸张、煤炭等。由于购买时省力省时，供应品又被视为工业日用品。业务咨询服务和维修保养服务属于业务服务类别，这些服务是根据某种合同提供的。

Case Fashion Supply Chain

Unit 7

Text A

Product Life Cycle and Its Implications

The product life cycle is a conceptual representation. It is a product aging process. Just as human-beings have a typical life cycle going from childhood, adolescence, youth, and old-age, so also products follow a similar route. Product life cycle is simply graphic portrayal of the sales history of a product from the time it is introduced to the time when it is withdrawn. According to Professor Philip Kotler, it is "an attempt to recognize distinct stages in the sales history of the product". To borrow the words of Mr. Kollat D.T., Mr. Blackwell R.D., and Robenson J.F., it is a "generalized model of sales and profits trends for a product class or category over a period of time". As a concept, it means three things:

(1) Products move through the cycle of Introduction, Growth, Maturity, and Decline at different speeds.

(2) Both sales volumes and unit profits rise correspondingly till the growth stage. However, in the period of maturity stage, sales volume rises but profits fall.

(3) The successful product management needs dynamic functional approach to meet the unique situations of sales and profitability.

The product aging process has four stages, namely, Introduction, Growth, Maturity, and Decline. A detailed analysis of each stage is a must in terms of basic features and implications.

1. Introduction

Whenever a new product is introduced, it has only a proved demand and not the effective demand. That is why sales are low and creeping very slowly. It may be the case with a product like instant coffee, frozen orange juice or a powdered coffee cream. This first stage of product life cycle is characterized by:

(1) Low and slow sales.

The product sales are the lowest and move up very slowly at snail's pace. The basic reasons for this are:

• Delays in expansion of production capacity;

• Delays in making available the product to consumers due to lack of retail outlets which are acceptable and adequate;

• Consumer resistance to change over from the established consumption behavioral patterns.

(2) Highest promotional expenses.

During this period of introduction or the development, the promotional expenses bear the highest proportion of sales. It is so because the sales are of smaller volume on one side and high level promotion efforts to create demand on the other. Demand creation is not an easy task as it is a matter of breaking the barriers and breaking new ice which is done by:

• Informing potential and present consumers of the new and unknown product;

• Inducing a trial of the product;

• Screening distribution net-work.

(3) Highest product prices.

The prices charged at the beginning are the highest possible because of:

• Lower output and sales absorbing fixed costs;

• Technological problems might not have been mastered fully;

• Higher margin to support higher doses of promotional expenses is a must for growth;

• Very few competitors or no competitors;

• Sales to higher income groups in a limited area for cultivating the effective demand.

2. Growth

Once the market has accepted the product, sales begin to rise. The prices may remain high to recover some of the development costs. With high sales and prices, profits rise sharply. This encourages competition leading to possible product improvement. Although the contribution to sales is sizeable from the high income group buyers, middle income group buyers do not contribute towards sales. The basic characteristics of this stage of product life cycle are:

(1) Sales rise faster.

The sales start climbing up at faster rate because of:

• Killing the consumer resistance to the product;

• The distribution network retail outlets is built to the needs;

• Production facilities are streamlined to meet the fast moving sales.

Thus, sales increase at an increasing rate over the period of time.

(2) Higher promotional expenses.

During the period of growth, the promotional strategy changes. The problem is no longer one of persuading the market to buy the product, but rather to make it to buy a particular brand.

The question is one of creating and maintaining and extending selective demand. The advertising moves towards brand identification and brand awareness, to have the effects of a brand image. Special offers, concessions, allowance to the stockiest and dealers are given to push a particular brand or brand group.

(3) Product improvements.

With the high sales and prices, profits rise sharply and because of this, there is greater incentive for the companies to enter the market. Competitors have the advantage of entering the market because research and development have already been completed by innovating firm at its costs. Once the originator has paved the pattern of market, competitors can become stronger by coming out with modified products. Along with product modification, they may reduce prices too. This makes the originators further improve the product and bring down the price to nab competition.

3. *Maturity*

Eventually, market becomes saturated because the house-hold demand is satisfied and distribution channels are full. Sales level off and over capacity in production becomes apparent. Competition intensifies as each manufacturer wants to ensure that he can maintain production at a level which gives him low unit costs. The greater the cost of production and the initial investment, the more important it is to maintain high output so as to cover fixed costs at lower rates of revenue. Lower prices are essential to stave off the competition. Though production costs are reduced, the margin of distributors may not taper off. The efforts are made to extend the maturity stage. That is why this period is much longer than the growth stage. The features of this stage of life cycle are:

(1) Sales increase at decreasing rate.

As most of the customers are knowing the uses of the product, the sales grow at failing rates giving an overall picture of "off level" situation. It shows that there is apparent gap in production level and sales level. This intensifies competition. Efforts are made to level the sales curve by extension strategies. There is little growth in the market as there is declaration in sales growth leading to market saturation. Therefore, demand mostly consists of repeat sales. Consequently competition intensifies, prices tend to fall and selling effort becomes aggressive. Profits, then, are squeezed. That is why the firms employ extension strategies to retain their market share. There can be at least five such extension strategies, which are briefly outlined below:

• Development of new markets

The first possibility is the development of new markets for existing products by isolating areas where the product is not used and modifying it to suit to those particular segment requirements. For instance, battery shavers were introduced to fulfil the need for electric shavers when the users are away from electricity supply. There has been a considerable effort to expand the usage of computers to meet the needs and budgets of small firms.

• Development of new uses

The second possibility is the development of new uses for the existing products such as the application of red LCD (Liquid Crystal Displays) , for example, in calculators and watches. Nylon is another example, a product which has gone through many expansions. Originally introduced for military purposes in the manufacture of parachutes and rope, it is now developed as a fibre, fabric in knit and woven form and gone into tyre manufacture.

• Development of more frequent use

This can be achieved either by altering its image or by emphasizing special characteristics like convenience and quality. Thus, turkeys have changed from "Christmas Treat" to "all year round food". Vitamin B capsules are popularized as a regular intake than as a curative dose.

• Development of wider range of products

This is another viable strategy. Today, we see practically an explosion in the flavours of ice-cream available in the market. Today, we get different classes of ice-cream, ranging from inexpensive everyday brands to very costly brands with unusual exotic combinations of flavours and colours.

• Development of style change

These style changes demonstrate the newness of the most recent product. Most of the consumer durable item manufacturers such as cars, sound gadgets, cameras, watches and the like go in for this strategy of creating new designs and models, making the consumers discard the earlier ones. Thus, Sony Corporation of Japan has been introducing new and latest models of television sets as ME-2026, ME-2036, ME-2066, ME-2096 and so on. Even Ambassador Mark I, Mark II, Mark III speak of technical improvements, reduction in prices to suit the needs of consumers.

(2) Normal promotional expenses.

During this period of maturity, the promotional expenses reach a normal ratio to sales. Most of the competitors spend very normal amount on promotion. Efforts are made to rationalize the existing budget. Though total expenditure does not expand, major share of the expenditure goes to distribution and brand promotion to keep the dealers' loyalty intact. Advertising emphasizes the difference between one brand and those of competitors. As a result, weaker competitors leave the market only to the larger and stronger manufacturers.

(3) Uniform and lower prices.

The prices charged by the producers are quite lower and uniform with a very narrow difference except for the real product differentiation. The strength and vitality of higher prices fade. That is why extension strategies are followed. The price is charged just to cover special costs in addition to the usual manufacturing expenses plus a low margin for the investment. It has an advantage of low margin over broad-based turnover.

4. Decline

In this terminal stage, sooner or later actual sales begin to fall under the impact of new product competition and changing consumer tastes and preferences. Prices and, hence, profits decline. It is stages where the market for the product has been superseded by a technological or style change that replaces the existing demand altogether. That is, the old products are rendered obsolete. For instance, the development of tough water based paint "oil-bond" has made significant inroads into the traditional market for oil-based varnish enamel paints. That is, alternatively, interest in the product may fade, leading to a rapid reduction in sales. The outstanding features of this stage of product life cycle are:

(1) Rapid fall in sales.

As the product is pretty old and new one is available, there is a change in the trend. People are interested in buying something new. The sales, therefore, fall sharply. Over production appears to be the major problem, which induces firms to close down.The total number of firms in the arena comes down. For instance, the number of companies manufacturing calculators is much less than what it was in 2017.

(2) Further fall in prices.

Rapid reduction in sales creates a fear and there will be intense competition to liquidate the stock at the earliest. There would be a new kind of competition to have enlarged share in such a decline stage to have maximum benefit.

(3) No promotional expenses.

Expenditure in support of product falls sharply as prices become keener for fast stock liquidation. Distribution network is reduced to the minimum with thorough rationalization. This is an advantage as product is known for good many years. It may enable the manufacturer to milk the product with profit though sales are scanty.

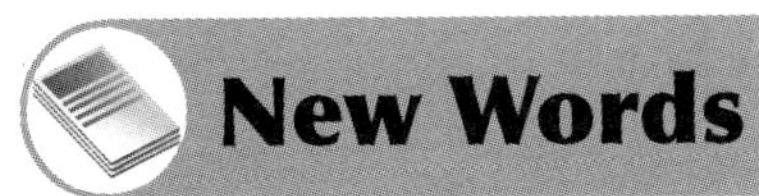

New Words

conceptual [kən'septʃuəl] *adj.* 观念的，概念的

adolescence [ˌædə'lesns] *n.* 青春期，青年期

portrayal [pɔː'treɪəl] *n.* 画像，肖像；描述

withdraw [wɪð'drɔː] *vt.* 退出；撤退，撤走

maturity [mə'tʃʊərəti] *n.* 成熟；完备

curve [kɜːv] *n.* 弧线，曲线

correspondingly [ˌkɒrə'spɒndɪŋli] *adv.* 相对地，比照地，相应地

dynamic [daɪ'næmɪk] *adj.* 动态的；动力的，动力学的；充满活力的

creep [kriːp] *vi.* 爬行，匍匐；缓慢地行进

expansion [ɪk'spænʃn] *n.* 扩张，扩大

resistance [rɪ'zɪstəns] *n.* 抵抗；反对；阻力

proportion [prə'pɔːʃn] *n.* 比，比率；比例

bear [beə] *vt.* 承担；忍受

inducing [ɪn'djuːsɪŋ] *adj.* 产生诱导作用的

charge [tʃɑːdʒ] *vi.* 索价；充电

cultivate ['kʌltɪveɪt] *vt.* 培养，栽培；耕作，种植

streamline ['striːmlaɪn] *vt.* 把……做成流线型；使现代化

concession [kən'seʃn] *n.* 让步，迁就；承认或允许

allowance [ə'laʊəns] *n.* 津贴，补贴；限额；折扣

incentive [ɪn'sentɪv] *n.* 动机，诱因，刺激
originator [ə'rɪdʒɪneɪtə] *n.* 发起人，创作者
pave [peɪv] *vt.* 铺设，为……铺平道路
modification [ˌmɒdɪfɪ'keɪʃn] *n.* 修改，修正，变更；改进
retain [rɪ'teɪn] *vt.* 保持，保留；记住
isolate ['aɪsəleɪt] *vt.* 使隔离，使孤立
shaver ['ʃeɪvə] *n.* 剃具，刮刀
parachute ['pærəʃuːt] *n.* 降落伞；缓降物
fibre ['faɪbə] *n.* 纤维
fabric ['fæbrɪk] *n.* 织物；布
knit [nɪt] *n.* 编织物；编织法
tyre ['taɪə] *n.* 轮胎
capsule ['kæpsjuːl] *n.* 胶囊；航天舱
curative ['kjʊrətɪv] *adj.* 治病的，有治病效力的
dose [dəʊs] *n.* 剂量，药量
viable ['vaɪəbl] *adj.* 可实施的，切实可行的
explosion [ɪk'spləʊʒən] *n.* 爆发；爆炸，炸裂
exotic [ɪg'zɒtɪk] *adj.* 异国的，外来的；异乎寻常的，奇异的
discard [dɪs'kɑːd] *vt.* 丢弃，抛弃
ration ['ræʃn] *n.* 定量，配给量
render ['rendə] *vt.* 给予，提供；使成为
obsolete ['ɒbsə'liːt] *adj.* 废弃的，老式的，已过时的
inroad ['ɪnrəʊd] *n.* 进展；侵袭
varnish ['vɑːnɪʃ] *n.* 清漆，罩光漆
enamel [ɪ'næml] *n.* 搪瓷；瓷釉
arena [ə'riːnə] *n.* 竞技场；场地
liquidate ['lɪkwɪdeɪt] *vt.* 清算，清偿；消除
scanty ['skænti] *adj.* （大小或数量）不足的，勉强够的

Phrases

product life cycle 产品生命周期
profit curve 利润曲线
sales volume 销售量
unit profit 单位盈利
instant coffee 即溶咖啡
at snail's pace 步履蹒跚
production capability 产能，生产能力
retail outlet 零售商店
promotional expense 推销费
level off 使平稳，使稳定
market saturation 市场饱和
market share 市场占有率
stave off 避开，挡开；延缓
taper off 逐渐变细，逐渐停止
go in for 参加，从事
except for 除……之外
sooner or later 迟早
close down（使）停业；（使）停产
in support of 支持

Abbreviation

LCD (Liquid Crystal Displays) 液晶显示器

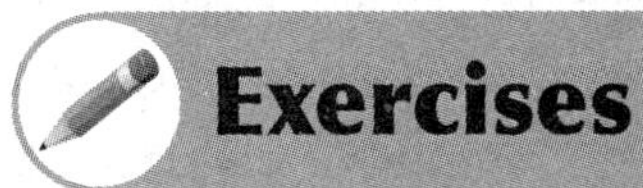

Exercises

EX. 1 Answer the following questions according to Text A.

(1) What is product life cycle according to Mr. Kollat D.T., Mr. Blackwell R.D., and Robenson J.F.?

(2) As depicted in Figure 7-1, how many stages does the product aging process have? And what are they?

(3) Why are sales low and creeping very slowly in the first stage of product life cycle?

(4) What are the characteristics of the first stage of product life cycle?

(5) What are the basic characteristics of the second stage of product life cycle?

(6) How does the promotional strategy change during the period of growth?

(7) What are the features of the third stage of product life cycle?

(8) During the period of maturity, what extension strategies are employed by the firms to retain their market share?

(9) Which extension strategy does the example "Nylon" illustrate?

(10) What are the outstanding features of the terminal stage of product life cycle?

EX. 2 Translate the following phrases from English into Chinese and vice versa.

(1) market saturation ______________________

(2) product life cycle ______________________

(3) market share ______________________

(4) profit curve ______________________

(5) production capability ______________________

(6) 零售店；零售网点 ______________________

(7) 推销费 ______________________

(8) 单位盈利 ______________________

(9) 花费，支出 ______________________

(10) 完好无损的；原封不动的 ______________________

EX. 3 **Translate the following into Chinese.**

Life cycle assessment (LCA, also known as life cycle analysis, ecobalance, and cradle-to-grave analysis) is a technique to assess environmental impacts associated with all the stages of a product's life from raw material extraction through materials processing, manufacture, distribution, use, repair and maintenance, and disposal or recycling. Designers use this process to help critique their products.

The goal of LCA is to compare the full range of environmental effects assignable to products and services by quantifying all inputs and outputs of material flows and assessing how these material flows affect the environment. This information is used to improve processes, support policy and provide a sound basis for informed decisions. The term life cycle refers to the notion that a fair, holistic assessment requires the assessment of raw-material production, manufacture, distribution, use and disposal including all intervening transportation steps necessary or caused by the product's existence.

EX. 4 **Fill in the blanks with the words given below.**

occurs	dynamic	suggests	production	invented
exports	cater to	maturing	developed	origin

The Product Life Cycle Theory

The product life cycle theory is an economic theory that was developed by Raymond Vernon in response to the failure of the Heckscher-Ohlin model to explain the observed pattern of international trade. The theory (1)________ that early in a product's life cycle, all the parts and labor associated with that product come from the area where it was (2)________. After the product becomes adopted and used in the world markets, production gradually moves away from the point of (3)________. In some situations, the product becomes an item that is imported by its original country of invention.The model applies to labor-saving and capital-using products that (4)________ high-income groups.

In the new product stage, the product is produced and consumed in the US; no export trade (5)________. In the (6)________ product stage, mass-production techniques are developed and foreign demand (in developed countries) expands; the US now (7)________ the product to other developed countries. In the standardized product stage, production moves to developing countries, which then export the product to (8)________ countries.

The model demonstrates (9)________ comparative advantage. The country that has the comparative advantage in the (10)________ of the product changes from the innovating (developed) country to the developing countries.

Text B

Product Life Cycle Management

Product life cycle management (PLM) is the succession of strategies by business management as a product goes through its life cycle. The conditions in which a product is sold changes over time and must be managed as it moves through its succession of stages.

The goals of PLM are to reduce time to market, improve product quality, reduce prototyping costs, identify potential sales opportunities and revenue contributions, and reduce environmental impacts at end-of-life. To create successful new products, the company must understand its customers, markets and competitors. PLM integrates people, data, processes and business systems. It provides product information for companies and their extended supply chain enterprise. PLM solutions help organizations overcome the increased complexity and engineering challenges of developing new products for the global competitive markets.

1. *Three assumptions of PLC management*

The concept of product life cycle (PLC) concerns the life of a product in the market with respect to business/commercial costs and sales measures. PLC proceeds through multiple phases, involves many professional disciplines, and requires many skills, tools and processes. PLC management makes the following three assumptions:

- Products have a limited life and thus every product has a life cycle.
- Product sales pass through distinct stages, each posing different challenges, opportunities, and problems to the seller.
- Products require different marketing, financing, manufacturing, purchasing, and human resource strategies in each life cycle stage.

All manufactured products have a limited life, and during this life they will pass through four product life cycle stages: Introduction, Growth, Maturity, and Decline. In each of these stages manufacturers face a different set of challenges. PLM is the application of different strategies to help meet these challenges and ensure that, whatever stage of the cycle a product may be going through, the manufacturer can maximize sales and profits for their product.

2. *Focusing on key business areas*

To effectively manage the product life cycle, organizations need to have a very strong focus on a number of key business areas.

- **Development**: Before a product can begin its life cycle, it needs to be developed. Research and new product development is one of the first and possibly most important phases of the manufacturing process that companies will need to spend time and money on, in order to make sure that the product is a success.
- **Financing**: Manufacturers will usually need significant funds in order to launch a new product and sustain it through the introduction stage, but further investment through the growth

and maturity stages may be financed by the profits from sales. In the Decline stage, additional investment may be needed to adapt the manufacturing process or move into new markets. Throughout the product life cycle, companies need to consider the most appropriate way to finance their costs in order to maximize profit potential.

• **Marketing**: During a product's life, companies will need to adapt their marketing and promotional activity depending on which stage of the cycle the product is passing through. As the market develops and matures, the consumer's attitude to the product will change. So the marketing and promotional activity that launches a new product in the introduction stage will need to be very different from the campaigns that will be designed to protect market share during the maturity stage.

• **Manufacturing**: The cost of manufacturing a product can change during its life cycle. To begin with, new processes and equipment mean costs are high, especially with a low sales volume. As the market develops and production increases, costs will start to fall; and when more efficient and cheaper methods of production are found, these costs can fall even further. As well as focusing on marketing to make more sales and profit, companies also need to look at ways of reducing cost throughout the manufacturing process.

• **Information**: Whether it's data about the potential market that will make a new product viable, feedback about different marketing campaigns to see which are most effective, or monitoring the growth and eventual decline of the market in order to decide on the most appropriate response, information is crucial to the success of any product. Manufacturers that efficiently manage their products along the product life cycle curve are usually those that have developed the most effective information systems.

Most manufacturers accept their products will have a limited life. While there may not be much they can do to change that, by focusing on the key business areas mentioned, product life cycle management allows them to make sure that a product will be as successful as possible during its life cycle stages, however long that might be.

3. Extending the product life cycle

Once the product is designed and put into the market, the offering should be managed efficiently for the buyers to get value from it. Before entering into any market, complete analysis is carried out by the industry for both external and internal factors including the laws and regulations, environment, economics, cultural values, and market needs. This term PLC is associated with every product that exists, however, due to a limited shelf life, the product has to expire. From the business perspective, as a good business, the product needs to be sold before it finishes its life. In terms of profitability, expiry may jolt the overall profitability of the business, therefore, there are a few strategies which are practiced to ensure that the product is sold within the defined period of maturity. Extending the product life cycle by improving sales, this can be done through:

• Advertising: Its purpose is to get additional audience and potential customers.

• Exploring and expanding to new markets: By conducting market research and offering the product (or some adapted form of it) to new markets, it is possible to get more customers.

• Reducing price: Many customers are attracted by price cuts and discount tags.

• Adding new features: Adding value to the product catches the attention of many buyers.

• Packaging: New, attractive, useful or eco-friendly packaging influence the target customers.

• Changing customer consumption habits: Promoting new trends of consumption can increase the number of customers.

• Special promotions: Raising interest by offering Jackpot and other offers.

• Heightening interest: Many of the following things attract many customers who match certain profiles: Eco-friendly production processes, good work conditions, funding the efforts of non-profit organizations (cancer cure, refugees, environment and animal protection, etc.) and the like.

Something important to notice is that all these techniques rely on advertising to become known. Advertising needs the others to target other potential customers and not the same over and over again.

4. Effective strategies to manage product life cycle

Product life cycle management allows companies to anticipate and manage their product's various business cycles. It involves using multiple pricing strategies along four stages of the product's life. There's the introduction stage, the growth stage, the peak stage, and finally the decline stage. Every product goes through these four stages. Some go through these four stages very quickly, while others take decades to reach their final end of life.

However, in some cases there's a fifth stage. Although this last stage is somewhat rare, it does occur. When it does, it is those companies who steal market share in the fourth stage that are ultimately able to achieve significant profits in the fifth. So, what are the most important strategies in this final stage of product life cycle management?

4.1 Assessing the product's future

Granted, the product itself is on a steady decline, but if the company has determined that this particular product might enter the fifth stage, then they might have the ability to capture market share in the fourth, and be the "last man standing" so to speak. In this case, the company must define future volumes, if and when that product will enter the fifth stage and what the company must do to steal market share in a declining market. These are some of the questions that must be answered:

• How long (in years) will customers continue to purchase the product?

• Will the company have access to critical parts and materials in order to continue manufacturing the product?

• Does the company have a competitive advantage? If so, how can the company use this advantage to steal market share in the fourth Stage?

4.2 Stealing market share in the fourth stage

Let's assume the company has determined that the product's decline period will last three more years, have one year where demand is extremely small or non-existent, followed by a fifth year of rebirth and growth. In this case, the company's market share on the product would be an inverse relationship to the product's decline in the fourth stage.

In essence, the company would be pushing out its competitors while grabbing additional market share in a declining market. However, this will only be successful if the company is tracking its market share in each of these three years during the decline stage:

• Company must track its increased market share during each of the three years.

• Company must continue to track customer consumption and ensure the product line will enter the fifth stage.

• Company must track gross profit during each year.

4.3 Preparing customers for the fifth stage

All this work must bear fruit in the fifth stage of product life cycle management. For this to be successful means the company must accept that raising the product's price might be a strategy to increase gross profit. Please note, raising pricing isn't paramount to success in this fifth stage, but an argument can easily be made that manufacturing costs have increased and therefore warrant an increased price. In this fifth stage the company can essentially dictate its product's price by explaining the increased costs, due to a lack of material availability, as well as the fact that the company is manufacturing a product other competitors have abandoned.

A number of companies may question the logic behind trying to steal market share in a declining market. However, when successful, companies are able to achieve significant returns on gross profit, returns that can help fund future product developments. A number of companies adopt this strategy and swear by the results.

Success depends upon a thorough understanding of the market, its customers and most importantly, the product's life. Granted, during this fourth and final stage, some competitors will be more than willing to abandon the market. However, they'll do so because they haven't taken the time to fully assess the product's life and its future returns.

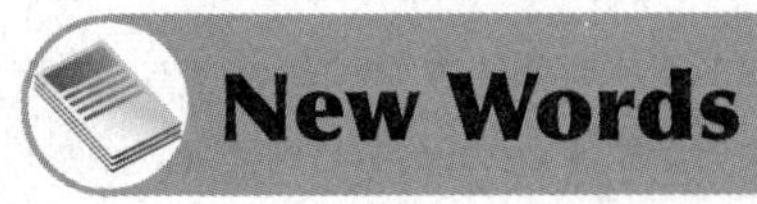

succession [sək'seʃn] *n.* 一系列，接连；继承人，继承权

concern [kən'sɜːn] *vt.* 涉及，关系到

proceed [prəʊ'siːd] *vi.* 进行，前进

monitor ['mɒnɪtə] *vt.* 监督，监控

extend [ɪk'stend] *vt.* 延伸，扩大，推广

expiry [ɪk'spaɪəri] *n.* 终止，满期，届期

jolt [dʒəʊlt] *vt.* 动摇；震动

eco-friendly ['iːkəʊ-ˌfrendlɪ] *adj.* 对生态环境友好的；不妨害生态环境的

jackpot ['dʒækpɒt] *n.* 头奖

heighten ['haɪtn] *vt.* （使）变高；（使）加强

refugee [ˌrefju'dʒiː] *n.* 避难者，难民

peak [pi:k] *n.* 最高点，顶点；尖端
granted ['græntɪd] *adv.* 不错，的确
steady ['stedi] *adj.* 稳定的，不变的
capture ['kæptʃə] *vt.* 捕获，占领；夺取；吸引
declining [dɪ'klaɪnɪŋ] *adj.* 衰退中的
non-existent [nɒn-ɪg'zɪstənt] *adj.* 不存在的
rebirth [ˌri:'bɜ:θ] *n.* 新生，再生；复兴
inverse [ˌɪn'vɜ:s] *adj.* 相反的，逆向的，倒转的
grab [græb] *vt.* 抢夺；夺取或抓住
paramount ['pærəmaʊnt] *adj.* 极为重要的，至高无上的
warrant ['wɒrənt] *vt.* 保证，担保；授权
dictate ['dɪkteɪt] *vt.* 指示，命令；口述
abandon [ə'bændən] *vt.* 放弃，抛弃
logic ['lɒdʒɪk] *n.* 逻辑，逻辑学
swear [sweə] *n.* 发誓，宣誓

Phrases

over time 随着时间的推移
key business areas 重点业务领域
to begin with 首先
laws and regulations 法规
cultural values 文化价值观
be associated with 和……联系在一起；与……有关
discount tags 折扣标签
catch the attention 吸引注意力
and the like 等等；诸如此类
rely on 依靠；信赖
on a steady decline 稳步下降
in essence 本质上，大体上
gross profit 毛利
push out 挤出；开除；除掉某人
bear fruit 奏效；结出果实

Abbreviations

PLM (Product Life Cycle Management) 产品生命周期管理
PLC (Product Life Cycle) 产品生命周期

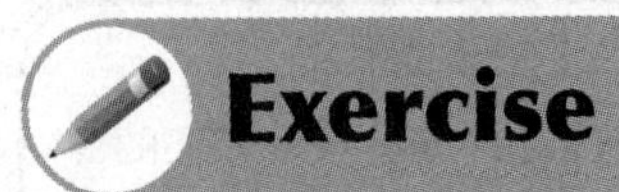

EX. Answer the following questions according to Text B.

(1) What is the goal of product life cycle management (PLM)?

(2) List one of the three assumptions made by PLM.

(3) What are the key business areas that organizations need to focus on to effectively manage the product life cycle?

(4) What factors are analyzed in a complete analysis carried out by the industry before a product enters into any market?

(5) List at least three techniques which can extend the product life cycle.

(6) What packaging may influence the target customers?

(7) If the fifth stage of product life cycle occurs, what companies are ultimately able to achieve significant profits?

(8) What are the most important strategies in the final stage of PLM?

(9) Suppose that the product's decline period will last three more years, what should the company track in each of these three years, to push out its competitors while grabbing additional market share?

(10) Why will some competitors be willing to abandon the market during the fourth and final stage?

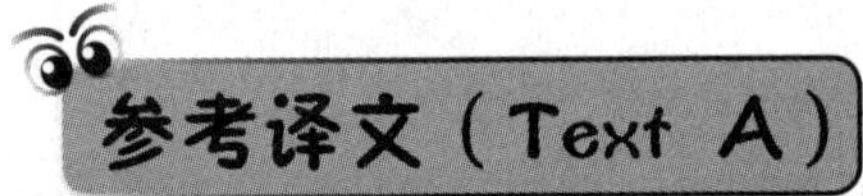

产品生命周期及其含义

产品生命周期是一个概念性的表述，是一个产品老化的过程。正如人类有一个典型的经历童年、青春期、青年和老年阶段的生命周期一样，产品也遵循类似的过程。产品生命周期简单地描述了产品从推出到退出的销售历史。菲利普·科特勒教授认为，产品生命周期是“识别产品销售历史上不同阶段的一次尝试”。借用科拉特、布莱克威尔和罗宾逊三位先生的话来说,产品生命周期是“某类产品在一段时间内的销售和利润趋势的广义模型”。作为一个概念，它有以下三个方面的含义：

（1）产品以不同的速度经历引进、发展、成熟和衰退的周期。

（2）销量和单位利润均相应地增长，直至发展阶段。但进入成熟阶段后，销量上升，而利润下降。

（3）成功的产品管理需要动态调节功能方法来满足销售和盈利的特殊情况。

产品老化过程有四个阶段，即引入期、发展期、成熟期和衰落期。就每个阶段的基本特征和含义而言，必须进行详细的分析。

1. 引入期

新产品无论什么时候引入，它都只是经过证实的需求，而不是有效需求。这就是为什么销量很低，增长非常缓慢的原因，速溶咖啡、冷冻橙汁或研磨奶油咖啡这样的产品可能会是这种情况。产品生命周期第一阶段的特点：

（1）销售低迷。

产品销量最低，且增长速度非常缓慢。其基本原因是：

• 产能扩张延迟；

• 缺乏可接受的和足够的零售网点导致向消费者提供产品的时间延迟；

• 消费者不愿改变既定的消费行为模式。

（2）推销费最高。

在产品推出和开发阶段，推销费用占销售收入的比例最高。因为一方面销量较小，另一方面促销力度较大，以创造需求。创造需求不是一项容易的任务，因为它是一个突破障碍并打破僵局的问题，需要通过以下方式来完成：

• 将新产品和未知产品告知潜在和现有的消费者；

• 诱导消费者试用产品；

• 筛选分销网络。

（3）产品价格最高。

产品的价格在开始时可能是最高的，因为：

• 承担固定成本的产量和销量都较低；

• 技术问题可能还没有被完全掌握；

• 要实现增长，必须提高利润率，以支持更多的推销费用；

• 竞争对手很少或没有竞争对手；

• 为了发展有效需求，在有限区域内向高收入人群销售。

2. 发展期

一旦市场接受了该产品，销售量就开始上升。为了收回部分开发成本，产品价格可能要保持在高位。由于销量和价格高，利润急剧上升。因此，各企业争先对产品进行可能的改进。高收入群体对销售额的贡献很大，中等收入群体的贡献并不大。产品生命周期这一阶段的基本特征：

（1）销售增长较快。

销售开始以更快的速度攀升，因为：

• 消除了消费者对产品的抵制情绪；

• 建立了满足客户需求的分销网络零售网点；

• 流线型的生产设施满足了快速增长的销售需求。

因此，销售额在一段时间内持续增长。

（2）推销费用增加。

在发展期阶段，推销策略发生了变化。现在面临的问题不再是说服市场购买产品，而是让市场购买某个特定的品牌，创造、维持和扩大选择性需求。广告要转向品牌识别和品牌意识，具备品牌形象的效果。为了推广某一品牌或某一品牌集团，向存货最充足者及经销商提供特惠、让利、补贴等。

（3）产品的改进。

随着销量的增加和价格的上涨，利润急剧上升，因此，企业进入市场的动力更大。竞争对手有进军市场的优势，因为研发成本已经由创新企业支付了。一旦原创企业铺设了市场模式，竞争对手就可以通过改进产品变得更加强大。随着产品的改进，他们可能还会降低价格。这使得原创企业进一步提高产品质量，并降低了产品价格，以获得竞争优势。

3. 成熟期

最终，由于家庭需求已得到满足和销售渠道也已饱和，市场趋于饱和，销售趋于平稳，产能明显过剩。由于每个制造商都希望确保自己能够维持生产水平，降低单位成本，竞争就加剧了。生产成本和初期投资越高，就越要保持高产量，从而以较低的收入弥补固定成本。低价是在竞争中暂时胜出的必要条件。虽然生产成本降低了，但经销商的利润可能不会减少。要尽力延长成熟期。这就是为什么成熟期比发展期长得多。生命周期这一阶段的特点是：

（1）销售额以递减速度增长。

由于大多数客户都知道产品的用途，所以销售增长率在下降，总体上呈现出“低水平”的情况，说明生产水平与销售水平存在明显差距。这使得竞争更为激烈，可尽力采用一些扩展策略将销售曲线拉平。市场几乎没有增长，因为销售增长已经导致市场饱和。因此，需求主要由重复销售构成。因此，竞争加剧，价格趋于下降，销售工作变得更为积极。于是，利润受到挤压。这就是这些公司采用扩展策略来保持市场份额的原因。至少有五种扩展策略，简要概述为：

• 开发新市场

第一种可能性是为现有产品开发新市场，隔离该产品未被使用的区域，并改进现有产品以适应这些特定的细分市场需求。例如，为了满足用户在没有电力供应的情况下对电动剃须刀的需求，引入电池剃须刀；为了满足小型公司的需求和预算，努力扩大计算机的用途范围。

• 开发新用途

第二种可能性是开发现有产品的新用途，例如，将现有的红色液晶显示屏应用到计算器和手表上。另一个例子是尼龙，这是一个已经经历多次扩展的产品。它最初用于制造军用降落伞和绳索，现在发展成为一种针织和编织品中的纤维、织物，并用于轮胎制造。

• 开发更高的使用频率

这可以通过改变产品的形象或强调产品的特性来实现，如强调产品的便利性和质量。因此，火鸡已经从“圣诞大餐”变成了“全年性食物”；维生素 B 胶囊已作为常规摄入品而不是治疗药品广受欢迎。

• 开发更多的产品种类

这是另一个可行的策略。例如，市场上冰淇淋口味激增。我们有各种各样的冰淇淋，有便宜的日常品牌，也有非常昂贵的品牌，其口味和颜色有着不同寻常的异国情调。

• 变换风格

风格的变化显示出近期产品的新颖之处。大多数耐用消费品制造商，如汽车、音响设备、照相机、手表等都采用这种策略，开发新设计和新型号，使消费者"喜新厌旧"。因此，日本索尼公司不断推出新式样和新型号的电视机，如 ME-2026、ME-2036、ME-2066，和 ME-2096 等。就连马克一世、马克二世、马克三世大使也谈到要改进技术，降低价格以满足消费者的需求。

（2）推销费用趋于正常。

在成熟期期间，推销费用与销售收入形成了正常的比例。大多数竞争对手在产品推销上的花费都趋正常，正在努力使现有预算合理化。虽然总支出没有增加，但支出的主要部分都用于分销和品牌推广，以保持经销商的忠诚度。广告也主要强调一个品牌和其他竞争品牌之间的区别。因此，实力较弱的竞争对手只能将市场留给规模更大、实力更强的制造商。

（3）统一低价。

除了真正的产品差异化之外，生产商收取的价格相对较低且统一，价格差别很小。价格上涨的势头和活力逐渐减弱，这就是要采用扩展策略的原因。除了通常的制造费用和较低的投资利润外，这个价格只是用来支付特殊成本。与大量的营业额相比，它具有利润率低的优势。

4. 衰落期

在最后这一阶段，实际销售迟早会受到新产品竞争和消费者口味偏好变化的影响。价格下降，利润也随之下降。在这个阶段，技术创新或风格变化已经完全代替了现有的需求，从而取代了产品市场。也就是说，旧产品被淘汰了。例如，硬水基涂料"油基黏结剂"的发展对传统的油基搪瓷涂料市场造成了巨大的冲击。换句话说，人们对该产品的兴趣可能会消退，导致销量迅速下降。产品生命周期这一阶段的突出特点是：

（1）销售额迅速下降。

由于产品太旧，又有新产品可用，销售趋势就发生了变化。人们对购买新产品兴趣盎然。因此，原产品销售量急剧下降。生产过剩似乎是主要问题，这导致许多企业倒闭。相互竞争的公司数量也下降了。例如，制造计算器的公司比 2017 年要少了很多。

（2）价格进一步下跌。

销售快速下降造成了一种恐惧，各企业争先在最早的时间内清空库存，从而形成激烈的竞争。在这样一个衰落阶段里，各企业将会形成一种新的竞争，扩大市场份额，以实现利益最大化。

（3）无推广费用。

由于价格随着快速清仓不断下降，推广产品的费用支出也在急剧下降。经过彻底的合理化考虑后，经销网络被缩小到最小范围。产品久负盛名，这是一个优势，它可以使制造商在销售不足的情况下，仍能从产品中获利。

Kit Kat: Revitalising a Brand Leader

Unit 8

Text A

Pricing Strategy

Pricing is the process whereby a business sets the price at which it will sell its products and services, and it may be part of the business' marketing plan. In setting prices, the business will take into account the price at which it could acquire the goods, the manufacturing cost, the market place, competition, market condition, brand, and quality of product.

Pricing is a fundamental aspect of financial modeling and is one of the 4 Ps of the marketing mix. The other 3Ps of the marketing mix are product, promotion, and place. Price is the only revenue generating element among the 4Ps, the rest being cost centers. However, the other Ps of marketing will contribute to decreasing price elasticity and so enable price increases to drive greater revenue and profits. Pricing can be a manual or automatic process of applying prices to purchase and sales orders, based on factors such as a fixed amount, quantity break, promotion or sales campaign, specific vendor quote, price prevailing on entry, shipment or invoice date, combination of multiple orders or lines, and many others. Automated systems require more setup and maintenance but may prevent pricing errors. The needs of the consumer can be converted into demand only if the consumer has the willingness and capacity to buy the product. Thus, pricing is the most important concept in the field of marketing. It is used as a tactical decision in response to comparing market situations.

1. Objectives of pricing

The objectives of pricing should consider:

• the financial goals of the company (i.e., profitability);

• the fit with marketplace realities (Will customers buy at that price?);

• the extent to which the price supports a product's market positioning and be consistent with the other variables in the marketing mix;

• the consistency of prices across categories and products.

Price is influenced by the type of distribution channel, the type of promotions, and the quality of the product. Price can act as a substitute for product quality, effective promotions, or an energetic selling effort by distributors in certain markets. From the marketer's point of view, an efficient price is a price that is very close to the maximum that customers are prepared to pay. In economic terms, it is a price that shifts most of the consumer economic surplus to the producer. A good pricing strategy would be the one which could balance between the price floor (the price below which the organization ends up in losses) and the price ceiling (the price by which the organization experiences a no-demand situation).

2. Pricing strategy

A business can use a variety of pricing strategies when selling a product or service. The price can be set to maximize profitability for each unit sold or from the market overall. It can be used to defend an existing market from new entrants, to increase market share within a market or to enter a new market. The firm's decision on the price of the product and the pricing strategy impacts the consumer's decision on whether or not to purchase the product. When firms are deciding to consider applying any type of pricing strategy they must be aware of the following reasons in order to make an appropriate choice which will benefit their business. The competition within the market today is extremely high, and for this reason, businesses must be attentive to their opponent's actions in order to have the comparative advantage in the market. The technology of internet usage has increased and developed dramatically, therefore, price comparisons can be done by customers through online access. Consumers are very selective regarding the purchases they make due to their knowledge of the monetary value. Firms must be mindful of these factors and price their products accordingly.

Broadly, there are six key pricing strategies mentioned in the marketing literature.

2.1 Premium pricing

Businesses use a premium pricing strategy when they're introducing a new product that has distinct competitive advantages over similar products. A premium-priced product is priced higher than its competitors. Premium pricing is most effective in the beginning of a product's life cycle. Small businesses that sell goods with unique properties are better able to use premium pricing. To make premium pricing palatable to consumers, companies try to create an image in which consumers perceive that the products have value and are worth the higher prices. Besides creating the perception of a higher quality product, the company needs to synchronize its marketing efforts, its product packaging and even the decor of the store must support the image that the product is worth its premium price.

2.2 Penetration pricing

Achieving an initial high volume of sales, with a new product, is the primary objective of penetration pricing. Instead of setting a high price to skim off small but profitable segments of the total market, a company can choose to use penetration pricing. Although this strategy calls for a product to be widely promoted, it allows the setting of a low initial price to enable the company to penetrate the market quickly and deeply. Using the penetration pricing strategy, the company can attract a large number of buyers quickly while it also captures a large share of the market. However, there are conditions that must be met:

Condition 1: The market for the product must be highly price sensitive so that a low price produces more market growth.

Condition 2: The market must be large enough to sustain low profit margins, and production and distribution costs must fall as sales volume increases.

Condition 3: The low price must help keep out the competition.

Condition 4: The company must be able to maintain its low-price position—otherwise, the price advantage will be only temporary. Once competitors enter the market, they may also lower prices.

2.3 Economy pricing

An economy pricing strategy sets prices at the bare minimum to make a small profit. Companies minimize their marketing and promotional costs. The key to a profitable economy pricing program is to sell a high volume of products and services at low prices. Used by a wide range of businesses including generic food suppliers and discount retailers, economy pricing aims to attract the most price-conscious consumers. With this strategy, businesses minimize the costs associated with marketing and production in order to keep product prices down. As a result, customers can purchase the products they need without frills.

While economy pricing is incredibly effective for large companies like Wal-Mart and Target, the technique can be dangerous for small businesses. Because small businesses lack the sales volume of larger companies, they may struggle to generate a sufficient profit when prices are too low. Still, selectively tailoring discounts to your most loyal customers can be a great way to guarantee their patronage for years to come.

2.4 Price skimming

Price skimming is a strategy of setting prices high by introducing new products when the market has few competitors. This method enables businesses to maximize profits before competitors enter the market, when prices then drop. Price skimming is a strategy that works for a new product that is also a new type of product, one that has no copycat competitors or substitutes, yet. Companies that create innovative new products can set high initial prices allowing them to "skim" revenues from the market. However, skimming pricing only works under certain conditions:

Condition 1: The product's quality and image must be strong enough to support its high price, and enough buyers must want and be willing to buy the product at the high price.

Condition 2: Costs involved in producing a smaller volume of the product cannot be so high that they "eat up" the advantage of charging more.

Condition 3: It cannot be easy for competitors to enter the market and swiftly undercut the high price.

With skimming pricing, the goal is to siphon off maximum revenues possible from the market prior to the introduction of substitutes or copycat offerings. Once the market has been skimmed, the company is free to lower the price drastically to capture low-end buyers while rendering competitors unable to compete on price.

2.5 Psychological pricing

Psychological pricing is a pricing strategy based on the theory that certain prices have a psychological impact. There's evidence that consumers tend to perceive "odd prices" as being nearly lower than they actually are, tending to round to the next lowest monetary unit. Thus, prices such as $1.99 are associated with spending $1 rather than $2. The theory that drives this is that lower pricing such as this institutes greater demand. Marketers use psychological pricing to encourage consumer to buy products based on emotions rather than on common-sense logic. For example, setting the price of a watch at $199 is proven to attract more consumers than setting it at $200, even though the true difference here is quite small. This is known as the "left-digit effect". One explanation for this trend is that consumers tend to put more attention on the first number on a price tag than the last. The goal of psychology pricing is to increase demand by creating an illusion of enhanced value for the consumer.

2.6 Bundle pricing

Businesses use bundle pricing to sell multiple products together for a lower price. This is an effective strategy to move unsold items that are simply taking up space. Bundling also creates the perception in the mind of the consumer that he's getting a very attractive value for his money. Bundle pricing works well for companies that have a line of complimentary products. For example, a restaurant could offer a free dessert with an entree on a certain day of the week. Older video games that are reaching the end of their lives are often sold with a Blu-ray to sweeten the deal. Companies need to study and develop pricing strategies that are appropriate for their goods and services. Certain pricing methods work for introducing new products whereas other strategies are implemented for mature products that have more competitors in the market.

Admittedly, there are many different and complex ways that pricing can be approached. However, the bottom-line rules of pricing are simple and straightforward. When it comes to pricing, the most important thing to remember is that prices must be set in a way that will cover costs and profits. With this in mind, pricing must be flexible, because prices should always be in line with changing costs, consumer demand, competitive pricing moves, and profit goals. When the time comes that there is a need to lower prices, the company should first find a way to lower costs, because pricing should always be done in a way that will assure sales and profit.

New Words

whereby [weə'baɪ] *adv.* 借此；通过……
generate ['dʒenəreɪt] *vt.* 形成，造成
elasticity [ˌiːlæ'stɪsəti] *n.* 弹性，弹力；灵活性，伸缩性
manual ['mænjuəl] *adj.* 用手的；手制的，手工的
invoice ['ɪnvɔɪs] *n.* 发货单；发票；（发货或服务）费用清单
willingness ['wɪlɪŋnəs] *n.* 自愿，乐意
tactical ['tæktɪkl] *adj.* 战术的，策略上的；有谋略的
energetic [ˌenə'dʒetɪk] *adj.* 精力充沛的，充满活力的
distributor [dɪ'strɪbjətə] *n.* 经销商；批发商，分发者
entrant ['entrənt] *n.* 参加者，新加入者
attentive [ə'tentɪv] *adj.* 细心的，注意的；周到的，殷勤的
monetary ['mʌnɪteri] *adj.* 货币的，金钱的；钱的
accordingly [ə'kɔːdɪŋli] *adv.* 因此，于是；相应地
palatable ['pælətəbl] *adj.* 可口的，美味的；宜人的，可接受的
synchronize ['sɪŋkrənaɪz] *vt.* 使同步，使同时
decor [deɪ'kɔː] *n.* 布置，装饰；布景
penetration [ˌpenɪ'treɪʃn] *n.* 渗透，穿透
sensitive ['sensətɪv] *adj.* 敏感的；感觉的
temporary ['tempərəri] *adj.* 短暂的，临时的，暂时的
generic [dʒə'nerɪk] *adj.* 一般的；类的，属性的
swiftly [swɪftli] *adv.* 迅速地，敏捷地
undercut [ˌʌndə'kʌt] *vt.* 廉价出售
siphon ['saɪfn] *vi.* 通过虹吸管吸出或抽取
low-end ['ləʊ-end] *adj.* 低档的，生产低档产品的
odd [ɒd] *adj.* 古怪的，奇数的
institute ['ɪnstɪtuːt] *vt.* 建立，制定；开始，着手
explanation [ˌeksplə'neɪʃn] *n.* 解释，说明；辩解
illusion [ɪ'luːʒn] *n.* 错觉；幻想；假象
complimentary [ˌkɒmplɪ'mentəri] *adj.* 赠送的，赞美的；表示敬意的，恭维的
dessert [dɪ'zɜːt] *n.* 甜点，餐后甜食
entree ['ɒntreɪ] *n.* 主菜；入场权
sweeten ['swiːtn] *vt.* 使……变甜，把……弄香
straightforward [ˌstreɪt'fɔːwəd] *adj.* 直截了当的，坦率的
assure [əʃʊə] *vt.* 向……保证，使……确信

Phrases

set the price 确定价格	at a bare minimum 最低限度
financial modeling 财务建模	without frill 无须矫饰，无须任何花架子
in response to 对……做出反应	price skimming 市场撇脂定价法
distribution channel 分销渠道	eat up 吃光；耗尽
price floor 价格下限	siphon off 吮吸，吸走
end up in losses 以损失告终	psychological pricing 心理定价
price ceiling 价格上限	common-sense logic 常识逻辑
online access 在线访问	left-digit effect 左位数效应
be mindful of 注意，留心	price tag 价格标签
premium pricing 溢价定价法	bundle pricing 捆绑定价策略
penetration pricing 渗透定价	bottom line rule 底线法则
skim off 从……挑选出	with... in mind 将……铭记在心
keep out 阻止进入	be in line with 与…… 一致；符合
economy pricing 经济学定价法	

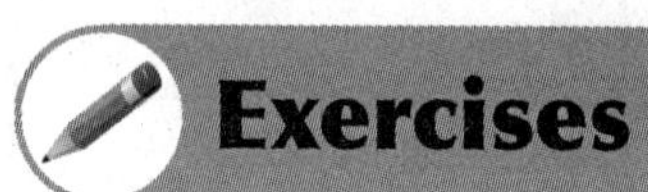

Exercises

EX. 1 Answer the following questions according to Text A.

(1) Which one is the revenue generating element among the 4Ps of the marketing mix?

(2) What is an efficient price from the marketer's point of view?

(3) How many key pricing strategies are there broadly mentioned in the marketing literature? And what are they?

(4) When do businesses use a premium pricing strategy?

(5) What does the company need to do to make premium pricing palatable to consumers?

(6) What is the primary objective of penetration pricing?

(7) Why is economy pricing likely to be dangerous for small businesses?

(8) What product does price skimming work for?

(9) What example can you list to show "left-digit effect"?

(10) Which one is the most effective way to move unsold items that are simply taking up space?

EX. 2 **Translate the following phrases from English into Chinese and vice versa.**

(1) bottom line rule ________
(2) distribution channel ________
(3) financial modeling ________
(4) penetration pricing ________
(5) premium pricing ________
(6) 市场撇脂定价法 ________
(7) 价格标签 ________
(8) 价格上限 ________
(9) 经销商；批发商，分发者 ________
(10) 发货单；发票 ________

EX. 3 **Translate the following into Chinese.**

In most skimming, goods are higher priced so that fewer sales are needed to break even. Selling a product at a high price, sacrificing high sales to gain a high profit is therefore "skimming" the market. Skimming is usually employed to reimburse the cost of investment of the original research into the product: commonly used in electronic markets when a new range, such as DVD players, are firstly sold at a high price. This strategy is often used to target "early adopters" of a product or service. Early adopters generally have a relatively lower price-sensitivity—this can be attributed to: their need for the product outweighing their need to economize; a greater understanding of the product's value, or simply having a higher disposable income.This strategy is employed only for a limited duration to recover most of the investment made to build the product. To gain further market share, a seller must use other pricing tactics such as economy or penetration. This method can have some setbacks as it could leave the product at a high price against the competition.

EX. 4 **Fill in the blanks with the words given below.**

alternatives	effects	employ	evident	concept
vary	negative	profitable	frequently	fundamental

Value-Based Pricing

Value-based pricing is pricing a product based on the value the product has for the customer and not on its costs of production or any other factor. This pricing strategy is (1)________ used where the value to the customer is many times the cost of producing the item or service. For instance, the cost of producing a software CD is about the same independent of the software on it, but the prices (2)________ with the perceived value the customers are expected to have.

The perceived value will depend on the (3)________ open to the customer. In business these alternatives are using competitors software, using a manual work around, or not doing an activity. In order to (4)________ value-based pricing, one must know its customers' business, one's business costs, and one's perceived alternatives. It is also known as perceived-value pricing.

Value-based pricing have many (5)________ on the business and consumers of the product. Value-based pricing is a (6)________ business activity and is the process of developing product strategies and pricing them properly to establish the product within the market. This is a key (7)________ for a relatively new product within the market, because without the correct price, there would be no sale. Having an overly high price for an average product would have (8)________ effects on the business as the consumer would not buy the product. Having a low price on a luxury product would also have a negative impact on the business as in the long run the business would not be (9)________. This can be seen as a positive for the consumer as they are not needing to pay extreme prices for the luxury product. There has been an (10)________ change in the marketing area within a business from cost plus pricing to the value.

Text B

How to Price Your Products

One of the secrets to business success is pricing your products properly. Price your products correctly and that can enhance how much you sell, creating the foundation for a business that will prosper. Get your pricing strategy wrong and you may create problems that your business may never be able to overcome.

"It's probably the toughest thing there is to do," says Charles Toftoy, associate professor of management science at George Washington University. "It's part art and part science."

There are a variety of different types of pricing strategies in business. However, there's no one surefire, formula-based approach that suits all types of products, businesses, or markets. Pricing your product usually involves considering certain key factors, including pinpointing your target customer, tracking how much competitors are charging, and understanding the relationship between quality and price.

1. How to price your products: Meeting business goals

1.1 Get clear about making money

The first step is to get clear about what you want to achieve with your pricing strategy: You want to make money. That's why you own a business. Making money means generating enough revenue from selling your products so that you can not only cover your costs, but take a profit and perhaps expand your business.

The biggest mistake many businesses make is to believe that price alone drives sales. Your ability to sell is what drives sales and that means hiring the right sales people and adopting the right sales strategy. The first thing you have to understand is that the selling price is a function of your ability to sell and nothing else. At the same time, be aware of the risks that accompany make poor pricing decisions. There are two main pitfalls you can encounter—under pricing and over pricing.

• Under pricing. Pricing your products for too low a cost can have a disastrous impact on your bottom line, even though business owners often believe this is what they ought to do in a down economy. Many businesses mistakenly under price their products attempting to convince the consumer that their product is the least expensive alternative hoping to drive up volume; but more often than not, it is simply perceived as "cheap". Remember that consumers want to feel that they are getting their "moneys worth" and most are unwilling to purchase from a seller they believe to have less value. Businesses also need to be very careful that they are fully covering their costs when pricing products. Reducing prices to the point where you are giving away the product will not be in the firm's best interest long term.

• Over pricing. On the flip side, over pricing a product can be just as detrimental since the buyer is always going to be looking at your competitors pricing. Pricing beyond the customer's desire to pay can also decrease sales. One pitfall is that business people will be tempted to price too high right out of the gate. They think that they have to cover all the expenses of people who work for them, the lease, etc. and this is what price it takes to do all that. However, the marketers are advised to put themselves in the customer's shoes. What would be a fair price to them? Many experts advise taking little surveys of customers with two or three questions on an index-card-sized form, asking them whether the pricing was fair.

1.2 Understand your other business priorities

There are other reasons to go into business. Understand what you want out of your business when pricing your products. Aside from maximizing profits, it may be important for you to maximize market share with your product—that may help you decrease your costs or it may result in what economists call "network effects", i.e., the value of your product increases as more people use it. A great example of a product having network effect is Microsoft's Windows operating system. When more people began to use Windows over rival products, more software developers made applications to run on that platform.

You may also want your product to be known for its quality, rather than just being the cheapest on the market. If so, you may want to price your product higher to reflect the quality. During a downturn, you may have other business priorities, such as sheer survival, so you may want to price your products to recoup enough to keep your company in business.

2. How to price your products: Factors to consider

There are many methods available to determine the "right" price. But successful firms use a combination of tools and know that the key factor to consider is always your customer first. The more you know about your customer, the better you'll be able to provide what they value and the more you'll be able to charge.

2.1 Know your customer

Undertaking some sort of market research is essential to getting to know your customer. This type of research can range from informal surveys of your existing customer base that you send out in e-mail along with promotions to the more extensive and potentially expensive research projects undertaken by third party consulting firms. Market research firms can explore your market and segment your potential customers very granularly—by demographics, by what they buy, by whether they are price sensitive, etc. If you don't have a few thousand dollars to spend on market research, you might just look at consumers in terms of a few distinct groups—the budget sensitive, the convenience centered, and those for whom status make a difference. Then figure out which segment you're targeting and price accordingly.

2.2 Know your costs

A fundamental tenet of pricing is that you need to cover your costs and then factor into a profit. That means you have to know how much your product costs. You also have to understand how much you need to mark up the product and how many you need to sell to turn a profit. Remember that the cost of a product is more than the literal cost of the item; it also includes overhead costs. Overhead costs may include fixed costs like rent and variable costs like shipping or stocking fees. You must include these costs in your estimate of the real cost of your product.

Many businesses either don't factor in all their costs and under price or literally factor in all their costs and expect to make a profit with one product and therefore overcharge. A good rule of thumb is to make a spread sheet of all the costs you need to cover every month, which might include the following:

• Your actual product costs, including labor and the costs of marketing and selling those products;

• All of the operating expenses necessary to own and operate the business;

• The costs associated with borrowing money (debt service costs);

• Your salary as the owner and/or manager of the business;

• A return on the capital you and any other owners or shareholders have invested;

• Capital for future expansion and replacement of fixed assets as they age.

List the dollar amount for each on your spreadsheet. The total should give you a good idea of the gross revenues you will need to generate to ensure you cover all those costs.

2.3 Know your revenue target

You should also have a revenue target for how much of a profit you want your business to make. Take that revenue target, factor into your costs for producing, marketing, and selling your product and you can come up with a price per product that you want to charge. If you only have one product, this is a simple process. Estimate the number of units of that product you expect to sell over the next year. Then divide your revenue target by the number of units you expect to sell and you have the price at which you need to sell your product in order to achieve your revenue and profit goals.

If you have a number of different products, you need to allocate your overall revenue target by each product. Then do the same calculation to arrive at the price at which you need to sell each product in order to achieve your financial goals.

2.4 Know your competition

It's also helpful to look at the competition—after all, your customer most likely will, too. Are the products offered comparable to yours? If so, you can use their pricing as an initial gauge. Then, look to see whether there is additional value in your product; do you, for example offer additional service with your product or is your product of perceived higher quality? If so, you may be able to support a higher price. Be cautious about regional differences and always consider your costs.

It may even be worthwhile to prepare a head-to-head comparison of the price of your products to your competitor's products. The key here is to compare net prices, not just the list (or published) price. This information could come from phone calls, secret shopping, published data, etc. Make notes during this process about how your company and products—and the competition—are perceived by the market. Be brutally honest in your evaluation.

2.5 Know where the market is headed

Clearly, you can not be a soothsayer, but you can keep track of outside factors that will impact the demand for your product in the future. These factors can range from something as simple as long-term weather patterns to laws that may impact future sales of your products. Also take into account your competitors and their actions. Will a competitor respond to your introduction of a new product on the market by engaging your business in a price war?

3. How to price your products: Deciding to raise or lower prices

One size does not fit all. You can only go so far pricing all your products based on a fixed markup from cost. Your product price should vary depending on a number of factors including:

- What the market is willing to pay;
- How your company and product are perceived in the market;
- What your competitors charge;
- Whether the product is "highly visible" and frequently shopped and compared;
- The estimated volume of product you can sell.

That opens the door to raising and/or lowering prices for your products. In order to make this call one way or the other, you should first understand what's already working. Analyze the profitability of your existing products, so you can do more of what works and stop doing what doesn't work. You want to find out which of your existing products are making money and which are losing money. You may be surprised at how many of your products are losing money.

You should also constantly re-evaluate your costs. To sell it right, you have to buy it right. If you are having a hard time selling a product at an acceptable profit, the problem may be that you are not buying the product right. It may be that your cost is too high rather than your price is too low.

3.1 When to raise prices-and how

You should always be testing new prices, new offers, and new combinations of benefits and premiums to help you sell more of your product at a better price. Test new offers each month. Raise the price and offer a new and unique bonus or special service for the customer. Measure the increase or decrease in the volume of the product you sell and the total gross profit dollars you generate.

It is a fact of life in business that you will have to raise prices from time to time as part of managing your business prudently. If you never raise your prices, you won't be in business for long. You have to constantly monitor your price and your cost so that you are both competitive in the market and you make the kind of money you deserve to make.

The best way to determine if the product is being priced correctly is to watch sales volumes immediately after making any change. This can be done by watching cash collections (if the business is cash or credit card based) or credit sales (if accounts receivables are used) for the weeks following. If a price increase is too high, customers will react pretty quickly. Also watching the competition can help. If you've made a positive change in prices; competitors are likely to follow suit.

But there is a right way and a wrong way to raise prices. You don't want to alienate your existing customer base by raising prices too steeply, especially during a recession. Rather than have a sudden increase, have a strategic plan over two to five years during which you gradually increase your price 5% to 10%.

In terms of raising the price, this is more easily accepted in "good" economic times. As the underlying cost of producing the product rises, the customer is prepared to accept the rise in the price to them. If the customer perceives that the firm's costs are going down while their price is going up, this will not be received well and is likely to backfire.

3.2 When to lower prices and how

You may realize that you have missed your target audience by pricing your products too high. You can always choose to discount your products or give customers something for free in order to get them to try your product or generate traffic to your storefront or website. You have to get people in and people like getting something for free or some kind of discount. You can make Wednesday senior citizen day when seniors get a 20% discount. Then maybe you can offer a student discount day. Then all you're doing is keeping the price the same, but to those people you're giving them a cut but it's not like you've lowered all prices.

Generally, lowering prices is not a good practice unless you are using this strategically to garner market share and have a price sensitive product or if all of your competitors are lowering their prices. An alternative to lowering price is to offer less for the same price which will effectively reduce your costs without appearing to reduce the value to the customer. Restaurants have found this particularly helpful in terms of portion sizes but this same strategy can be applied to service industries as well.

4. Monitor your pricing

Another key component to pricing your product right is to continuously monitor your prices and your underlying profitability on a monthly basis. It's not enough to look at overall profitability of your company every month. You have to focus on the profitability (or lack of profitability) of every product you sell. You have to make absolutely sure you know the degree to which every product you sell is contributing to your goal of making money each month.

Here are some other practices to help you price right:

• Listen to your customers. Try to do this on a regular basis by getting feedback from customers about your pricing. Let them know you care about what they think.

• Keep an eye on your competitors. If you don't have deep pockets and can not afford to hire a market research team, hire some college students to go out on a regular basis and monitor what your competitors are doing.

• Have a budget action plan in place. Try to have a plan for your pricing that extends out three to six months in the future.

You owe it to yourself and to your business to be relentless in managing your product pricing. Remember, how you set the price of the products could be the difference between the success and failure of your business.

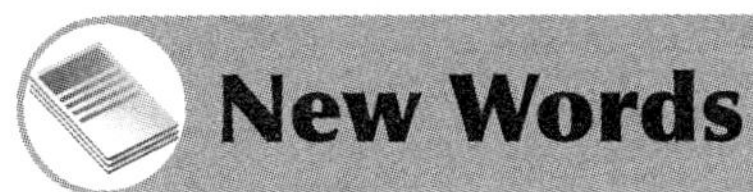

New Words

surefire ['ʃʊəfaɪə] *adj.* 准不会有错的，一定成功的

formula ['fɔːmjələ] *n.* 公式，准则

pinpoint ['pɪnpɔɪnt] *vt.* 确定，准确地指出

accompany [ə'kʌmpəni] *vt.* 附加，补充；陪伴，陪同

pitfall ['pɪtfɔːl] *n.* 陷阱，诱惑，圈套

disastrous [dɪ'zæstrəs] *adj.* 损失惨重的；灾难性的

mistakenly [mɪ'steɪkənli] *adv.* 错误地，被误解地

underprice [ˌʌndə'praɪs] *vt.* 将定价调低，削价抢生意

overprice [ˌəʊvə'praɪs] *vt.* 将……标价过高；索价过高

convince [kən'vɪns] *vt.* 使相信，说服

detrimental [ˌdetrɪ'mentl] *adj.* 有害的，不利的

lease [liːs] *n.* 租约，租契；租期

downturn ['daʊntɜːn] *n.* 低迷时期

sheer [ʃɪə] *adv.* 完全地，全然；垂直地，陡峭地

recoup [rɪ'kuːp] *vt.* 偿还，补偿，收回

granularly ['grænjʊləli] *adv.* 精细地

tenet ['tenɪt] *n.* 原则；信条，教义

markup ['mɑːkʌp] *n.* 涨价；成本加价率

literal ['lɪtərəl] *adj.* 照字面的，原义的，逐字的

overcharge [ˌoʊvə'tʃɑːdʒ] *vt.* 对……要价过高，向……乱讨价

spreadsheet ['spredʃiːt] *n.* 电子表格程序

shareholder ['ʃeəhəʊldə] *n.* 股东；股票持有者

calculation [ˌkælkju'leɪʃn] *n.* 计算，盘算；估计

gauge [geɪdʒ] *n.* 评估，测量的标准或范围

cautious ['kɔːʃəs] *adj.* 小心的，谨慎的

brutally ['bruːtl] *adv.* 残忍地，野蛮地

soothsayer ['suːθseɪə] *n.* 占卜者，预言家
prudently ['pruːdntli] *adv.* 谨慎地，慎重地
deserve [dɪ'zɜːv] *vt.* 值得，应得；应受
alienate ['eɪliəneɪt] *vt.* 使疏远，离间
steeply [stiːp] *adv.* 险峻地，陡峭地；急剧地
recession [rɪ'seʃn] *n.* 经济衰退，不景气；后退
underlying [ˌʌndə'laɪɪŋ] *adj.* 潜在的，含蓄的
backfire [ˌbæk'faɪə] *vi.* 适得其反，事与愿违的结果；发生回火
storefront ['stɔːfrʌnt] *n.* 店面（房），铺面（房）
garner ['gɑːnə] *vt.* 获得，储存
relentless [rɪ'lentləs] *adj.* 不懈的，坚韧的，不屈不挠的

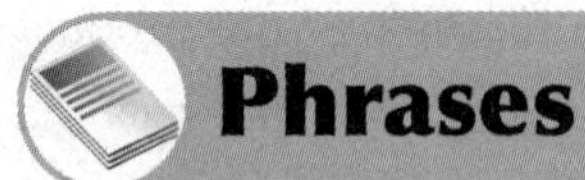

Phrases

associate professor 副教授
get clear about 弄清楚
be aware of 意识到
bottom line 底线；结果；首要之事
drive up 使……上升
be perceived as 被视为，被认为是
be unwilling to 不愿意
give away 失去；泄露；赠送
on the flip side 反过来说
put in others' shoes 设身处地为别人着想
go into business 经商，从事商业
aside from 除……之外
network effect 网络效应
send out 发出，发送
consulting firm 咨询公司
make a difference 有影响，起（重要）作用
figure out 想出，解决；计算出
factor into 考虑到
turn a profit 扭亏为盈
overhead costs 管理费用；营业间接成本
rule of thumb 拇指规则，经验法则
fixed asset 固定资产
come up with 想出，提出
be comparable to 与……可比较的，比得上……的
be cautious about 谨慎对待……，当心……
keep track of 记录；与……保持联系，跟踪
follow suit 跟着做，照着做；如法炮制
keep an eye on 注意，留心；照管，照看
owe... to 应归功于

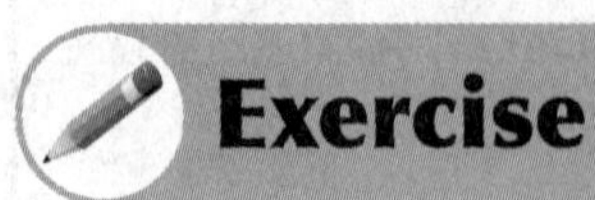

Exercise

EX. Answer the following questions according to Text B.

(1) What drives sales, price alone or the ability to sell?
(2) What are the two main pitfalls one business encounter while making pricing decisions?
(3) Why does under pricing the products have a disastrous impact?

(4) What will occur when a network effect is present?
(5) What is an essential way to know your customer?
(6) What is a fundamental tenet of pricing?
(7) If the products offered by competitors are comparable to yours, what can you do?
(8) Why is raising the price more easily accepted by the customer in "good" economic times?
(9) What is an alternative to lowering price?
(10) Can you list any other practices to price the product right? And what are they?

参考译文（Text A）

定价策略

定价是企业设定销售产品和服务的价格的过程，它可能是企业营销计划的一个部分。在制定价格时，企业会考虑商品的售价、制造成本、市场位置、竞争、市场状况、品牌和产品质量。

定价是财务建模的一个基本方面，是营销组合的四个 P 之一。营销组合的其他三个 P 是产品、促销和分销渠道。价格是四个 P 中唯一产生收入的元素，其余均是成本中心。然而，营销组合中的其他 P 将有助于降低价格波动，从而使价格上涨，产生更大的收入和利润。定价可以是将价格应用于购买和销售订单的人工或自动过程，并以诸如固定金额、数量突破、促销或销售活动、特定供应商报价、入市时的普遍价格、发货或发票日期、多个订单或多个产品线组合等因素为基础。自动化系统需要更多的设置和维护，但可以防止定价错误。只有当消费者愿意并有能力购买产品时，消费者的需求才能转化为产品需求。因此，定价是市场营销中最重要的概念。它被用作一种战术决策，以应对市场的比较情况。

1. 定价的目标

定价的目标应考虑：

• 公司的财务目标（即盈利能力）；
• 符合市场现实（客户会以这个价格购买吗？）；
• 价格在多大程度上支持产品的市场定位，并与营销组合中的其他变量保持一致。
• 产品类别和产品价格的一致性

价格受分销渠道类型、促销类型和产品质量的影响。价格可以替代说明产品质量，有效的促销，或经销商在某些市场的积极销售努力。从市场营销人员的角度来看，有效价格是非常接近客户愿意支付的价格上限。从经济学的角度来说，它是将消费者的大部分经济盈余转移到生产者的一个价格。一个好的定价策略应该是能够平衡价格下限（低于这个价格，企业最终会亏损）和价格上限（即使企业的产品处于无市场需求状态的价格）的策略。

2. 定价策略

企业在销售产品或服务时可以使用多种定价策略。设定价格旨在使每个销售单元或从整体市场中获取的利润最大化。它可以用来防止新的企业进入现有市场，用来增加市场份额或进入一个新的市场。企业对产品价格和定价策略的决定影响着消费者是否购买产品的决策。当企业决定采用任何类型的定价策略时，他们必须意识到原因，以便做出对其业务有利的适当选择。当今市场内部的竞争非常激烈，因此企业必须注意竞争对手的行动方案，才能在市场中获得相对优势。互联网应用技术已经有了极大的提高和发展，因此，消费者可以通过在线访问的方式来比较价格。由于消费者了解钱的价值，他们在购买时都会精挑细选。企业必须注意这些因素，并相应地对产品定价。

一般来说，市场营销文献中提到的关键性定价策略有以下六种。

2.1 溢价定价

当企业推出一种新产品时，他们使用一种溢价定价策略，这种新产品与同类产品相比具有明显的竞争优势。高售价产品的定价高于竞争对手的产品。溢价定价在产品生命周期的初期最为有效。出售具有独特属性的商品的小企业能够更好地使用溢价定价。为了让高价位更容易让消费者接受，企业试图创造一种形象，让消费者认为产品有价值，值得更高的价格。除了给人一种高质量产品的印象，企业还需要同步其营销力度，产品包装，甚至店内的装饰都必须支持产品物有所值的形象。

2.2 渗透定价

通过新产品实现最初的高销量，是渗透定价的主要目标。企业可以选用渗透定价法从整个市场中攫取虽小但可盈利的份额，而不是设定一个高价格。虽然这一策略要求产品得到广泛推广，但它可以设定一个较低的初始价格，使企业能够迅速而深入地渗透市场。采用渗透定价策略，企业既能快速吸引大量买家，又能抢占较大的市场份额。但是，必须满足以下条件：

条件 1）：产品的市场必须对价格高度敏感，这样低价才能带来更多的市场增长。

条件 2）：市场规模必须足够大，以维持较低的利润率，生产和分销成本必须随着销量的增长而下降。

条件 3）：低价必须有助于阻止竞争。

条件 4）：企业必须能够保持其低价地位，否则价格优势将只是暂时的。一旦竞争者进入市场，他们也可能降低价格。

2.3 经济定价

经济定价策略将价格设定在最低限度，以获得少量利润。企业将营销和促销成本降到最低。一个盈利的经济定价方案的关键是要以较低的价格销售大量的产品和服务。包括普通食品供应商和折扣零售商在内的许多企业都在使用经济定价，目的是吸引对价格最敏感的消费者。通过这种策略，企业可以将与营销和生产相关的成本最小化，从而降低产品价格。因此，顾客可以购买他们需要的产品，而不需要虚张声势。

尽管对沃尔玛和塔吉特这样的大企业来说，经济定价非常有效，但对小企业来说，这种方法可能是危险的。由于小企业缺乏大企业的销量，当价格过低时，它们可能难以产生足够的利润。不过，精心地为最忠实的顾客调整折扣，可能是保证他们在未来几年继续光顾你的好办法。

2.4 撇脂定价

撇脂定价是在市场竞争对手很少的情况下，通过推出新产品来制定高价一种策略。这种方法使企业能够在竞争对手进入市场之前实现利润最大化，而竞争对手进入市场之后，价格就会下降。撇脂定价是一种适用于新产品的策略，这种新产品也是一种新类型的产品，还没有模仿的竞争者或替代品。创造革新产品的企业可以设定较高的初始价格，从而“攫取”市场收入。然而，撇脂定价只在某些情况下有效：

条件 1)：产品的质量和形象必须足以支撑其高昂的价格，并且有足够多的买家想要并愿意以较高的价格购买该产品。

条件 2)：生产小批量产品的成本不能高到“吃掉”高价带来的优势。

条件 3)：竞争对手进入市场并迅速降低价格是易做到的。

采用撇脂定价的目的是在替代品或仿制品进入市场之前，从市场上尽可能多地攫取收入。一旦市场被“撇脂”，该企业就可以大幅降价，以吸引低端买家，同时让竞争对手无法在价格上展开竞争。

2.5 心理定价

心理定价是一种定价策略，其理论基础是某些价格能产生心理影响。有证据表明，消费者倾向于认为“奇数价格”几乎低于其实际价格，奇数价格倾向于四舍五入到下一个最低的货币单位。因此，像 1.99 美元这样的价格经常与花费 1 美元而不是 2 美元联系在一起。产生这一现象的理论是，像这样的较低价格会带来更大的需求。营销人员利用心理定价来鼓励消费者基于情感而不是常识逻辑来购买产品。例如，事实证明，将一块手表的价格定在 199 美元比定在 200 美元更能吸引消费者，尽管两者之间的真正差别很小。这就是所谓的“左位数效应”。这种趋势的解释是，消费者往往更关注价格标签上的第一个数字，而不是最后一个数字。心理定价的目的是通过为消费者创造一种价值提升的错觉来增加需求。

2.6 捆绑定价

企业使用捆绑定价，旨在以更低的价格销售多个产品。这是一个有效的策略，以推动那些占着大量空间的未售产品的销售。捆绑销售还会让消费者产生这样一种感觉：他的钱花得值。捆绑定价对于拥有一系列免费产品的公司来说非常有效。例如，餐厅可以在一周的某一天上主菜时配上免费的甜点；那些即将寿终正寝的老款电子游戏通常会附带蓝光光盘销售，以使交易更有吸引力。企业需要研究和开发适合其产品和服务的定价策略。某些定价方法适用于推出新产品，而其他策略适用于市场上竞争对手较多的成熟产品。

诚然，可以采用许多不同和复杂的方法进行定价。然而，定价的底线是简单和直接的。说到定价，需要记住的最重要的一点是，设定的价格必须能涵盖成本和利润。记住，定价必须是灵活的，因为价格应该始终与不断变化的成本、消费者需求、有竞争力的定价方案、利润目标保持一致。当需要降低价格的时候，企业应该首先找到降低成本的方法，因为定价应该始终以确保销售和利润的方式进行。

Case Apple's Premium Pricing Strategy and Product Differentiation Strategy

Unit 9

Text A

Retail Marketing Strategies

A retail marketing strategy refers to how a store sell its goods to its target customers. Each type of retail business has to make decisions about all the details of its marketing mix. A marketing mix consists of the product, price, place, promotion, and packaging. Internet marketing strategies and those for stores that people shop at in person must be developed to meet the needs of potential customers. A retail marketing strategy is first outlined in a business plan.

Common retail marketing strategies involve how products and stores are positioned and differentiated. A differentiation strategy focuses on products that can stand out from the others competing for the attention and dollars of the target market. For example, a furniture store may offer hand-made products or other items very different from what competing stores are offering. Of course, the product shouldn't only be different, it has to be something that targeted customers want and need. Retail market differentiation must set stores and products apart in order to create strong branding. A retailer needs to decide as to what it wants to achieve for its customers. He has to decide the target market and then select the appropriate combination of product, price, place, and promotion. Here are six best retail marketing strategies.

1. Retail positioning

This involves choice of target market and differential advantage. Targeting allows retailers to tailor the marketing mix, which includes product assortment, service levels, store locations, prices and promotion, to the needs of their chosen customer segments. Differentiation provides a reason to the customer to shop at one store rather than at another. The customer should have distinct expectations from the store when he walks into it, which should be different from the expectations that he has when he walks into another store. Retail positioning comes from novelty in the processes of shopping offered to the customers and novelty in the product assortment or both.

1.1 Novelty in the process offered to the shopper

The way a store facilitates a shopper to make his choice of products and brands, the way he is able to access the items in the store, and the way he makes his payments, determine a customer's satisfaction with a store. But a customer does not want a similar treatment for all his purchases and on all occasions when he visits the store. For some products, his choice of brand may be very clear, and a salesperson's attempt to help him would only irritate him. But for some other products, the same customer would solicit help of salespersons in making a choice among brands and would welcome a salesperson's attempt to influence his purchase. For some purchases, the customer would like his favourite brand to be placed prominently on the shelf. But when he does not have a clear brand choice, he would not mind some clutter on the shelves because he wants all the brands to be available. Most customers would prefer to be allowed to pay their bills as early as possible but on some occasions they would be more tolerant of delays than on others. Customers would be finicky about delays in making payments when they are rushing home after office but they would be more relaxed during their weekend shopping trips. While it is not easy to distinguish between customers and their purchase occasions, the retailer will have to make judgments about the expectations of a customer when he walks into the store.

It will be a good idea to allocate a particular salesperson to a customer, i.e., when a customer walks in he is always served by a particular salesperson rather than different salespersons depending on what he proposes to buy. Under the new arrangement, all salespersons would have to know enough about all the product categories but would know more about the purchasing behavior of a set of customers allocated to them.

1.2 Novelty in the product/product assortment offered to the shopper

A retail shop has to be known for being of a certain type. A store may be famous for being very prompt in stocking the latest or the most fashionable product. Another may be known for stocking all possible variety in a category and yet another may be famous for stocking the most premium brands.

A store would become too unwieldy if it tries to have too many different types of assortments. A store which stocks the latest products in a category will also be able to stock the most premium brands of the category but the attention of the company will be divided and it will be difficult to handle relationships with diverse suppliers whose business philosophies are different. Such a strategy will also send conflicting signals to customers as to what the store really stocks well.

2. Location of the retail store

For some products like groceries, consumers do not like to go to a far away store. Therefore, store location has great influence on sales performance of such products. A retailer has to decide whether it will be a standalone store in a city, or will it open stores to cover a designated area like a city, state or country. A retailer may decide to open one store in each city. The retailer has to buy from distributors to replenish its stocks. Or it decides to open as many stores as a city can sustain, and moves to another city and again opens as many stores as that city can sustain. Therefore, it covers cities one by one, instead of opening one store in each city. It opens a distribution centre in each city. The distribution centre receives supplies for all the stores in the city in a single truck from each supplier. Smaller lots of each of these supplies are loaded on trucks bound for each store. The retailer buys from the manufacturer directly, and does not have to buy from distributors.

A retailer's choice of a city depends upon factors like its congruence with its chosen target market, the level of disposable income, the availability of suitable sites, and level of competition. A retailer's choice of a particular site in a city depends on level of existing traffic passing the site, parking facilities, presence of competitors and possible opportunities to form new retailing centres with other outlets. When two or more non-competing retailers agree to site outlets together, the retailing centre can draw more customers than what each individual store would have been able to do. More than proximity to customers, the location of a store is important in terms of how often the target customers are likely to visit the site as they live their lives. The lifestyle of the target customers, and the goods and services that they buy will decide whether they will visit the site or not, and how often. Being in the place which the customer will visit in pursuance of his lifestyle will ensure that the customer will walk into the store. This aspect is important because customers are combining purchases of different genre of goods and combining purchases of goods and pursuance of entertainment.

3. *Product assortment and services*

A retailer has to decide on the breadth of its product assortment, and also its depth. A retailer may have a broad product assortment, but within each product line, it can stock a shallow product range. Or it can have a narrow product assortment, but within each product line, it can stock a deep product range. Therefore, a retailer's choice of product assortment ranges from stocking one deep product line to stocking a broad range of products including toys, cosmetics, jewellery, clothes, electrical goods, and household accessories. A retailer begins with one or limited product lines and gradually broadens product assortment to be able to sell more products to customers who come to its store.

Petrol stations start out as fuel providers, and expand by adding provision stores or food outlets to maximize the revenue that can be obtained from the customer. Some stations on the highway may also add a Cineplex to make their retail outlet a one-stop entertainment and utility centre for the customer. By expanding its product assortment, a retailer reduces price sensitivity of customers. A traveller stops at a petrol station because he can buy an assortment of products, and not because its fuel cost is low. A retailer's decision of the product assortment that he will stock will depend on its positioning strategy, the expectation that its customers have come to have of it, and also on the profitability of product lines that it carries.

It may be prompted to drop slow moving unprofitable lines unless they are necessary to conform with the range of products expected by its customers. A retailer also has to decide whether it will sell only manufacturer brands, or it will have its own label or store brands. Most manufacturers may sell their own label brands products to compliment manufacturer brands.

Retailers need to consider the nature and degree of customer service. Degree of service can vary from customers being expected to search for their items to elaborate displays and suggestions from sales personnel. Retail outlets for expensive items like cars provide elaborate services in the forms of product displays, test drives and arrangement of loans, whereas in a discount store, customers would have to select their items, sometimes from heaps of merchandise. Service levels have to be higher when customer knowledge levels are low; expertise is required to buy the right product (that the customer lacks), and the products are expensive (money spent in relation to customer's disposable incomes are high). The retailer can also use service levels as a means of differentiating his offer when the product assortment is similar to those of competitors. For instance, a cosmetics store can employ its personnel as grooming advisors to help a customer choose relevant products from the store.

4. Price

A retailer may choose to compete purely on price, but price can be a differential advantage only when a retailer has immense buying power, and has been able to control cost. A retailer may favor everyday low prices rather than higher prices supplemented by price discounts.

Such a retailer is patronized by customers who prefer predictable low prices rather than occasional price discounts. A retailer may sell no-frill products, which are basic commodities such as bread and soft drinks that are sold in rudimentary packaging at low prices. It appeals to the price conscious shopper who wants standard products at low prices. Some retail items may be priced very competitively to generate more demand for other items. Such products may often be sold below cost and are called "loss leader". The idea is that the customers get attracted to the low price of the "loss leader" and walk in the store to buy the item but may end up buying many more items. The items chosen for inclusion should be widely known and bought on frequent basis.

5. Promotion

Retail promotion includes advertising, public relation, publicity, and sales promotion. The goal is to position the store in consumers' minds. Retailers design ads, stage special events, and develop promotions aimed at their markets.

A store's opening is a carefully orchestrated blend of advertising, merchandising, goodwill and glitter. All the elements of an opening—press coverage, special events, media advertising and store displays—are carefully planned. Retail advertising is carried out at the local level, although retail chains can advertise nationally. Local advertising by retailers provides specific information about their stores, such as location, merchandise, hour, price, and special sale. In contrast, national retail advertising generally focuses on image. A popular retail advertising practice is cooperative advertising. Under cooperative advertising, manufacturers pay retailers to feature their products in store mailers or the manufacturer develops a TV or print ad campaign and includes the name of the retailers carrying the product at the end. Many retailers are avoiding media advertising in favour of direct-mail or frequent shopper programmes. The frequent shopper programmes offer perks ranging from gift certificates to special sales for most frequent shoppers. Direct-mail and catalogue programmes may be a cost effective method of increasing store loyalty and spending by core customers.

6. Store atmosphere

Store atmosphere is created by the design, colour, and layout of a store. A retailer works on both exterior and interior designs to create an appropriate store atmosphere. The store atmosphere should prompt target customers to visit the store and stimulate them to buy once they are in the store.

External designs include architectural design, sign, window display, and use of color that create identity for a retailer. The image which is projected should be consonant with the ethos of the store. For instance, a kids' store is usually bright, vibrant (may be in the shape of Mickey Mouse) and colourful to attract the child and make him want to buy things in the store. Such a store should generally have lots of space for the child to move around and explore his world. Even the salespeople should match the child's temperament. They should be playful. Interior design like store lighting, fixtures, and fittings as well as layout affect store atmosphere. If a store has narrow aisles, it appears congested and unclean, the customers may not like to spend too much time in such an environment. A poorly lit store is uninviting. Colour, sound, and smell affect mood of customers, and customers stay longer in stores which are colourful, play good music and smell good. People attribute different meanings to different colors, and a retailer uses colors to create the desired atmosphere in the store. Music can be used to create a relaxed atmosphere, and make the customers linger on in the store.

Creating a retail marketing plan or strategy is done by taking a business's strategic plan and goals and applying the marketing mix to reach those goals. A marketing mix consists of decisions about the product, price, place, promotion, and packaging. After deciding what it plans on doing for each category of the marketing mix, the business should then consider its retail marketing strategies based on those decisions. Business plans are a common place to find a business's retail marketing plan or strategy. In general, a business plan is created when a start-up company searches for partnerships or applies for financing opportunities. The company must be able to display a strong marketing strategy to prove it will likely be successful. The business plan must show that the marketing plan is in line with the business's goals and seems realistic, and does not conflict with the business's mission and goals.

New Words

position [pə'zɪʃn] *vt.* 定位；安置，把……放在适当位置

hand-made ['hænd'meɪd] *adj.* 手工制的

differential [ˌdɪfə'renʃl] *adj.* 差别的，有区别的

tailor ['teɪlə] *vt.* 专门制作；定做

assortment [ə'sɔːtmənt] *n.* 杂烩；各种各样

novelty ['nɒvlti] *n.* 新奇，新颖

facilitate [fə'sɪlɪteɪt] *vt.* 促进，促使；使便利

irritate ['ɪrɪteɪt] *vt.* 激怒，使烦恼

solicit [sə'lɪsɪt] *vt.* 恳求；征求

prominently ['prɒmɪnəntli] *adv.* 显著地

clutter ['klʌtə] *n.* 杂乱的东西；杂乱

tolerant ['tɑːlərənt] *adj.* 忍受的；容忍的，宽容的

distinguish [dɪ'stɪŋgwɪʃ] *vt.* 区分，辨别

allocate ['æləkeɪt] *vt.* 拨……（给），划……（归）；分配……（给）

standalone ['stændəˌləʊn] *adj.* 单独的，独立的

designate ['dezɪgneɪt] *vt.* 命名；指定，选定

replenish [rɪ'plenɪʃ] *vt.* 补充，重新装满

sustain [sə'steɪn] *vt.* 使保持，使稳定持续

congruence ['kɒŋgruəns] *n.* 合适，相称；一致

disposable [dɪ'spəʊzəbl] *adj.* 用后即丢弃的，一次性的；可任意处理的

outlet ['aʊtlet] *n.* 专营店，经销店；折扣品经销店

proximity [prɒk'sɪməti] *n.* （时间或空间）接近，邻近，靠近

pursuance [pər'sjuːəns] *n.* 执行，进行，实行

genre ['ʒɒnrə] *n.* （文学、艺术等的）体裁，类型

utility [juː'tɪləti] *n.* 实用，效用；公用事业

sensitivity [ˌsensə'tɪvəti] *n.* 敏锐的感觉，悟性；敏感

supplement ['sʌplɪmənt] *v.* 增补，补充

patronize ['peɪtrənaɪz] *vt.* 光顾；赞助，资助

rudimentary [ˌruːdɪ'mentri] *adj.* 基础的，基本的；未充分发展的

stage [steɪdʒ] *vt.* 举办，举行；组织；上演

orchestrate ['ɔːrkɪstreɪt] *vt.* 策划；精心安排

goodwill [ˌgʊd'wɪl] *n.* 信誉，商誉；友好，善意

glitter ['glɪtə] *v.* 闪亮，闪耀；闪现

perk [pɜːk] *n.* 额外利益；津贴；特权

layout ['leɪaʊt] *n.* 布局，布置；设计，安排

consonant ['kɒnsənənt] *adj.* （与……）一致的，符合的，和谐的

ethos ['iːθɑːs] *n.* （某团体或社会的）道德思想，道德观

vibrant ['vaɪbrənt] *adj.* 充满生机的，生气勃勃的；精力充沛的

playful ['pleɪfl] *adj.* 有趣的；爱嬉戏的，爱玩的

fitting ['fɪtɪŋ] *n.* （设备或家具的）小配件，附件

aisle [aɪl] *n.* 走道，过道

linger ['lɪŋgə] *vi.* 继续存留；流连，逗留

congested [kən'dʒestɪd] *adj.* 拥挤的，挤满的；（交通）堵塞的

uninviting [ˌʌnɪn'vaɪtɪŋ] *adj.* 无吸引力的，不诱人的	start-up ['stɑːt-ʌp] *adj.* （新企业等））开办阶段的，启动时期的
	mission ['mɪʃn] *n.* 使命，任务

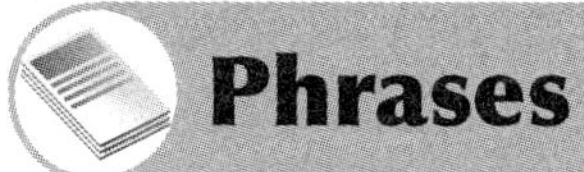

Phrases

retail marketing strategy 零售营销策略
marketing mix 市场营销组合
in person 亲自，本人；直接
stand out from 脱颖而出
compete for（为……）争夺，竞争
set apart 分开；区别，使与众不同
as to 关于
be tolerant of 宽容，容忍
be finicky about 挑剔
specialize in 专攻，专门研究
be prompt in 在……方面及时的，迅速的
sales performance 销售业绩
be bound for 准备到……去，开往……，驶向……
product line 产品线，产品系列
provision store 供应店
conform with 合乎，符合
no-frill product 廉价商品
heaps of 大量的，许多
in rudimentary 在初级阶段
appeal to 对……产生吸引力；呼吁，恳求
loss leader 亏本出售的商品；招揽顾客的廉价品
end up 结束，告终
press coverage 新闻报道
be consonant with 符合，与……一致
attribute...to 把……归因于……

Exercises

EX. 1 Answer the following questions according to Text A.

(1) What does a retail marketing strategy refer to?
(2) What does retail positioning come from?
(3) What factors determine a customer's satisfaction with a store?
(4) What factors does a retailer's choice of a city depend upon?
(5) How does a retailer's choice of product assortment range?
(6) In what situations do service levels have to be higher?
(7) May a retailer favor everyday low prices or higher prices supplemented by price discounts?
(8) What is the difference between local retail advertising and national retail advertising?
(9) What elements inside a store may affect mood of customers?
(10) What must the business plan show in terms of the marketing plan?

EX. 2 **Translate the following phrases from English into Chinese and vice versa.**

(1) loss leader ______________
(2) product line ______________
(3) retail marketing strategy ______________
(4) provision store ______________
(5) sales performance ______________
(6)（为……）争夺，竞争 ______________
(7) 廉价商品 ______________
(8) 用后即丢弃的，一次性的 ______________
(9) 信誉，商誉 ______________
(10) 食品杂货店，食品杂货 ______________

EX. 3 **Translate the following into Chinese.**

Location is the mantra in real estate; it also applies to retail. It's important to select the right place to conduct business with your target market. Retailers generally select their location based on where their target market shops. For many retailers, this means creating a presence at a shopping mall or a retail-heavy area. Some retailers choose to only offer an online store. This can be based on a number of factors, such as saving on rent and other overhead expenses. Depending on the product or service they're selling, a brick-and-mortar location may not be necessary if the target market mostly shops online.

The location of the business needs to fit into the overall marketing strategy. In the case of the small business that sells environmentally friendly women's clothing, they may consider an online-only store. Because their target market cares about their clothes being made in an environmentally conscious way, they also may care about reducing greenhouse gas emissions and waste. As a result, they may choose to do much of their shopping online and may value retailers that tout their environmentally conscious practices. As a result, this small business could benefit from not having a retail store because their target market would not buy from it.

EX. 4 **Fill in the blanks with the words and phrase given below.**

specialize	annual	consumable	range	in addition to
common	transactions	physical	convenience	variety

Different Types of Retail Outlets

The types of retail outlets vary greatly and depend on what kind of goods and services they sell. Goods can (1)________ from long-lasting hardline items such as cars and furniture to perishables like groceries, drinks and baked goods. Those (2)________ products include toiletries, clothes and shoes. Another category of retail items is art, which includes books, musical instruments and fine art.

Department stores are one of the most (3)________ retail stores in the United States. Examples include Target and Macy's, where customers can purchase a wide (4)________ of goods all in one place. Big box stores are a kind of retailer that (5)________ in one kind of product, such as furniture, electronics and home goods. Examples of big box stores include Best Buy and Ikea.

Some retailers focus on price, such as discount stores. These retailers sell their products and services at a lower cost to increase the number of sales they make. Some of these stores offer their own in-house brands, (6)________ other brands. Wal-Mart is an example of a discount store. Warehouse stores also focus on providing their customers with low prices. For many warehouse companies, such as Costco, customers need to purchase an (7)________ membership in order to take advantage of their low prices.

Local neighborhood stores, or mom-and-pop shops, are smaller retail locations run by entrepreneurs and small business owners. They usually have just one location and offer a niche product or service. Some mom-and-pop shops, such as (8)________ stores or corner stores, offer a variety of products within the same category, like groceries.

Many retailers don't have a (9)________ location and only operate online. These can range from large, multinational corporations like Amazon to small, one-person businesses. Online retailers conduct purchase (10)________ through an e-commerce platform and ship their customers' goods to their homes.

Text B

Content Marketing Strategies Boost Customer Loyalty

In an industry where many companies rely on selling products that are the same or similar to competitors' offerings, retailers are embracing content marketing as a means to stand out from the crowd and provide value to the customer.

Leading retailers such as Pet360, Boohoo, Beachmint, and Blinds.com understand that content marketing strategies can only turn into revenue if the content makes the brand relatable to the consumer.

To successfully engage customers with content, retailers are banking on numerous delivery vehicles, such as the e-commerce website, digital publications, and social media. Merchants also are tapping a variety of content types to deliver their brand message, including but not limited to: blog posts, how-to guides, videos, advertisements, images, and infographics.

1. The state of content marketing in retail

Content marketing has become a priority investment for B2B organizations over the past few years, but has only recently become a focus for retailers looking to foster customer loyalty. In fact, only 39% of B2C content marketers have a documented content strategy, according to a report from the Content Marketing Institute and Marketing Profs.

With the advent of social media, the average consumer can gather product reviews and information from sources more relatable to them than any mass medium. Thus, traditional advertising is taking on a less prominent role in the daily consumption habits of the consumer, according to Michael Brenner, Head of Strategy at Newscred.

"One of the big aspects of confusion is the notion that content marketing is an individual piece of content or a different kind of ad, as opposed to a mentality or culture," Brenner said. "Whether via print, radio, TV and now the Internet, advertisers as brands have simply shifted their approach to continuously trying to get that promotional message in front of our consumers using whatever mass medium they've been shifting towards. The retailers that are getting it right are realizing that they need to create stories and tell them in a larger, more consistent way than just promoting what they do through traditional advertising."

In particular for retailers with niche products or a long timeline between purchases, content marketing can create frequent touch points with shoppers in between purchase periods.

"If I'm an underwear retailer, a customer is only going to shop for underwear a couple times a year," said Jason Goldberg, VP of Commerce Strategy at Razorfish. "If the customer is only going to come to us twice a year when they need underwear, I don't have a great opportunity to build the relationship with that customer and my brand. I need to give the customer more reasons to visit me more often, and it can not all be to replenish my drawer."

2. *Video content enhances the visual experience*

Video has become one of the most popular content marketing vehicles, offering a 360-degree online view of products that otherwise could only be experienced in-store. Retail site visitors who view videos stay on the site two minutes longer on average and are 64% more likely to purchase than other site visitors, according to comScore research.

"One of the impediments to buying from certain product categories online is that you're not sure exactly what you're going to get," Goldberg said in an interview with Retail TouchPoints. "You've lost the ability to see that item on the mannequin in the store, try clothes on for yourself, or see exactly how big that television is and whether it's going to fit in your living room. Video is a much more immersive way to help customers have confidence that what they're ordering is what they want."

Retailers are using a variety of video types, depending on their brand goals and product lines. Videos can provide product information, how-to guides, user-generated feedback, cross-sell ideas and more. Blinds.com, for example, created a library of videos designed to illustrate how to choose the right window treatment, and how to measure and install the products. While the content initially added value to the website, it wasn't until Blinds.com enlisted the services of video commerce solution provider LiveClicker that the content could be managed and measured for effectiveness.

"Before we were working with LiveClicker, we had minimal information available to us, and I didn't necessarily know what that information was telling me," said Robert Reed, Video Producer at Blinds.com. "I could see the number of plays and I couldn't see much detail beyond that. Because we can see these metrics now, we can be more strategic and put videos in a particular order or put them in a certain place on the site that increases conversion rates."

Comparing Q1 2013 to Q1 2014, the video engagement rate on the Blinds.com website increased by 99%. Revenue increased by 92%, while orders and conversion rates both increased by approximately 70%.

"There's so many different ways that you can try to help customers through additional measuring and installation to show them that this is something they can do themselves," Reed said. "Video is a great way to help customers come to the realization that these processes aren't that hard to put together."

Other retailers use video solutions to promote their products, but also strive to differentiate their brands from the rest of the pack. Women's fashion retailer Boohoo built up its own video channel, Boohoo TV, to accompany the retail site, giving consumers detailed video guides on how to wear clothing from the Boohoo brand. The television site includes information regarding fashion trends, a section dedicated to BoohooMAN, the retailer's menswear collection, as well as advertisements promoting the brand clothing and lifestyle.

The value of Boohoo TV doesn't end with the videos, as the retailer implemented the Amplience video merchandising solution to create digital commerce experiences.The online video merchandising solution enables Boohoo TV to merchandise products directly alongside the video channel, creating a direct link from brand-building content to product collections. The solution is designed to streamline the buying process and increase average order value, giving consumers relevant purchasing options on a sidebar while they browse new trends.

3. The benefits of professional vs. amateur video

Professionally produced video optimized for e-commerce outperforms user-generated (UGC) video by 30%, delivering a 24.7% lift compared to an 18.7% lift for the UGC video, according to comScore.

"A lot of people say that video doesn't have to be professionally done, and I think there's a place for UGC video," said Robert Rose, Chief Strategist at the Content Marketing Institute. "But I'm actually a big believer that the better the video quality is, the better it is for the brand. A lot of brands have taken the advice that video can be shot using an iPhone, and then when they go through with it the video ends up looking unprofessional and not very good."

Brenner shared similar sentiments, advising that brands need to understand the economics behind their video strategies in order to make them work. He recommended retailers hire videographers and trained directors that not only know how to use video to tell a story effectively, but also help create a content-centric culture throughout the organization.

"Consumers are choosing what they want to watch and when they want to watch it," Brenner explained. "Why do we consume more video? We're becoming a more visual society and I think it's becoming harder to entertain us. It's not that people don't read print, it's just that if you want to be entertained, we're more easily and quickly entertained through moving visual content."

4. *Engaging the consumer throughout the purchasing process*

Video content is certainly not the only successful vehicle retailers are using to build their brands. Other content marketing strategies are helping retailers such as Pet360 drive their e-commerce strategies. Additionally, retailers and publishing departments are converging more frequently to create digital and print publications for consumers to read during their shopping journeys.

These content marketing methods are designed to help retailers connect with the consumer throughout numerous touch points and throughout the purchasing process, even when they are not considering purchasing an item. The retailers that are implementing these methods successfully are getting a leg-up against the competition.

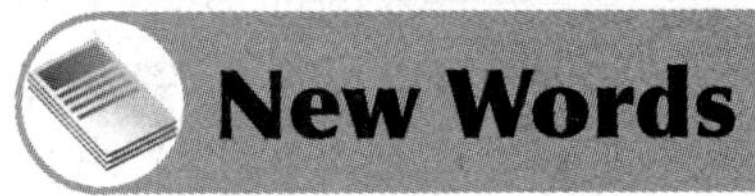

New Words

embrace [ɪm'breɪs] *vt.* 接受；拥抱

relatable [rɪ'leɪtəbl] *adj.* 有关系的

merchant ['mɜːtʃənt] *n.* 商人；批发商

infographics ['ɪnfəʊ'græfɪks] *n.* 图表设计，资讯图像；信息图像

priority [praɪ'ɔːrəti] *n.* 优先事项；优先；优先权

foster ['fɔːstə] *vt.* 促进，助长；培养

notion ['nəʊʃn] *n.* 观念，信念

mentality [men'tæləti] *n.* 心态，思想状况

continuously [kən'tɪnjuəsli] *adv.* 连续不断地

consistent [kən'sɪstənt] *adj.* 一致的；连续的；持续的

timeline ['taɪmlaɪn] *n.* 时间表

impediment [ɪm'pedɪmənt] *n.* 妨碍，阻碍，障碍

mannequin ['mænɪkɪn] *n.* 时装模特；(用于陈列服装的)人体模型

immersive [ɪ'mɜːsɪv] *adj.* 沉浸式的，使人沉醉的；身临其境的

cross-sell [krɒs-'sel] *n.* 交叉销售

install [ɪn'stɔːl] *vt.* 安装；设置

enlist [ɪn'lɪst] *vt.* 争取，谋取（帮助、支持或参与）

effectiveness [ɪ'fektɪvnəs] *n.* 效力；有效性

metrics ['metrɪks] *n.* 衡量指标

menswear ['menzweə] *n.* 男服（尤用于商店中）

implement ['ɪmpləmənt] *vt.* 使生效；贯彻，执行，实施

relevant ['reləvənt] *adj.* 相关的，有重大关系的

browse [braʊz] *v.* （在商店里）随便看看；浏览

amateur ['æmətə] *n.* 业余爱好者；生手；外行

optimize ['ɒptɪmaɪz] *vt.* 使最优化；充分利用

outperform [ˌaʊtpə'fɔːm] *vt.* （效益上）超过，胜过

strategist ['strætədʒɪst] *n.* 战略家，善于筹划部署的人

sentiment ['sentɪmənt] *n.* 观点；情绪；感情

videographer [vɪdɪ'ɒgrəfə] *n.* 摄像师，摄影师

converge [kən'vɜːdʒ] *vi.* 汇集，聚集，集中

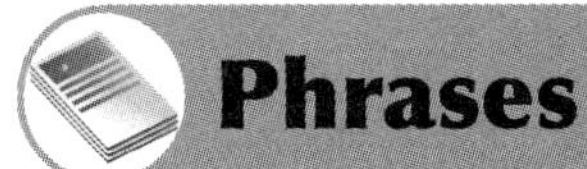

Phrases

bank on 指望，依靠

digital publication 数字出版物；数字出版

customer loyalty 客户忠诚度

with the advent of 随着……的到来

take on a role 承担起某种作用；扮演角色

daily consumption habit 日常消费习惯

as opposed to 与……形成对照

touch point 接触点，触点

on the site 在现场

try on 试穿；试戴

fit in 适合，适应，融入（群体）

conversion rate 折算率；汇率

strive to 争取；努力

dedicate to 把（时间、力量等）用在……

go through with 做完，完成；贯彻执行

get a leg-up against 获得一臂之力，以对抗……

Abbreviations

CMS (Content Management System) 内容管理系统

B2B (Business-to-Business) 企业对企业电子商务

B2C (Business-to-Consumer) 企业对用户电子商务

VP (Vice President) 副总裁

UGC (User Generated Content) 用户生成内容，即用户原创内容

Exercise

EX. Answer the following questions according to Text B.

(1) To successfully engage customers with content, what delivery vehicles are retailers banking on?

(2) What is one of the big aspects of confusion as to content marketing, according to Michael Brenner, Head of Strategy at Newscred?

(3) What can content marketing create, in particular for retailers with niche products?

(4) Why is video one of the most popular content marketing vehicles?

(5) What is one of the impediments to buying from certain product categories online, according to Jason Goldberg, VP of Commerce Strategy at Razorfish?

(6) How can video enhance customers' experience, according to Jason Goldberg, VP of Commerce Strategy at Razorfish?

(7) What is the purpose of the online video merchandising solution being designed?

(8) According to com.Score, which video is more effective, professionally produced video or user-generated (UGC) video?

(9) What did Brenner recommend regarding video?

(10) Why are various content marketing methods designed?

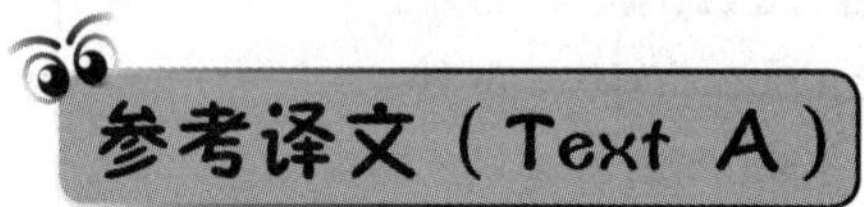

零售营销策略

零售营销策略是指商店如何向目标顾客销售商品。每种类型的零售企业都必须决定其营销组合的所有细节。营销组合包括产品、价格、渠道、促销和包装。为满足潜在客户的需求，企业必须开发网络营销策略和实体店营销策略，并在商业计划中首先对零售营销策略加以概述。

常见的零售营销策略包括产品和商店的定位和差异化。差异化战略重点关注能够在吸引目标市场注意力和金钱这一竞争中脱颖而出的产品。例如，家具店可能会提供手工制作的产品或其他与竞争对手截然不同的产品。当然，产品不应该只是与众不同，它必须是目标客户想要和需要的东西。零售市场的差异化必须把商店和产品分开，以创建强大的品牌。零售商需要决定为客户实现什么目标。他们必须确定目标市场，然后选择合适的营销组合方案，将产品、价格、渠道和促销四要素有机组合起来。以下是六种最佳的零售营销策略。

1. 零售定位

这包括目标市场的选择和差异化优势。根据目标市场允许零售商根据他们所选客户群体的需求，调整营销组合，包括产品分类、服务水平、商店位置、价格和促销。差异化为顾客提供了在一家商店购物而不是在其他商店购物的理由。当顾客走进一家商店时，他应该对这家商店有不同于其他商店时的期望。零售定位既要考虑顾客购物过程的新颖性，也要考虑产品分类的新颖性，或者两者兼而有之。

1.1 购物过程的新颖性

商店帮助顾客选择产品和品牌，顾客获得商品的方式以及他付款的方式决定了顾客对商店的满意度。但是，顾客不希望他在购买所有商品时，以及他每次进入商店时都得到类似的接待。对于某些产品，他对品牌的选择可能非常明确。这时，销售人员给他提供的帮助可能只会令他不悦。但对于其他一些产品，顾客会寻求售货员的帮助，以便在品牌中做出选择。顾客欢迎售货员提供信息，帮助他们购物。对于一些商品，顾客希望他最喜欢的品牌放在货架上最显眼的地方。但当他没有明确的品牌选择时，他不会介意货架上的杂乱，因为他希望所有的品牌他都能买到。大多数顾客更愿意尽早付款，但在某些情况下，他们会比其他人更能容忍拖延。顾客在下班后急着赶回家时，会对付款延迟有苛责。但在周末购物时，他们会更放松。虽然区分顾客和他们的购买场合并非易事，但零售商在顾客走进商店时必须对他的期望做出明确的判断。

给客户指定一个特定的销售人员，这是一个好主意。也就是说，当一个客户走进来时，他总是由一个特定的销售人员来服务，而不是根据他打算购买的物品由不同的销售人员提供服务。根据新的安排，所有销售人员都必须对所有产品有足够的了解，而且对分配给他们的客户的购买行为有更充分的了解。

1.2 提供给顾客的产品/产品分类的新颖性

零售店必须以某种类型而闻名。一家商店可能因及时贮备最新或最时髦的产品而闻名。而另一家商店可能因为贮备某类产品的所有种类而闻名，还有一些商店可能因为贮存最高档的品牌而闻名。

如果一家商店试图拥有太多不同类型的分类，那么它将缺乏灵活性。如果一个商店既要储存一个品类中的最新产品，又要储存该品类中最高档的品牌，那就会分散注意力，很难处理与有着不同经营理念的供应商之间的关系。这样的策略还会给顾客发出矛盾的信号，使他们无法得知这家商店真正的存货是什么。

2. 零售店的位置

对于像食品杂货这样的商品，消费者不喜欢去很远的商店。因此，店面位置对这类产品的销售业绩有很大的影响。零售商须决定是在某个城市开设一家独立的商店，在城市、州或国家等指定地区开设商店，还是在每个城市开一家店。零售商必须从分销商那里进货以补充库存，决定在一个城市能开多少家店就开多少家，然后搬到另一个城市，并在那个城市尽可能多开店。因此，它并不是在每个城市只开一家店，而是在多个城市陆续开店，并在每个城市开设配送中心。配送中心用一辆卡车从每个供应商那里收到该城市所有商店的供应品。这些小批量的供应品被装载到开往每个商店的卡车上。零售商直接从制造商购买，而不需要从分销商处购买。

零售商对城市的选择取决于诸多因素，如与所选目标市场的一致性、可支配收入水平、合适地点的可用性和竞争水平等。零售商在城市中选择一个特定的地点时要考虑许多因素，如该地点的现有交通量、停车设施、竞争对手，以及其他门店形成新的零售中心的可能性。当两家或两家以上的非竞争零售商同意将门店集中在一起时，零售中心所能吸引的顾客数量将超过每家单独门店所能吸引的顾客数量。选择商店的位置时，除了靠近顾客，目标顾客在日常生活中去该地点的频率也很重要。目标客户的生活方式，以及他们购买的商品和服务将决定他们是否会去该地点，以及去的频率。将商店的位置确定在顾客按照自己的生活方式会去的地方，这将确保顾客会走进商店。这一点很重要，因为顾客会将购买不同类型的商品和追求娱乐结合起来。

3. 产品分类及服务

零售商必须决定产品分类的广度和深度，他们可能有一个广泛的产品分类。在每个产品线中，可以储存浅的产品系列，或窄的产品分类，和深的产品系列。因此，零售商的产品种类范围很广，从一条浅的产品线到广泛的产品线，包括玩具、化妆品、珠宝、服装、电子产品和家用配件。零售商从一条或几条有限的产品线开始，逐渐扩大产品种类，以便向前来其商店的顾客销售更多的产品。

加油站一开始是提供燃料的，然后通过增加供应商店或食品店来扩大规模，以最大限度地增加从顾客那里获得的收入。高速公路上的一些车站还可能增加一个电影院，使他们的零售店成为客户的一站式娱乐和公用事业中心。通过扩大产品种类，零售商降低了顾客对价格的敏感度。出行的人在加油站停车是因为他可以买到各种各样的产品，而不是因为它的燃料成本低。零售商对库存产品种类的决定将取决于它的定位策略、顾客对它的期望，以及它所拥有的产品线的盈利能力。

零售商可能会被迫放弃一些无利可图的滞销产品线，除非这些产品线符合客户所期望的范围。零售商还必须决定是否只销售制造商品牌，还是拥有自己的商标或商店品牌。大多数制造商可能会出售自有商标的品牌产品，以打造和推广自身的品牌。零售商需要考虑客服性质和水平。服务程度可以不同，从客户自己搜寻商品到精美的展示和销售人员的建议等。汽车等昂贵商品的零售店提供精心设计的服务，包括产品展示、试驾和贷款安排。而在折扣店，顾客有时候必须从成堆的商品中挑选商品。

当客户对产品的了解程度较低，需要专业知识来购买合适的产品（客户缺少的产品），且产品昂贵（相对于客户可支配收入而言，花费较高）时，服务水平必须更高。

当产品分类与竞争对手相似时，零售商还可以将服务水平用作区分其供应商品或服务的一种手段。例如，化妆品商店可以雇佣员工作为美容顾问，帮助顾客从商店中选择相关产品。

4. 价格

零售商可能会选择纯粹依靠价格进行竞争，但只有当零售商拥有巨大的顾客购买力，并且能够控制成本时，价格才能成为差异化优势。零售商可能倾向于每天低价，而不是以价格折扣为补充的高价。

更喜欢可预测的低价而非偶尔打折产品的顾客通常会光顾这样的零售店。零售商可以销售一些廉价产品。它们都是一些基本商品，如面包和饮料等，以较低的价格和基本包装出售。这样的零售店吸引了那些希望以低价购买标准产品的、有价格意识的顾客。一些零售商品的价格可能很有竞争力，以增加顾客对其他商品的需求。这类产品通常会以低于成本的价格出售，被称为“招揽顾客的廉价品”。其理念是，顾客被低价的“招揽顾客的廉价品”吸引，从而走进商店购买商品，但最终可能会购买更多商品。选择列入的商品应该是顾客熟知并经常购买的商品。

5. 促销

零售促销包括广告、公关、宣传和促销，其目标是在消费者心中定位这家商店。零售商设计广告，举办特别的活动，并针对他们的市场开发促销活动。

一家商店的开业是经过精心策划的，它融合广告、商品展销，打造商誉和招揽顾客等多种元素。开业的所有要素，如新闻报道、特别活动、媒体广告和商店展示都要经过精心策划。零售广告是在当地进行的，尽管零售连锁店可以在全国范围内做广告。零售商在本地的广告为顾客提供商店的具体信息，如地点、商品、营业时间、价格和特价信息。相比之下，全国性的零售广告通常注重打造商店形象。一个流行的零售广告做法是合作性广告。在合作性广告模式下，制造商付钱给零售商，让他们在商店的邮件中展示自己的产品，或者开发一个电视或平面广告，并在最后呈现销售该产品的零售商的名称。许多零售商正在避免媒体广告，转而采用直邮或常客计划。常客计划为最经常光顾的顾客提供从礼券到特价商品等各种优惠。直邮和目录计划可能是提高商店忠诚度和核心客户支出的一种低成本的有效方法。

6. 商店氛围

商店氛围是由商店的设计、色彩和布局来创造的。一位零售商会从商店外部和内部设计入手，创造一个适当的商店氛围。商店氛围应促使目标客户来店参观，并刺激他们在店里购物。

外部设计包括建筑设计、标志、橱窗展示和色彩的使用，创造标志性特征。外部形象应该与商店的氛围相吻合。例如，儿童商店通常是明亮、充满活力的（可能是米老鼠的形状）和丰富多彩的，以吸引孩子，并促使他们想在商店买东西。这样的商店一般应该有足够的空间，让孩子们能四处走动，探索他们的世界。甚至，销售人员的形象也应该符合孩子的气质，应该是好玩的。店内灯光、设施、配件以及布局等室内设计都会影响商店氛围。如果一家商店通道狭窄，看起来拥挤且不干净，顾客可能不会在这样的环境中花费太多的时间。而且，灯光昏暗的商店不太招顾客喜欢。色彩、声音和气味影响顾客的心情，顾客在色彩鲜艳、音乐好听、气味好的商店逗留的时间更长。人们对不同的颜色赋予不同的含义，零售商使用不同的颜色来营造商店氛围。音乐也可以用来营造一种轻松的氛围，让顾客流连忘返。

通过制定企业的战略计划和目标，并应用营销组合来实现这些目标，零售营销计划或策略可以得以制定。营销组合包括关于产品、价格、渠道、促销和包装等方面的决策。在决定了每种营销组合元素的具体实施方案后，企业应该基于这些决定考虑其零售营销策略。通常，我们可以在企业计划书中找到一家企业的零售营销计划或战略。一般来说，当一家初创公司寻找合作伙伴或申请融资机会时，就会制定一份企业计划书。该企业必须能够展示强有力的营销策略，以证明它可能会成功。企业计划书必须表明其营销计划与企业的目标相一致，并且看起来是现实可行的，并且不与企业的使命和目标相冲突。

Case A Tailored Fit: How Boohoo Used Digital Marketing to Drive Sales and Grow Revenue

Unit 10

Text A

Sales Promotion

Sales promotion is one of the elements of the promotional mix. Sales promotion uses both media and non-media marketing communications for a pre-determined, limited time to increase consumer demand, stimulate market demand or improve product availability. Examples include contests, coupons, freebies, loss leaders, point of purchase displays, prizes, product samples, and rebates. Sales promotion is implemented to attract new customers, to hold present customers, to counteract competition, and to take advantage of opportunities that are revealed by market research. It is made up of activities, both outside and inside activities, to enhance company sales. Outside sales promotion activities include advertising, publicity, public relations activities, and special sales events. Inside sales promotion activities include window displays, product and promotional material display and promotional programs such as premium awards and contests. Sales promotion includes several communications activities that attempt to provide added value or incentives to consumers, wholesalers, retailers, or other organizational customers to stimulate immediate sales. These efforts can attempt to stimulate product interest, trial, or purchase.

1. Characteristics of sales promotion

Sales promotion represents a variety of techniques used to stimulate the purchase of a product or brand. Sales promotion has a tactical, rather than strategic role in marketing communications and brand strategy. Researchers identified a set of common characteristics of sales promotion, including:

It has short-term effects and duration;

It operates and influences only the last phase of the purchase process;

It exhibits a secondary role in relation to other forms of marketing communication;

It performs an accessory role regarding the products core benefits;

It is not a single technique. It is a set of techniques used for a specific purpose.

2. *Two types of sales promotion*

Sales promotions can be directed at either the customer, sales staff, or distribution channel members (such as retailers). Sales promotions targeted at the consumer are called consumer sales promotions. Sales promotions targeted at retailers and wholesale are called trade sales promotions. Both manufacturers and retailers make extensive use of sales promotions.

2.1 Consumer sales promotions

Consumer sales promotions are short term techniques designed to achieve short term objectives, such as to stimulate a purchase, encourage store traffic or simply to build excitement for a product or brand. Traditional sales promotions techniques include:

Price deal: A temporary reduction in the price, such as 50% off.

Loyal reward program: Consumers collect points, miles, or credits for purchases and redeem them for rewards.

Cents-off deal: It offers a brand at a lower price. Price reduction may be a percentage marked on the package.

Price-pack/Bonus pack deal: The packaging offers a consumer a certain percentage more of the product for the same price (for example, 25% extra). This is another type of deal in which customers are offered more of the product for the same price. For example, a sales company may offer their consumers a bonus pack in which they can receive two products for the price of one. In these scenarios, this bonus pack is framed as a gain because buyers believe that they are obtaining a free product. The purchase of a bonus pack, however, is not always beneficial for the consumer. Sometimes consumers will end up spending money on an item they would not normally buy had it not been in a bonus pack. As a result, items bought in a bonus pack are often wasted and are viewed as a "loss" for the consumer.

Coupons: Coupons have become a standard mechanism for sales promotions.

Loss leader: The price of a popular product is temporarily reduced below cost in order to stimulate other profitable sales.

Free-standing insert (FSI): A coupon booklet is inserted into the local newspaper for delivery.

Checkout dispensers: On checkout the customer is given a coupon based on the products purchased.

Mobile couponing: Coupons are available on a mobile phone. Consumers show the offer on a mobile phone to a salesperson for redemption.

Online Interactive Promotion Game: Consumers play an interactive game associated with the promoted product.

Rebates: Consumers are offered money back if the receipt and barcode are mailed to the producer.

Contests/sweepstakes/games: The consumer is automatically entered into the event by purchasing the product.

Aisle interrupter: A sign that juts into the aisle from the shelf.

Dangler: A sign that sways when a consumer walks by it.

Dump bin: A bin full of products dumped inside.

Bidding portals: Getting prospects.

Glorifier: A small stage that elevates a product above other products.

Lipstick Board: A board on which messages are written in crayon.

Necker: A coupon placed on the "neck" of a bottle.

Electroluminescent: Solar-powered, animated light in motion.

Kids eat free specials: Offers a discount on the total dining bill by offering 1 free kids meal with each regular meal purchased.

Sampling: Consumers get one sample for free, after their trial and then could decide whether to buy or not.

New technologies have provided a range of new opportunities for sales promotions. Loyalty cards, personal shopping assistants, electronic shelf labels, and electronic advertising displays allow for more personalized communications and more targeted information at the point of purchase. For example, shoppers may receive alerts for special offers when they approach a product in a specific aisle.

2.2 Trade sales promotions

Trade allowances: Short term incentive offered to induce a retailer to stock up on a product.

Dealer loader: An incentive given to induce a retailer to purchase and display a product.

Trade contest: A contest to reward retailers that sell the most product.

Point-of-purchase displays: Used to create the urge of "impulse" buying and selling your product on the spot.

Training programs: Dealer employees are trained in selling the product.

Push money: Also known as "spiffs". An extra commission paid to retail employees to push products.

Trade discounts (also called functional discounts): These are payments to distribution channel members for performing some function.

3. Consumer thought process

3.1 Meaningful savings: Gain or loss

Many discounts are designed to give consumers the perception of saving money when buying products, but not all discounted prices are viewed as favorable to buyers. Therefore, before making a purchase, consumers may weigh their options as either a gain or a loss to avoid the risk of losing money on a purchase. A "gain" view on a purchase results in chance taking. For example, if there is a buy-one-get-one discount that seems profitable, a shopper will buy the product. On the other hand, a "loss" viewpoint results in consumer aversion to taking any chances. For instance, consumers will pass on a buy-three-get-one discount if they believe they are not benefiting from the deal. Specifically, consumers will consider their options because the sensation of loss is 2.5 times greater than the sensation of gain for the same value.

3.2 Impulse buying

Impulse buying results from consumers' failure to weigh their options before buying a product. It is any purchase that a shopper makes that has not been planned. For example, if a consumer has no intention of buying a product before entering a store, but purchases an item without any forethought, that is impulse buying. Product manufactures want to promote and encourage this instant purchase impulse in consumers. Buyers can be very quick to make purchases without thinking about the consequences when a product is perceived to be a good deal. Therefore, sales companies increasingly implement promotional campaigns that will be effective in triggering consumer impulse buying behavior to increase sales and profit.

3.3 Comparing prices

Many consumers read left-to-right, and therefore, compare prices in the same manner. For example, if the price of a product is $93 and the sales price is $79, people will initially compare the left digits first (9 and 7) and notice the two digit difference. However, because of this habitual behavior, consumers may perceive the ($14) difference between $93 and $79 as greater than the ($14) difference between $89 and $75. As a result, consumers often mistakenly believe they are receiving a better deal with the first set of prices based on the left digits solely. Because of that common misconception, companies capitalize on this sales pricing strategy more often than not to increase sales.

3.4 Right digit effect

The right digit effect focuses on the right digits of prices when the left digits are the same. In other words, prices like $45 and $42 force consumers to pay more attention to the right digits (the 5 and 2) to determine the discount received. This effect also implies that consumers will perceive larger discounts for prices with small right digit endings, than for large right digit endings. For example, in a $32-to-$31 price reduction, consumers will believe to have received a greater deal than a $39-to-$38 price reduction. As a result, companies may use discounts with smaller right digits to mislead consumers into thinking they are receiving a better deal and increasing profit. However, consumers also are deceived by the infamous 9-ending prices. The right digit effect also relates to consumers' tendency to identify 9-ending prices as sale (rather than regular) prices or to associate them with a discount. For example, a regular price of $199 is mistakenly viewed as a sale or discount by consumers. Sales companies most commonly use this approach because the misinterpretation of consumers usually results in an increase of sales and profit.

3.5 Framing effect

The framing effect is the phenomenon that occurs when there is a change in an individual's preference between two or more alternatives caused by the way the problem is presented. In other words, the format in which something is presented will affect a person's viewpoint. This theory consists of three subcategories: risky choice framing, attribute framing, and goal framing. Risky choice framing references back to the gain-or-loss thought processes of consumers. Consumers will take chances if the circumstance is profitable for them and avoid chance-taking if it is not. Attribute framing deals with one key phrase or feature of a price discount that is emphasized to inspire consumer shopping. For example, the terms "free" and "better" are used commonly to lure in shoppers to buy a product. Goal framing places pressure on buyers to act hastily or face the consequences of missing out on a definite price reduction. A "limited time only" deal, for example, attempts to motivate buyers to make a purchase quickly, or buy on impulse, before the time runs out.

3.6 Outside forces

Although there are aspects that can determine a consumer's shopping behavior, there are many outside factors that can influence the shoppers' decision in making a purchase. For example, even though a product's price is discounted, the quality of that product may dissuade the consumer from buying the item. If the product has poor customer reviews or has a short "life span", shoppers will view that purchase as a loss and avoid taking a chance on it. A product can also be viewed negatively because of consumers' past experiences and expectations. For example, if the size of a product is misleading, buyers will not want to buy it. An item advertised as "huge", but is only one inch tall, will ward off consumers. Also, the effects of personal characteristics, such as consumers' gender, subjective norms, and impulsivity can also affect a consumer's purchase intentions. For example, a female will, generally, purchase a cosmetic product more often than a male. In addition, some shoppers may be unable to buy a product because of financial constraints. Neither a discounted price nor a bonus pack has the ability to entice consumers if they cannot afford the product.

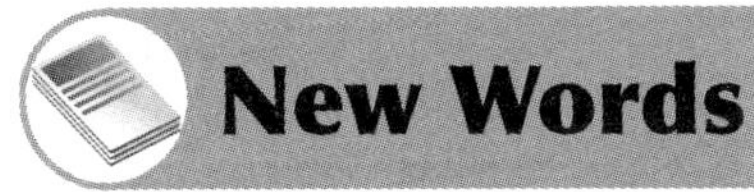

pre-determined ['pri-dɪ'tɜ:mɪnd] *adj.* 事先预定的；事先安排的

freebie ['fri:bi] *n.* （常指公司或商店提供的）免费品

rebate ['ri:beɪt] *n.* 退还款；折扣

counteract [ˌkaʊntər'ækt] *vt.* 抵制，抵抗；抵消

incentive [ɪn'sentɪv] *n.* 激励，刺激；鼓励

sweepstake ['swi:psteɪk] *n.* 抽奖促销，凭姓名抽奖

duration [dju'reɪʃn] *n.* 持续时间；期间

redeem [rɪ'di:m] *v.* 补救，弥补；掩饰……之不足

bonus ['bəʊnəs] *n.* 奖金，红利；额外津贴，意外收获

beneficiary [ˌbenɪ'fɪʃiəri] *n.* 受益者，受惠人

booklet ['bʊklət] *n.* 小册子

dispenser [dɪ'spensə] *n.* 配药员；分配者

redemption [rɪ'dempʃn] *n.* 补偿；赎回；（证券等）兑现

interactive [ˌɪntər'æktɪv] *adj.* 交互式的；互动的

receipt [rɪ'si:t] *n.* 收据，收条

barcode ['bɑːkəʊd] *n.*（商品的）条形码
dangler ['dæŋglə] *n.* 悬摆物，悬挂物
glorifier ['glɔːrɪfaɪə] *n.* 赞美者，颂扬者
elevate ['elɪveɪt] *vt.* 提高，使提升
wobbler ['wɒblə] *n.* 不稳定的人；思想动摇的人
jiggle ['dʒɪgl] *v.*（使）上下急动，左右摇摆
crayon ['kreɪən] *n.* 彩色铅笔（或粉笔、蜡笔）
electroluminescent [ɪ'lektrəʊluːmɪ'nesənt] *adj.* 场致发光的；电荧光的
alert [ə'lɜːt] *n.* 警戒；警报
commission [kə'mɪʃn] *n.* 佣金；回扣；手续费
aversion [ə'vɜːʒn] *n.* 厌恶，憎恶
sensation [sen'seɪʃn] *n.* 感觉，知觉；感觉能力
forethought ['fɔːθɔːt] *n.* 远虑；先见
trigger ['trɪgə] *vt.* 引起，触发
solely ['səʊlli] *adv.* 仅，只，唯；单独地
misconception [ˌmɪskən'sepʃn] *n.* 错误的认识，误解
deceive [dɪ'siːv] *vt.* 欺骗，蒙骗，诓骗
infamous ['ɪnfəməs] *adj.* 臭名远扬的，声名狼藉的
misinterpretation [ˌmɪsɪn'tɜːrprɪteiʃn] *n.* 错误解释；错误判读
inspire [ɪn'spaɪə] *vt.* 激励，鼓舞；赋予灵感
lure [ljuə] *vt.* 劝诱，引诱，诱惑
hastily ['heɪstli] *adv.* 急速地；仓促地；草率地
norm [nɔːm] *n.* 常态，正常行为，规范；标准，准则
impulsivity [ɪmpʌl'sɪvəti] *n.* 冲动性，冲动；冲动型
constraint [kən'streɪnt] *n.* 限制，限定；约束

Phrases

promotional mix 促销组合
non-media marketing communications 非媒体营销传播
perform an accessory role 扮演辅助角色
make an extensive use of 广泛使用
consumer sales promotion 消费者促销
trade sales promotion 贸易促销
loyal reward program 忠诚用户回馈服务
cents-off deal 降价出售
bonus pack deal 附加赠送；加量不加价
price-back deal 原价降低，原价多售，原价打折
checkout dispenser 收银台
point-of-sale display 销售点展示
loyalty card 积分卡
trade allowance 交易折让
stock up 贮备，囤积
on the spot 在现场；立即；当场
push money 给推销员的佣金
functional discount 职能折扣
more often than not 往往，通常
right digit effect 右位数效应
framing effect 框架效应
risky choice framing 风险决策框架
attribute framing 特征框架效应
goal framing 目标框架

place pressure on 给……施加压力
miss out on 错过，错失了
on impulse 凭冲动，一时兴起
dissuade... from 劝阻……远离
take a chance on... 冒险
ward off 防止；避开

Abbreviations

POP (Point-of-Purchase) 采购点
FSI (Free-Standing Insert) 夹页广告

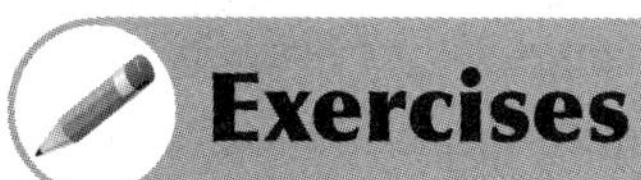

Exercises

EX. 1 Answer the following questions according to Text A.

(1) What do outside and inside sales promotion activities include respectively?
(2) What are common characteristics of sales promotion?
(3) What are the two types of sales promotions?
(4) What is price-pack/bonus pack deal?
(5) What is loss leader?
(6) What is push money in terms of trade sales promotion techniques?
(7) Why may consumers perceive the difference between \$93 and \$79 as greater than the difference between \$89 and \$75?
(8) What does the right digit effect imply?
(9) What is the Framing Effect? And what categories does this theory consist of?
(10) Which personal characteristics can affect a consumer's purchase intentions?

EX. 2 Translate the following phrases from English into Chinese and vice versa.

(1) consumer sales promotion ____________________
(2) point-of-sale display ____________________
(3) bonus pack deal ____________________
(4) push money ____________________
(5) stock up ____________________
(6) 交易折让 ____________________

(7) 贸易促销 ________________________
(8) 忠诚用户回馈服务 ________________________
(9) 交互式的；互动的 ________________________
(10) 抽奖促销，凭姓名抽奖 ________________________

EX. 3 **Translate the following into Chinese.**

A sales promotion is any type of reduced pricing or bonus deal offered to customers to encourage them to make a purchase. Sales promotions exist in every different type of sales, and may be something as simple as a reduced price at the grocery store or a low interest rate on an auto loan. An advertised sales promotion can be a great way to get customers to come into a business and end up spending additional money. A sales promotion at a business may be a scheduled event, such as a weekly or monthly price reduction, or it may occur at different times throughout the year. It is completely up to the company as to when they will offer promotional pricing on goods or services. Sales promotions often occur at the changes of the seasons, where the type of merchandise sold may change, and companies will want to move old merchandise quickly to make room for new items to sell at full price.

EX. 4 **Fill in the blanks with the words given below.**

slumping	lasting	draw	prominently	induce
awareness	offered	showcasing	inundated	tactics

In-Store Promotions

An in-store promotion is a marketing strategy that is meant to bring people into the store and to purchase specific items that are part of the in-store promotion. These strategies most often come directly from manufacturers, or they may be (1)________ by the store itself. The idea is to generate additional revenue due to the extra sales of the products involved, or even to (2)________ a brand switch when offered by the manufacturer. Stores most often use such strategies to drive traffic into the store, to eliminate too much stock, or to create additional revenues when sales are (3)________. Often, however, the main emphasis comes from brand manufacturers attempting to create brand (4)________, while building brand equity in-store.

Driving the effort of in-store promotion, many (5)________ are utilized to entice people to buy the product itself or to buy into the brand. Signs, banners, coupons, TV screens, and other in-store brand mediums are often displayed in an attempt to (6)________ attention to the brand message and induce preference for the brand. Shoppers are often (7)________ with the messages throughout the shopping experience. Product displays are another common form of in-store promotion, which are usually placed (8)________ in the middle or end of an aisle, (9)________ the product while minimizing distraction. Oftentimes, such displays are found as the front of the store near cash registers as well, in an attempt to leave a (10)________ impression as customers prepare to exit the store.

Promotional Mix

In marketing, the promotional mix describes a blend of promotional variables chosen by marketers to help a firm reach its goals. It has been identified as a subset of the marketing mix. It is believed that there is an optimal way of allocating budgets for the different elements within the promotional mix to achieve best marketing results, and the challenge for marketers is to find the right mix of them. The promotional mix typically contains four elements: advertising (paid, non-personal communication through mass media), personal selling (a paid personal communication to inform and persuade customers to purchase), sales promotion (to provide added value or incentives to consumers, wholesalers, retailers, or other organizational customers to stimulate immediate sales), and public relations (a broad set of communication efforts to create and maintain favorable relationship between organization and stakeholder).

Promotion mix shall depend on nature of the product market, promotional budget, costs and availability of promotional methods, overall marketing strategy, buyer readiness stage and product life stage. Promotion strategy may be "push" (use of a company's sales force and trade promotion activities to create consumer demand for a product. The producer promotes the product to wholesalers, the wholesalers promote it to retailers, and the retailers promote it to consumers), "pull" (high spending on advertising and consumer promotion to build up consumer demand for a product, consumers will ask their retailers for the product, the retailers will ask the wholesalers, and the wholesalers will ask the producers) or a combination of the two (It focuses both on the distributor as well as the consumers, targeting both parties directly).

1. Advertising

Advertising informs, persuades and at times entertains. Advertising can be of numerous types—competitive or comparative advertising (showing comparison with another brand, like Zen with Sentro), reinforcement advertising (assures current users about quality), reminder advertising (brand is still around with same quality attributes, like Bourn Vita during the Second World War), institutional advertising (to promote corporate image, ideas, and political issues—like Reliance Power ad for supremacy of family agreement), advocacy advertising (Tata Tea's ad asking questions to a political candidate), pioneer or primary demand advertising (stimulates the main demand for a product), in-film advertising (In the movie *Chalte Chalte*, actor Shah Rukh Khan acting as a driver, recommends other drivers to also use Castrol CRB like him), national advertising (Amul Butter, being sold throughout India, is being advertised through various media), transit advertising (ad placed in Metro or local trains) and so on.

Various media are available for advertising—newspapers, magazines, direct mail, radio,

TV, Internet, yellow pages, outdoor, etc. It is up to the advertiser to decide which one or ones to make use of. The ad message would be given differently on different media, due to media characteristics. Advertising effectiveness can be judged through pretest, and posttest.

2. Personal selling

Personal selling is a process which includes seven steps—prospecting (developing a list of potential customers), pre-approach (prepares customer profile about his needs, present use and reaction to current brand), approach (contacting to deliver value), presentation (to create a desire to buy the product), overcoming objections (regarding price, quality, use, after-sales service, warranty, etc.), closing the sale (asking the prospect to buy the product) and follow up (to see that order was properly executed).

For personal selling the firm requires salespeople, who may be order getters (persuading current and new customers to buy) and order takers (seeking repeat sales). To increase effectiveness of salespeople, the marketing manager decides on sales territories and sales quota. The effectiveness of sales force depends upon performance appraisal. Information can be sought through the call reports, customer feedback and invoices.

Some of the firms, instead of personal selling, go in for vending machines, which are cheaper to install and operate and flexible in location. Mother Dairy, weighing machines at railway stations, metro stations, ATMs operated by banks, coffee and tea machines operated by Hindustan Unilever and Nestle are good examples.

3. Sales promotion

Sales promotions are short-term incentives to encourage the purchase or sale of a product or service. Sales promotion as a technique of promotion has been developed to supplement and coordinate advertising and personal selling efforts of a firm. It is any short-term incentive used by a firm to increase the sales of its product.

It consists of all those promotional activities that help in enhancing sales through non-repetitive and one-time communication. It is aimed at stimulating market demand and consumer purchasing. It focuses the selling efforts on a selected small group of people.

3.1 Objectives

A firm undertakes sales promotion with the following objectives:

Increasing the buying response of ultimate consumers;

Increasing the selling efforts and intensity by dealers as well as by sales personnel;

Supplementing and co-ordinating the efforts of advertising and personal selling;

Introduction of new products and brands, and acquainting the customers about the use of product;

Acquainting the customers about the utility of the product;

Affecting instant purchase and attracting new customers;

Increasing sales during slack periods and increasing profits of the firm;

Improving the corporate image of the firm;

Others—improving market share, obtaining dealer outlets, meeting competition.

Sales promotion includes several communications and activities that attempt to provide added value or incentives to consumers, wholesalers, retailers, or other organizational customers to stimulate immediate sales.

These efforts can attempt to stimulate product interest, trial, or purchase. While developing a sales promotion strategy, it is important to keep these in mind: consumer attitudes and buying patterns, firm's brand strategy, competitive strategy, advertising strategy, stage in PLC, and government regulations.

3.2 Tools and programmes designed for consumers

Tools & Programmes for consumers include the following:

Sample (free samples given to consumers);

Demonstrations or instructions (Vacuum cleaner);

Coupon (a certificate that reduces the price, a dentist to charge no consultation fee, if coupon is presented);

Money-refund orders (makemytrip.com gives Rs. 300 cash back on purchase of air ticket, if purchase is made through ICICI Credit card);

Premium (gift) offers (Liril gave a soap box almost free with two soap cakes. Hindustan Lever offered a "Sun silk" sachet free with its detergent powder Rin. Kwality Walls tied up with Cadbury to give free a 5 Star with the purchase of Kwality ice-cream);

Price-off (Rs. 4 on a Brooke Bond tea pack of 500 grams);

Contests / quizzes / sweepstakes (Sage Publication on every Sunday asks question, of whose answers are in that very newspaper and gives books in prize);

Trading stamps (issued by retailers to customers who buy goods from there, Bangalore Central gives a stamp worth Rs. 600 on purchase of Rs. 5,000, which can be used after next purchase of Rs. 1,200);

Fairs and Exhibitions (trade shows, fashion shows or parades, fairs and exhibitions, Lever Lame sponsored Fashion Week for many years);

Exchange scheme (Exchange the old product with new by paying less , like exchange of old Black & White Television for Colour Television by paying rupees 8,000 only);

Sale (Annual clearance sale of Jainsons). The list is not exhaustive.

3.3 Tools and programmes designed for dealers/distributors

Tools and programmes for dealers/distributors sales promotion includes:

Free display (of material at the point of purchase);

Retail demonstrations (arranged by manufactures for preparing and distributing the products as a retail sample, like, Nescafe Instant Coffee was served to consumers for trying the sample on the spot of demonstration regarding the method of using the product);

Trade deals (offered to encourage retailers to give additional selling support to the product, e.g., tooth paste sold with 30% to 40% margin);

Buying allowance (Sellers give buying allowance of a certain amount of money for a product bought);

Buy-back allowance (offered to encourage repurchase of a product immediately after an initial trade deal is over. A buy back is a resale opportunity);

Free goods (Seller gives free goods, e.g., one piece free with two, or two pieces free with 10);

Advertising and display allowance (to popularise the product and brand name, like calendar, key ring, crockery, etc.);

Contests (for salesmen);

Dealer loader (A gift for an order is a premium given to the retailer for buying certain quantities of goods or for special display done by the retailer);

Training for salesmen (to give them a better knowledge of a product and how to use it).

4. Public relations

Public relations are used to build rapport with employees, customers, investors, and the general public. Almost any organization that has a stake in how it is portrayed in the public arena employs some level of public relations. There are a number of public relations disciplines falling under the banner of corporate communications, such as analyst relations, media relations, investor relations, internal communications, and labor relations. Most of them include the aspect of peer review to get visibility.

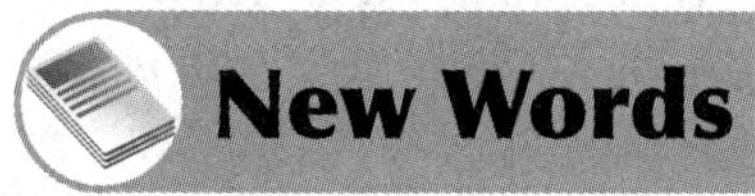

New Words

subset ['sʌbset] *n.* 子集；分组，小组

optimal ['ɑːptɪməl] *adj.* 最优的，最佳的

entertain [ˌentə'teɪn] *vt.* 招待，款待；使有兴趣，娱乐

comparative [kəm'pærətɪv] *adj.* 比较的，相比的

reinforcement [ˌriːɪn'fɔːsmənt] *n.* 巩固，加强，强化

reminder [rɪ'maɪndə] *n.* 提醒物；提示

institutional [ˌɪnstɪ'tuːʃənl] *adj.* 制度上的；惯例的；机构的

supremacy [sjuː'preməsi] *n.* 至高无上；最高权威

advocacy ['ædvəkəsi] *n.* （对某思想或信念的）拥护，支持，提倡

candidate ['kændɪdət] *n.* 候选人，申请人

transit ['trænzɪt] *n.* 运输；经过；中转

pretest ['priːtest] *n.* （学习或做某事前的）预先测试

posttest ['pəʊstest] *n.* 后测，后测验

presentation [ˌpriːzen'teɪʃn] *n.* 展示会，介绍会，发布会

objection [əb'dʒekʃn] *n.* 反对，异议

execute ['eksɪkjuːt] *vt.* 实行，执行，实施

territory ['terətɔːri] *n.* 领域，（某人负责的）地区

quota ['kwəʊtə] *n.* 限额；配额；定额

appraisal [ə'preɪzl] *n.* 评价；鉴定

vending ['vendɪŋ] *n.* 贩卖，售卖

coordinate [kəʊ'ɔːdɪneɪt] *vt.* （使）协调；（使）一致

non-repetitive ['nɒn-rɪ'petətɪv] *adj.* 非重复的

acquaint [ə'kweɪnt] *vt.* 使熟悉，使了解
slack [slæk] *adj.* 萧条的；松弛的，懈怠的
demonstration [ˌdemən'streɪʃn] *n.* 示范，演示
instruction [ɪn'strʌkʃn] *n.* 用法说明，操作指南
charge [tʃɑːdʒ] *v.* 要价，收费
refund ['riːfʌnd] *n.* 退款，返还款；偿还金额
sachet [sæ'ʃeɪ] *n.* （塑料或纸质）密封小袋
detergent [dɪ'tɜːdʒənt] *n.* 洗涤剂，去垢剂
fair [feə] *n.* 集市，商品交易会，展销会
exhaustive [ɪg'zɔːstɪv] *adj.* 彻底的，全面的；详尽的
popularise ['pɒpjuləraɪz] *vt.* 使大众化，普及
crockery ['krɑːkəri] *n.* 陶器，瓦器
rapport [ræ'pɔː] *n.* 融洽，和谐
visibility [ˌvɪzə'bɪləti] *n.* 可见性，可见度；明显性

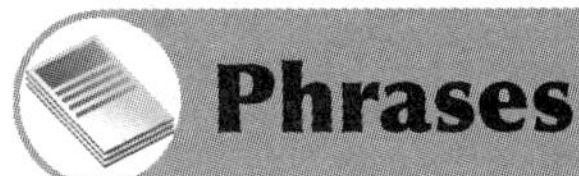

Phrases

be identified as 被识别为……，被确认为……
competitive advertising 竞争性广告
comparative advertising 比较性广告
reinforcement advertising 强化性广告
reminder advertising 提示性广告
corporate image 企业形象
advocacy advertising 倡议广告
pioneer or primary demand advertising 先锋或基本需求广告
in-film advertising 植入广告
national advertising 全国性广告
transit advertising 交通工具上的广告
follow up 跟进；采取措施
sales quota 销售定额
sales force 销售人员，推销人员
performance appraisal 绩效评估
go in for 赞成；对……感兴趣
vending machine 售货机
metro station 地铁站
keep... in mind 记住，记着
detergent powder 洗衣粉；清洁剂
tie up with 和……有密切关系
annual clearance sale 年度清仓大甩卖
buying allowance 购买折让
buy-back allowance 回购津贴
public relations 公关工作（或活动）；公共关系
have a stake in 在……有利害关系
public arena 公共场所或公共竞技场
under the banner of 在……的旗帜下；为了……的事业
peer review 同行评议

Abbreviations

ATM (Automatic Teller Machine) 自动取款机
PIC (Programmable Interrupt Controller) 可编程中断控制器
ICICI (Industrial Credit and Investment Corporation of India) 印度工业信贷投资银行

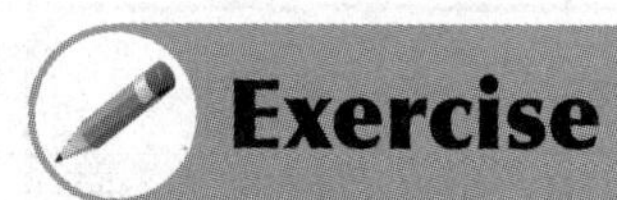

EX. Answer the following questions according to Text B.

(1) What are the four elements typically contained in the promotional mix?
(2) What factors shall promotional mix depend on?
(3) What are the numerous types of advertising?
(4) Why is workplace conflict inevitable?
(5) Can you list at least three objectives of sales promotion? And what are they?
(6) Can you list at least five tools and programmes designed for consumers? And what are they?
(7) Can you list one example to show what is coupon?
(8) Can you list at least five tools and programmes designed for dealers/distributors?
(9) What is the purpose of offering buy-back allowance?
(10) Can you list any public relations disciplines falling under the banner of corporate communications?

参考译文（Text A）

促　　销

促销是促销组合的要素之一。促销利用媒体和非媒体营销传播手段，在预先确定的有限时间内增加消费者需求，刺激市场需求或提高产品的可用性。促销方式包括竞赛、优惠券、免费赠品、为招揽顾客亏本销售的商品、购买点展示、奖品、产品样本和回扣。促销是为了吸引新客户、留住现有客户、应对竞争并利用市场调查研究所展现的机会。它由包括外部和内部活动在内的各种活动组成，以促进公司销售。外部促销活动包括广告、宣传、公关活动、特殊销售活动等。内部促销活动包括橱窗展示、产品和促销材料展示以及奖品、竞赛等。促销活动包括一些传播活动，其旨在为消费者、批发商、零售商或其他组织客户提供增值或激励，以刺激即时销售。这些努力可能尝试着刺激顾客对产品产生兴趣、试用或购买。

1. 促销的特点

促销代表了用以刺激购买某个产品或品牌的各种技巧。在营销传播和品牌战略中，促销具有战术作用，而不是战略作用。研究人员确定了促销活动的一系列共同特点，包括：

它具有短期效果且持续时间短；

它只对采购过程的最后阶段起作用并产生影响；

相对于其他形式的营销传播，它发挥着次要作用；

在产品核心利益方面，它起着辅助作用；

它不是一种单一的技术，而是用于特定目的的一组技术。

2. 两种类型的促销

促销活动可以针对客户、销售人员或分销渠道人员（如零售商）。针对消费者的促销活动称为消费者促销；针对零售商和批发的促销活动称为贸易促销。制造商和零售商都在广泛利用促销活动。

2.1 消费者促销

消费者促销是短期手段，旨在实现短期销售目标，例如刺激购买、推动商店客流量或者仅仅是为某种产品或某个品牌造势。传统的促销手段包括：

价格优惠：暂时降价，如打五折；

忠诚奖励计划：消费者通过购物积分，并将其兑换成奖品；

降价出售：以更低的价格提供某个品牌的产品，降价幅度可以在包装上标明。

原价多售/优惠装：在相同的价格下，优惠装可以为消费者提供更高的产品比例（如25%的额外优惠）。这是另一种以同样的价格向顾客提供更多产品的优惠措施。例如，一家销售公司可能会给他们的消费者提供一个优惠装，其中，消费者可以以一个产品的价格获得两个产品。在这种情况下，这个优惠装被界定为一种收益，因为顾客相信他们正在获得一个免费的产品。然而，购买优惠装商品并不总是对消费者有利。有时，消费者最终会把钱花在一些他们通常不会购买的商品上（如果这些商品不是优惠包装的话，他们不会购买）。因此，购买的优惠装中的商品常常被浪费，而且被视为消费者的“损失”。

优惠券：优惠券已经成为促销的标准机制；

亏本销售品：暂时降低受欢迎的产品价格，使其低于成本价，以刺激其他可赢利的产品销售；

夹页广告：将优惠券小册子夹入当地发行的报纸；

收银台领券：在结账时，顾客根据所购买的商品从商家获得一张优惠券；

移动优惠券：顾客可以在手机上获得优惠券，并通过手机向销售人员展示并且要求兑换优惠券；

在线互动推广游戏：消费者参与和推广产品相关的互动游戏；

返利：如果把收据和条形码邮寄给生产商，消费者就可以得到退款；

竞赛/抽奖/游戏：消费者通过购买产品自动进入各项活动；

过道中断器：从货架上凸出到过道上的标志；

吊牌：当消费者经过吊牌时，它会摇摆；

减价货品柜：一个装满减价产品的货品柜；

竞价门户：获取潜在客户；

美化者：将产品提升到其他产品之上的小舞台；

口红板：用蜡笔写信息的板；

瓶颈券：放在瓶口上的优惠券；

电致发光：太阳能驱动的动态光；

儿童免单的特价餐：在总餐费上提供折扣，每购买一份常规餐，就提供一份免费的儿童餐；

抽样：消费者可以免费得到一个样品，并在试用后，决定是否购买该类产品。

新技术为促销活动提供了一系列新的机会。积分卡、个人购物助理、电子货架标签和电子广告允许在顾客购买时进行更为个性化的交流并给顾客提供更有针对性的信息。例如，当购物者接触到某一特定通道的商品时，可能会收到特价商品的提示信息。

2.2　贸易促销

贸易补贴：鼓励零售商购买并储备某种商品的短期激励措施；

设备赠送：诱导零售商购买并展示产品的一种激励手段；

贸易竞赛：奖励销售产品最多的零售商的竞赛；

采购点展示：用于制造“冲动”购物的强烈欲望，并营造现场销售产品的氛围；

培训活动：经销商员工接受产品销售方面的培训；

佣金：向推销产品的零售员工支付的额外佣金；

贸易折扣（也称为功能折扣）：支付给分销渠道人员的酬金，因为他们履行了职责。

3. 消费者思维过程

3.1　有意义的节约：收益或损失

许多折扣旨在让消费者在购买产品时产生一种省钱的感觉，但并不是所有的折扣价格都被认为对购买者有利。因此，在购买之前，消费者可能会权衡他们的选择是盈利还是亏损，以避免在购买时出现亏钱的风险。认为此次购物行为是在“赚钱”的想法会促使购物者去冒险。例如，如果购物者认为“买一送一”的折扣看起来有利可图，他们就会购买该产品。但是，如果消费者认为此次购物行为是在“赔钱”，他们就不愿冒险去买。例如，如果消费者认为他们没有从交易中获益，他们就会放弃“买三送一”的折扣。具体来说，消费者会考虑他们的选择，因为对于同样的价值，消费者“损失”的感觉比“收益”的感觉大 2.5 倍。

3.2　冲动购买

冲动性购买是由于消费者在购买产品之前未能权衡他们的选择。它是购物者没有计划的任何购买行为。例如，如果消费者在进入商店之前无意购买任何商品，但最终却在没有任何预先考虑的情况下购买了商品，这就是冲动性购买。产品制造商希望能促进和激发消费者的这种即时购买冲动。当一件商品被认为是物美价廉时，购买者可以很快买下该商品，而不考虑后果。因此，销售公司越来越多地开展促销活动，期望有效地激发消费者的冲动购买行为，以增加销售量和利润。

3.3　比较价格

许多消费者阅读的方式是从左至右，因此，他们以同样的方式比较价格。例如，如果一个产品的价格是 93 美元，而销售价格是 79 美元，人们首先会比较左边的数字（9 和 7），然后注意到两个数字间的差异。然而，由于这种习惯性行为，消费者可能会认为 93 美元和 79 美元之间（14 美元）的差异比 89 美元和 75 美元之间（14 美元）的差异味更大。因此，仅根据左边的数字，消费者常常会错误地认为，他们更能在第一组价格中获益。由于这种普遍的误解，公司往往利用这种销售定价策略来提高销售额。

3.4　右位数效应

当价格的左位数相同时，右位数效应集中在价格的右位数上。换句话说，像 45 美元和 42 美元这样的价格迫使消费者更多地关注右位数字（5 和 2）来确定商家提供的折扣。这一效应还意味着，消费者会认为以右位数小结尾的商品价格会比以右位数大结尾的价格有更大的折扣。例如，消费者会认为他们在 32 美元至 31 美元的降价中得到的好处要大于从 39 至 38 美元的降价中获得的好处。因此，企业可能会使用较小的右位数折扣来误导消费者，让他们以为自己获得了更多的好处，从而增加公司的利润。然而，消费者也被臭名昭著的 9 结尾价格所欺骗。右位数效应还使消费者倾向于将 9 结尾价格视为促销价格（而非常规价格），或者将其与折扣联系在一起。例如，199 美元这一正常价格被消费者误认为是促销价或折扣价。销售公司最经常使用这种方法，因为消费者的误解通常会带来销售额和利润的增加。

3.5　框架效应

框架效应是一种现象。当一个人在两种或两种以上的选择之间的偏好由于问题的呈现方式而发生变化时，框架效应这一现象就会出现。换句话说，呈现内容的方式会影响一个人的观点。该理论包括三个子范畴：风险选择框架、特征框架和目标框架。风险选择框架涉及消费者的得失思维过程。如果环境对消费者有利，他们就会冒险；反之，他们就会避免冒险。特征框架处理的是价格折扣中的一个关键性措辞或特征，对其加以强调，从而鼓励消费者购物。例如，“免费”和“更好”这两个词通常用来吸引消费者购买产品。目标框架给购物者施加压力，迫使他们匆忙购物，否则就会承担错失明确降价的后果。例如，“限时”优惠策略试图刺激购物者在活动时间结束之前快速或冲动购买。

3.6　外部力量

虽然决定消费者购物行为的因素有多方面，但也有很多外部因素可以影响消费者的购买决定。例如，即使一个产品的价格打折，该产品的质量可能会使消费者对该产品望而却步。如果顾客对该产品的评价很差，或者该产品“寿命”很短，消费者就会将购买行为视为一种损失，并避免冒险。由于消费者过去的经验和期望，产品也可能会招致冷遇。例如，如果产品的规格有误，购买者也会失去购买意愿。一件被宣传为“巨大的”但实际上只有一英寸高的商品会吓跑消费者。此外，个人特征，如消费者的性别、主观标准和冲动性也会影响消费者的购买意图。例如，一般来说，女性比男性更经常地购买化妆品。此外，一些购物者会因为经济拮据而无法购买产品。如果消费者买不起这种产品，无论是折扣价还是优惠装都无法诱使他们产生购买行为。

Case　Frito-Lay Enhances In-store Promotion via Augmented Reality App

Unit 11

Text A

Advertising

Advertising is an audio or visual form of marketing communication that employs an openly sponsored, non-personal message to promote or sell a product, service or idea. Sponsors of advertising are typically businesses wishing to promote their products or services. Advertising is differentiated from public relations in that an advertiser pays for and has control over the message. It differs from personal selling in that the message is non-personal, i.e., not directed to a particular individual. Advertising is communicated through various mass media, including traditional media such as newspapers, magazines, television, radio, and new media such as blogs, social media. The actual presentation of the message in a medium is referred to as an advertisement or "ad" for short. Commercial ads often seek to generate increased consumption of their products or services through "branding", which associates a product name or image with certain qualities in the minds of consumers. On the other hand, ads that intend to elicit an immediate sale are known as direct-response advertising. Non-profit organizations may use free modes of persuasion, such as a public service announcement. Advertising may also be used to reassure employees or shareholders that a company is viable or successful.

1. Types of advertising

Advertising is an integral part of an integrated marketing communications plan that also includes public relations and direct sales. Businesses have many choices of where and how to advertise, and each has its benefits and drawbacks. You can contact different media companies yourself and compare prices and data or hire a professional marketing company that doesn't represent any of the media but has reliable knowledge of them all. These companies can help you choose the best type of advertising and specific providers of it to give you the most for your advertising budget.

1.1 Online advertising

Online advertising is a form of promotion that uses the Internet for the expressed purpose of delivering marketing messages to attract customers. Online ads are delivered by an ad server. Examples of online advertising include contextual ads that appear on search engine results pages, banner ads, in pay per click text ads, rich media ads, social network advertising, online classified advertising, advertising networks and e-mail marketing, including e-mail spam. A newer form of online advertising is Native Ads; they go in a website's news feed and are supposed to improve user experience by being less intrusive. However, some people argue this practice is deceptive.

1.2 Cell Phone and mobile advertising

A relatively new form of advertising compared to the others, but one that's dominating the media mix, uses cell phones, iPads, Kindles, and other portable electronic devices with internet connectivity. Current trends in mobile advertising involve major use of social media such as Twitter. Right now, this is the toughest nut to crack. This kind of advertising is not only disruptive, but can leave the customers with a lot of ill will. If you do it, do it right. For a while, native advertising was a good way to get into the feed, but even that has come under scrutiny for being deceptive.

1.3 Print advertising

Once a huge driver of sales, print is taking a back seat to the many digital forms of advertising now available to marketers. However, if there is one thing that's certain about advertising, it's that being different is good. And when consumers tire of digital ads, a return to printed pieces and the tactile feeling and permanence they provide is definitely in the cards. Typically, print can be split into three subcategories.

1.3.1 Periodical advertising

If it's in a magazine, a newspaper, or anything else that comes out at regular intervals, then it's periodical advertising. For decades, print ads were the gold standard for advertisers and their clients. To grab the center spread of a big magazine or the back cover of a newspaper meant millions of people were seeing the message.

1.3.2 Brochures, leaflets, flyers, handouts, and point-of-sale advertising

Although some of these media can be placed within the pages of newspapers and magazines, they are treated as a separate entity, usually because they have less chance of being seen. From something that sits on a counter or customer service desk to a glossy car brochure, small print media offer a more intimate and long-form way of engaging the consumer. Use this approach when you have more information than you can cram into a print ad.

1.3.3 Direct mail advertising

Either of the techniques mentioned above can be incorporated into direct mail. It simply means that your printed pieces are mailed direct to the consumer. This is a technique that has been, and continues to be, abused by inferior marketing agencies that have turned the craft into junk mail. If it is creative and intelligently conceived and executed, direct mail can be a fantastic way to engage the customer. Do not count it out.

1.4 Guerrilla advertising

Also known as ambient media, guerrilla advertising (or marketing) has become prominent over the last 20 years. It is a broadly used term for anything unconventional, and usually invites the consumer to participate or interact with the piece in some way. Location is important, as is timing. The driving forces behind guerrilla advertising or marketing are creative ideas and innovation, not a large budget. Quite often, you will ask for forgiveness rather than permission with these campaigns, and they will spread via word of mouth and social media.

1.5 Broadcast advertising

A mass-market form of communication including television and radio, broadcast advertising has, until recently, been the most dominant way to reach a large number of consumers. Broadcast advertising has really taken a beating over the last few years, especially with the rise of DVRs and "ad skipping" technology. However, it is still a popular way to reach millions of people, especially when the Super Bowl comes around.

Television advertising is one of the most expensive types of advertising; networks charge large amounts for commercial airtime during popular events. The annual Super Bowl football game in the United States is known as the most prominent advertising event on television—with an audience of over 108 million and studies showing that 50% of those only tuned in to see the advertisements. During the 2014 edition of this game, the average thirty-second ad cost $4 million, and $8 million was charged for a 60-second spot. Virtual advertisements may be inserted into regular programming through computer graphics. It is typically inserted into otherwise blank backdrops or used to replace local billboards that are not relevant to the remote broadcast audience. Radio advertisements are broadcast as radio waves to the air from a transmitter to an antenna and thus to a receiving device. Airtime is purchased from a station or network in exchange for airing the commercials. While radio has the limitation of being restricted to sound, proponents of radio advertising often cite this as an advantage. Radio is an expanding medium that can be found on air, and also online. According to Arbitron, radio has approximately 241.6 million weekly listeners, or more than 93% of the US population.

1.6 Outdoor advertising

Billboards, also known as hoardings in some parts of the world, are large structures located in public places which display advertisements to passing pedestrians and motorists. Most often, they are located on main roads with a large amount of passing motor and pedestrian traffic; however, they can be placed in any location with large numbers of viewers, such as on mass transit vehicles and in stations, in shopping malls or office buildings, and in stadiums. The form known as street advertising first came to prominence in the UK by Street Advertising Services to create outdoor advertising on street furniture and pavements, working with products such as Reverse Graffiti, air dancers and 3D pavement advertising, for getting brand messages out into public spaces. Sheltered outdoor advertising combines outdoor with indoor advertisement by placing large mobile, structures (tents) in public places on temporary bases. The large outer advertising space aims to exert a strong pull on the observer, the product is promoted indoors, where the creative decor can intensify the impression. Mobile billboards are generally vehicle mounted billboards or digital screens. These can be on dedicated vehicles built solely for carrying advertisements along routes preselected by clients. They can also be specially equipped cargo trucks or, in some cases, large banners strewn from planes.

1.7 Public service advertising

Unlike traditional commercials, Public Service Advertisements (PSA) are primarily designed to inform and educate rather than sell a product or service. PSAs traditionally appear on TV and radio, but are also heavily promoted online.

1.8 Product placement advertising

Covert advertising is when a product or brand is embedded in entertainment and media. For example, in a film, the main character can use an item or other of a definite brand, as in the movie *Minority Report*, where Tom Cruise's character John Anderton owns a phone with the Nokia logo clearly written in the top corner, or his watch engraved with the Bulgari logo. Another example of advertising in film is in *I, Robot*, where the main character played by Will Smith mentions his Converse shoes several times, calling them "classics", because the film is set far in the future. *I, Robot* and *Spaceballs* also showcase futuristic cars with the Audi and Mercedes-Benz logos clearly displayed on the front of the vehicles. Cadillac chose to advertise in the movie *The Matrix Reloaded*, which as a result contained many scenes in which Cadillac cars were used. Similarly, product placement for Omega Watches, Ford, VAIO, BMW and Aston Martin cars are featured in recent James Bond films, most notably *Casino Royale*. In *Fantastic Four: Rise of the Silver Surfer*, the main transport vehicle shows a large Dodge logo on the front. *Blade Runner* includes some of the most obvious product placement; the whole film stops to show a Coca-Cola billboard.

2. Functions of advertising

Advertising permeates the Internet, network television, daily newspapers, and roadside billboards. Products, services, and ideas are sold through advertising, enabling businesses to attract customers for their wares. Internet advertising is rapidly displacing print advertising, due to its convenience of use, cost effectiveness, and ease of distribution.

2.1 Identifying brands

Products, services, and ideas are sold through businesses that are differentiated by their brand identities. Brand identity is communicated to the public via advertising. Consumers build emotional relationships with certain brands with which they become increasingly familiar through the years, thanks to advertising.

2.2 Information

Advertising supplies the necessary information to consumers so that they know what is available and where to buy it. It broadcasts information on products, services and ideas sold on the open market through a variety of media portals. It reveals the special features being sold, what color and size the product is and which stores carry it.

2.3 Persuasion

Powerful, visual advertising presentations compel consumers to purchase goods, services and ideas as a way to achieve emotional fulfillment. Persuasion is the core mission of advertising. Advertising tells you how the product, service or idea you are considering will improve your life. According to Jeremiah O'Sullivan R, author of *The Social and Cultural Effects of Advertising*, advertising feeds on the concepts of ideology, myth, art attraction. Advertising infuses images and ideas into products and services, just as the meanings of products and services are infused into images and ideas, notes O'Sullivan.

2.4 Previewing new trends

Previews about the virtues of new products, services and ideas motivate consumers to obtain them because they don't want to be left out. Advertising lets consumers in on up-and-coming trends and new markets. They offer coupons, rebates and trial offers on new products, services or ideas to recruit new customers and induce existing customers to try things. Advertisers preview new or improved products, services and ideas to consumers in order to appeal to their sense of wanting to be in the know about leading edge trends. Previewing new trends is a technique employed by advertisers that capitalizes on consumers' desires to "keep up with the Jones" by owning the latest and greatest product, service or idea.

2.5 Demand

The demand generated by advertising, public relations, and sales promotion "pulls" the goods or services through channels of distribution, notes "Reference for Business". One of the powerful functions of advertising is to generate consumer demand for specific products, services and ideas through ad campaigns that target the audiences that are most likely to buy them. Products, services and concepts are sold in volume, according to the consumer demand for them.

2.6 Customer base

Consistent quality advertising increases consumer loyalty for a product, service or idea. Advertising seeks to maintain the current customer base by reinforcing purchasing behavior with additional information about the benefits of brands. The goal of advertising is to build and reinforce relationships with customers, prospects, retailers, and important stakeholders.

2.7 Competitive pricing

Advertising displays consumer goods with competitive prices relative to the current market, thus educating consumers about what things should cost. Advertising lets you know what the competition is doing, when the next sale is, and how you can receive the latest coupon or rebate and seeks to assure you that you are receiving the best value for your money. A number of goals and objectives are employed in advertising and can be both short or long term in nature. Short-term goals and objectives pertain to the ad copy itself. Ads are designed to introduce certain concepts and must also be convincing. Long-term advertising goals pertain to desired effects. The key to successful advertising is knowing how much to allocate toward specific types of advertising. You also need to properly identify your target audience so you are reaching the right consumers.

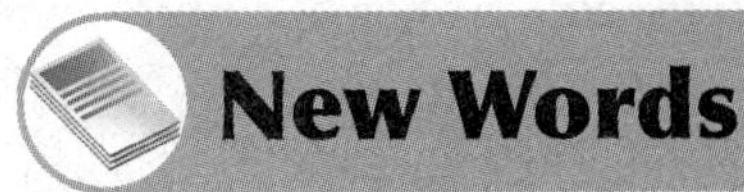

New Words

visual ['vɪʒuəl] *adj.* 视觉的；视力的
openly ['əʊpənli] *adv.* 公开地，毫不隐瞒地
elicit [i'lɪsɪt] *vt.* 引出，诱出；探出
entity ['entəti] *n.* 实体；独立存在物
reassure [ˌriːə'ʃɔː] *vt.* 使……安心，打消……的疑虑
integral ['ɪntɪgrəl] *adj.* 必需的，不可或缺的
drawback ['drɔːbæk] *n.* 缺点，不利条件
contextual [kən'tekstʃuəl] *adj.* 与语境相关的；与上下文有关的
spam [spæm] *n.* 滥发的电邮，垃圾电邮
intrusive [ɪn'truːsɪv] *adj.* 侵扰的；侵入的，闯入的
deceptive [dɪ'septɪv] *adj.* 欺骗性的，骗人的；误导的
connectivity [ˌkɑːnek'tɪvəti] *n.* 连接（度）；联结（度）
inferior [ɪn'fɪriə] *adj.* 较差的，次的；比不上……的
conceive [kən'siːv] *v.* 想象，设想；想出（主意、计划等）
fantastic [fæn'tæstɪk] *adj.* 极好的，了不起的
ambient ['æmbiənt] *adj.* 周围的；氛围的
prominent ['prɑːmɪnənt] *adj.* 杰出的，突出的；显眼的，显著的
dominant ['dɑːmɪnənt] *adj.* 首要的；占支配地位的，占优势的
airtime ['eətaɪm] *n.* （广播或电视节目的）播放时间
virtual ['vɜːtʃuəl] *adj.* 事实上的，实际上的；虚拟的
transmitter [træns'mɪtə] *n.* 发射机，发射台；传送者，传输者
antenna [æn'tenə] *n.* 天线；触角
covert ['kʌvət] *adj.* 秘密的，隐蔽的，暗中的
logo ['ləʊgəʊ] *n.* 商标，标识
engrave [ɪn'greɪv] *v.* 在……上雕刻（字或图案）
showcase ['ʃəʊkeɪs] *v.* 在玻璃橱窗陈列；使展现
permeate ['pɜːmieɪt] *v.* 渗透，弥漫，扩散
compel [kəm'pel] *v.* 强迫，迫使；使必须
ideology [ˌaɪdi'ɑːlədʒi] *n.* 思想（体系）；思想意识，意识形态
infuse [ɪn'fjuːz] *vt.* 注入；使获得
virtue ['vɜːtʃuː] *n.* 美德，德行；优点
recruit [rɪ'kruːt] *v.* 吸收（新成员）；征募（新兵）
reinforce [ˌriːɪn'fɔːs] *v.* 巩固，加强，强化；充实；使更强烈
stakeholder ['steɪkhəʊldə] *n.* 参与人，参与方；有权益关系者，利益相关者
convincing [kən'vɪnsɪŋ] *adj.* 令人信服的，有说服力的

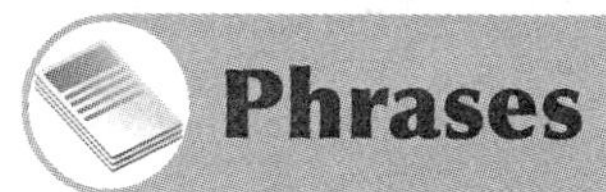

Phrases

marketing commercials 营销广告
in that 因为，原因是
have control over 能控制……，对……进行控制
mass media 大众传媒
social media 社交媒体
be referred to as 被称作，被称为
for short 作为简称，作为缩写
search engine（计算机）搜索引擎
banner ads（互联网上的）通栏广告，横幅广告
rich media ads 富媒体广告
portable electronic device 便携式电子设备
ill will 恶意，憎恨，敌意
under scrutiny 受到审查
take a back seat 让权于他人，退居次要位置
periodical advertising 期刊广告
at regular intervals 定期，每隔一定时间
junk mail 垃圾广告邮件
count out 不把……算入；不包括
guerrilla advertising 游击式广告
driving force 驱动力
word of mouth 口碑营销
take a beating 受打击；投资失败
receiving device 接收设备，接收装置
mass transit vehicle 公共交通车辆
exert a strong will on 对……施加强烈的意志
product placement advertising 植入式广告
be embedded in 嵌入
media portals 媒体门户网站
feed on 以……为食；以……为能源
leave out 遗漏，省去；不考虑
trial offer 试用机会
keep up with the Jones 攀比，赶时髦

Abbreviations

DVR (Digital Video Recorder) 硬盘录像机
3D (3 Dimensions) 三维，三个维度
PSA (Public Service Advertisement) 公益广告

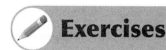

Exercises

EX. 1 Answer the following questions according to Text A.

(1) How is advertising differentiated from public relations?
(2) What is online advertising?

(3) Why is mobile advertising the toughest nut to crack?

(4) Which subcategory of print advertising has been abused by inferior marketing agencies that have turned the craft into junk mail?

(5) What are the driving forces behind guerrilla advertising?

(6) Why do some proponents of radio advertising often cite the limitation of being restricted to sound as an advantage?

(7) Where are the billboards most often located?

(8) What is covert advertising or product placement advertising?

(9) What are the concepts that advertising feeds on, according to Jeremiah O'Sullivan R?

(10) What is previewing new trends?

EX. 2 **Translate the following phrases from English into Chinese and vice versa.**

(1) banner ads ____________

(2) junk mail ____________

(3) marketing commercials ____________

(4) mass media ____________

(5) media portals ____________

(6) 公共交通车辆 ____________

(7) 富媒体广告 ____________

(8) 社交媒体 ____________

(9) 口碑营销 ____________

(10) 传单 ____________

EX. 3 **Translate the following into Chinese.**

Advertising is always present, though people may not be aware of it. In today's world, advertising uses every possible media to get its message through. It does this via television, print (newspapers, magazines, journals, etc.), radio, press, internet, direct selling, hoardings, mailers, contests, sponsorships, posters, clothes, events, colours, sounds, visuals and even people (endorsements).

The advertising industry is made of companies that advertise, agencies that create the advertisements, media that carry the ads, and a host of people like copy editors, visualizers, brand managers, researchers, creative heads and designers who take it the last mile to the customer or receiver. A company that needs to advertise itself and/or its products hires an advertising agency. The company briefs the agency on the brand, its imagery, the ideals and values behind it, the target segments and so on. The agencies convert the ideas and concepts to create the visuals, text, layouts and themes to communicate with the user. After approval from the client, the ads go on air, as per the bookings done by the agency's media buying unit.

EX. 4 **Fill in the blanks with the words given below.**

likely	toss	stagnant	prospects	relate
purchase	name	fun	practice	growing

Online Advertising

The term online advertising is simply a term that relates to advertising online, or advertising over the Internet. In (1)________ online advertising is about getting your website in front of the people who are interested in your product or service. All you have to do is to find the best terms and phrases that people search for , who would like to (2)________ exactly your goods and services. If you can do this, then your online advertising will be successful, however, if you select the terms and phrases that do not (3)________ to the goods you are selling, then your keyword based online advertising efforts will (4)________ fail. It really is as simple as that.

Online advertising is (5)________ at 15% per year, checkout our online advertising newsarticle about this statistical truth. The facts are very simple, advertising is (6)________ yet online advertising is growing, so therefore it must work. Small businesses do not (7)________ their advertising dollars into the wind just for fun. There are many ways to advertise online with video, articles, paid or organic placement, and banner advertising, to (8)________ a few. If you are serious about your advertising (9)________ both locally and nationally or internationally you need to consider your options as it relates to advertising online with mobile smartphones. Online advertising programs are going through the roof for all that is mobile advertising—so jump in and have (10)________!

Text B

Theories of Advertising Effects

Advertising messages are all around us, yet the mechanism which leads from exposure to brand advertising through to sales is not entirely clear. Studies have repeatedly demonstrated a clear association between advertising and sales response. Yet the exact process that leads from the consumer of being exposed to an advertising message through to a purchase or behavioral response is not entirely clear.

The advertising and marketing literature suggests a variety of different models to explain how advertising works. These models are not competing theories, but rather explanations of how advertising persuades or influences different types of consumers in different purchase contexts. They identified four broad classes of model: cognitive information models, pure affect models, hierarchy of effect models, integrative models, and hierarchy-free models.

1. Cognitive information models

Advertising researchers have a long-standing interest in understanding both the degree and type of cognitive elaboration that occurs when consumers are exposed to persuasive messages. Cognitive information models assume that consumers are rational decision-makers and that advertising provides consumers with information utility by reducing the need to search for other information about a brand. For example, an advertisement in the Yellow Pages or an online directory means that the consumer does not have to travel from store to store in search of a product or service. Consumers process this information at a cognitive level before forming an attitude to the brand and purchase intent. A cognition is any thought that surfaces during the elaboration of the information.

A common theme in cognitive information models is that the net favorability of cognitive responses has a direct influence on attitude strength. In the cognitive information models, the general path to persuasion is as follows:

Ad cognition→ Attitude to ad (A_{ad}) → Brand cognition → Attitude to brand(A_b) →Purchase Intention (PI)

Theoretical works, combined with empirical studies, suggest that advertising information is more useful for experience goods (experiential services) than for search goods (tangible products). Research studies also suggest that consumers who are involved in the purchase decision are more likely to actively seek out product information and actively process advertising messages while low-involvement consumers are more likely to respond at an emotional level.

2. Pure affect models

Pure affect models suggest that consumers shape their preferences to a brand based on the feelings and attitudes elicited by exposure to an advertising message. When consumers view an advertisement, they not only develop attitudes towards the advertisement and the advertiser, but also develop feelings and beliefs about the brand being advertised.

Pure affect models help to explain the consumer's emotional responses to advertising and brands. These models suggest that simple exposure to a brand is sufficient to generate purchase intention. Exposure in the form of advertising messages leads to an attitude to the advertisement (A_{ad}) which transfers to the attitude to the brand (A_b) without any further cognitive processing. Exposure it not restricted to physical contact; rather it can refer to any brand-related contact such as advertising, promotion or virtual brands on websites.

In pure affect models, the path to communication effectiveness is represented by the following:

Attitude to ad (A_{ad}) → Attitude to Brand (A_b) → Purchase Intention (PI).

This path is also known as the peripheral route to persuasion. Empirical research in the pure affect sphere suggests that advertising messages do not need to be informative to be effective, however consumers must like the advertising execution for the message to be effective. In addition, ad liking and advertiser credibility may be especially important for corporate image advertising (compared to product-related advertising).

3. Hierarchy of effects models

Hierarchical models are linear sequential models built on an assumption that consumers move through a series of cognitive and affective stages culminating in the purchase decision. The common theme among these models is that advertising operates as a stimulus and the purchase decision is a response. A number of hierarchical models can be found in the literature including Lavidge's Hierarchy of Effects, DAGMAR and AIDA and other variants. And, of these models, the AIDA model is one of the most widely applied.

The AIDA model proposes that advertising messages need to accomplish a number of tasks designed to move the consumer through a series of sequential steps from brand awareness through to action (purchase and consumption).

Awareness—The consumer becomes aware of a category, product or brand (usually through advertising)

↓

Interest—The consumer becomes interested by considering the brand's fit with the consumer's lifestyle

↓

Desire—The consumer develops a favorable (or unfavorable) disposition towards the brand

↓

Action—The consumer forms a purchase intention or actually makes a purchase

As consumers move through the hierarchy of effects they pass through both a cognitive processing stage and an affective processing stage before any action occurs. Thus the hierarchy of effects models all include Cognition (C)—Affect (A)—Behavior (B) as the core steps in the underlying behavioral sequence. The underlying behavioral sequence for all hierarchy models is as follows:

Cognition (Awareness/learning) → Affect (Feeling/interest/desire)→ Behavior (Action e.g., purchase/consumption/usage/sharing information).

The literature offers numerous variations on the basic path to persuasion. The basic AIDA model is one of the longest serving models. Contemporary hierarchical models often modify or expand the basic AIDA model, resulting in additional steps, however, all follow the basic sequence which includes Cognition—Affect—Behavior. Some of these newer models have been adapted to accommodate consumer's digital media habits. Selected hierarchical models follow:

Basic AIDA model: Awareness→ Interest→ Desire→ Action;

Modified AIDA model: Awareness→ Interest→ Conviction →Desire→ Action;

AIDAS Model: Attention → Interest → Desire → Action → Satisfaction;

AISDALSLove model: Awareness→ Interest→ Search →Desire→ Action → Like/dislike→ Share → Love/ Hate;

Lavidge et al.'s Hierarchy of Effects: Awareness→ Knowledge→ Liking→ Preference→ Conviction→ Purchase;

DAGMAR Model: Awareness → Comprehension → Attitude/Conviction → Action;

Rossiter and Percy's Communications Effects: Category Need → Brand Awareness → Brand Preference (Ab) → Purchase Intent→ Purchase Facilitation.

All hierarchical models indicate that brand awareness is a necessary precondition to brand attitude, brand preference or brand purchase intention. The process of moving consumers from purchase intention to actual sales is known as conversion. While advertising is an excellent tool for creating awareness, brand attitude and purchase intent, it usually requires support from other elements in the promotion mix and the marketing program to convert purchase intent into an actual sale. Many different techniques can be used to convert interest into sales including special price offers, special promotional offers, attractive trade-in terms, guarantees or a strong call-to-action as part of the advertising message.

4. Integrative Models

Integrative models assume that consumers process advertising information via two paths—both cognitive (thinking) and affective (feeling) simultaneously. These models seek to combine the type of purchase with the consumer's dominant mode of processing. Integrative models are based on research findings indicating that congruence between personality and the way a persuasive message is framed. That is, aligning the message framing with the recipient's personality profile may play an important role in ensuring the success of that message. In a recent experiment, five advertisements (each designed to target one of the five personality traits) were constructed for a single product. Findings suggest that advertisements were evaluated more positively when they aligned with participants' motives. Tailoring persuasive messages to the personality traits of the targeted audience can be an effective way of enhancing the message's impact.

There are many integrative frameworks. Two of the more widely used models are the grids developed by Foote, Cone, Belding (FCB) and another devised by Rossiter and Percy, and which is an extension of the FCB approach. These planning grids are very popular with advertising practitioners because of their ease of application.

The FCB planning grid has two dimensions, involvement and information processing. Each dimension has two values, representing extremes of a continuum, specifically involvement (high/low) and information processing (thinking/feeling). The FCB planning grid gives rise to a number of implications for advertising and media strategy.

Quadrant 1: High-involvement/rational purchases: In the first quadrant consumers learn about a product through advertising after which they develop a favorable (or unfavorable) disposition to the product which may or may not culminate in a purchase. This approach is considered optimal for advertising high ticket items such as cars and household furniture. When this is the dominant approach to purchasing, advertising messages should be information-rich and media strategy should be weighted towards media such as magazines and newspapers capable of delivering long-copy advertising.

Quadrant 2: High-involvement/emotional purchases: In the second quadrant, audiences exhibit an emotional response to advertisements which transfers to products. This approach is used for products such as jewellery, expensive perfumes and designer fashion where consumers are emotionally involved in the purchase. When this mode of purchasing is evident, advertising should be designed to create a strong brand image and media should be selected to support the relevant image. For example, magazines such as *Vogue* can help to create an up-market image.

Quadrant 3: Low-involvement/rational purchases: The third quadrant represents routine low-involvement purchases evident for many packaged goods such as detergents, tissues and other consumable household items. Consumers make habitual purchases, and after consumption the benefit of using the brand is reinforced which ideally results in long-term brand loyalty (re-purchase). Given that this is a rational purchase, consumers need to be informed or reminded of the product's benefits. Advertising messages should encourage repeat purchasing and brand loyalty while media strategy should be weighted towards media that can deliver high frequency required for reminder campaigns such as TV, radio and sales promotion.

Quadrant 4: Low-involvement/emotional purchases: In the final quadrant, consumers make low-involvement, relatively inexpensive purchases that make them feel good. Impulse purchases and convenience goods fall into this category. The purchase leads to feelings of satisfaction which, in turn, reinforces the purchase behavior. When this approach is the dominant purchase mode, advertising messages should "congratulate" customers on their purchase choice and the media strategy should be weighted towards options that reach customers when they are close to the point-of-purchase such as billboards, sales promotion and point-of-sale displays. Examples of this approach include "McDonald's— You Deserve a Break Today" and "L'Oreal—Because You're Worth It".

5. Hierarchy-free models

Many authors have treated reason (rational processes) and emotion (affective processes) as entirely independent. Yet, other researchers have argued that both reason and emotion can be employed simultaneously, to process advertising information. Hierarchy-free models draw on evidence from psychology and consumer neuroscience which suggest that consumers process information via different pathways rather than in any linear/sequential manner. Thus, hierarchy-free models do not employ any fixed processing sequence. These models treat advertising as part of the brand totality. Some hierarchy-free models treat brands as "myth" and advertising as "myth-making" while other models seek to tap into the consumer's memories of pleasant consumption experiences (e.g., the MAC–Memory-Affect-Cognition model). Hierarchy-free models are of increasing interest to academics and practitioners because they are more customer-centric and allow for the possibility of consumer co-creation of value.

New Words

mechanism ['mekənɪzəm] *n.* 机制，原理

exposure [ɪk'spəʊʒə] *n.* 暴露，揭露

behavioral [bɪ'heɪvjərəl] *adj.* 关于行为的

affect [ə'fekt] *n.* 感情，情感

integrative ['ɪntɪgreɪtɪv] *adj.* 综合的，整体化的

elaboration [ɪˌlæbə'reɪʃən] *n.* 详尽阐述，精心制作

assume [ə'suːm] *v.* 假定，假设；认为

rational ['ræʃnəl] *adj.* 合理的，理性的，明智的

intent [ɪn'tent] *n.* 意图，意向；目的

surface ['sɜːfɪs] *vi.* 浮到水面；显露

favorability [ˌfeɪvərə'bɪləti] *n.* 倾向性

peripheral [pə'rɪfərəl] *adj.* 次要的；附带的；外围的

credibility [ˌkredə'bɪləti] *n.* 可信性，可靠性

linear ['lɪniə] *adj.* 线的，直线的

sequential [sɪ'kwenʃl] *adj.* 按次序的，顺序的，序列的

culminate ['kʌlmɪneɪt] *vi.* 达到顶点，达到高潮；告终

stimulus ['stɪmjələs] *n.* 促进因素，激励因素

fit [fɪt] *n.* 适合，适宜

disposition [ˌdɪspə'zɪʃn] *n.* 性格，性情；倾向

accommodate [ə'kɑːmədeɪt] *vt.* 适应，调节

facilitation [fə'sɪlɪteɪʃn] *n.* 容易，便利，简易化；促进

precondition [ˌpriːkən'dɪʃn] *n.* 先决条件，前提

conversion [kən'vɜːʒn] *n.* 转变，转换；转化

simultaneously [ˌsaɪml'teɪniəsli] *adv.* 同时地

grid [grɪd] *n.* 网格，方格；栅栏

extreme [ɪk'striːm] *n.* 极端，极度，极限

continum [kən'tɪnəm] *n.* 连续体

quadrant ['kwɑːdrənt] *n.* 四分之一圆周；象限

perfume [pə'fjuːm] *n.* 香水，芳香

evident ['evɪdənt] *adj.* 清楚的，显而易见的，显然的

detergent [dɪ'tɜːdʒənt] *n.* 洗涤剂，去垢剂

tissue ['tɪsjuː] *n.* （尤指用作手帕的）纸巾，手巾纸

pathway ['pæθweɪ] *n.* 路径，途径

tap [tæp] *v.* 利用，开发，发掘

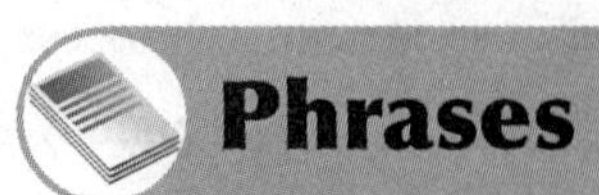

be exposed to 暴露于，面临

behavioral response 行为反应

cognitive information model 认知信息模型

pure affect model 纯情感模型

hierarchy of effect model 效果模型层级

integrative model 整合模型

hierarchy-free model 无层次模型

cognitive elaboration 认知阐释

in search of 寻找，寻求	give rise to 造成，引起，导致
at a cognitive level 在认知层面	high ticket item 高价物品
at an emotional level 在情感层面	be capable of 有能力，能够
be built on 以……为基础	congratulate on 祝贺
form a purchase intention 形成购买意向	draw on 凭借，利用；动用
align... with... 使……与……一致，相符	tap into 充分利用或挖掘
personality trait 性格特点	

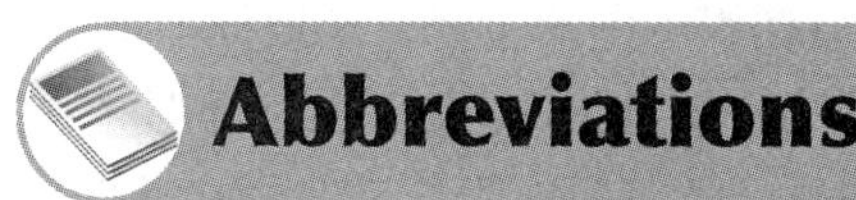

Abbreviations

AIDI (Awareness-Interest-Desire-Action) 意识—兴趣—欲望—行动
MAC (Memory-Affect-Cognition) 记忆—情感—认知

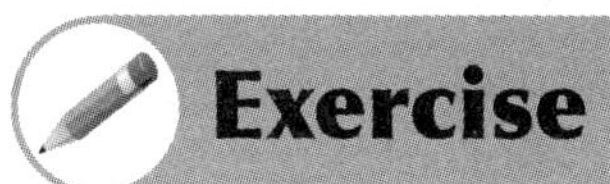

Exercise

EX. Answer the following questions according to Text B.

(1) What are the different models that the advertising and marketing literature suggests to explain how advertising works?
(2) What do cognitive information models assume?
(3) What is the common theme in cognitive information models?
(4) What is the general path to persuasion in the cognitive information models?
(5) What is the path to communication effectiveness in pure affect models?
(6) What assumption are hierarchical models built on?
(7) What does the AIDA model propose?
(8) What should advertising messages and media strategy be like, when high involvement/ rational purchase is the dominant approach to purchasing?
(9) What should advertising messages and media strategy be like when high involvement/ rational purchase is evident?
(10) Why are hierarchy-free models of increasing interest to academics and practitioners?

参考译文（Text A）

广 告

广告是一种视听形式的营销传播方式，它使用公开赞助的、非个人的信息来推广或销售产品、服务或想法。广告赞助商通常是希望推广其产品或服务的企业。广告与公共关系的不同之处在于，广告客户付费并控制信息。它不同于个人销售，因为其信息是非个人的，即信息并不针对某个特定的人。广告通过各种大众传媒传播，包括传统媒体，如报纸、杂志、电视、广播，以及博客、社交媒体等新媒体。信息在媒体中的实际呈现被称为广告。商业广告通常寻求通过“品牌创建”来增加顾客对其产品或服务的消费。“品牌创建”指的是在消费者心中创建产品名称或形象与产品之间的联系。那些旨在引起即时销售的广告被称为直接反应广告。非营利组织可以使用免费的说服方式，如公共服务公告。广告也可以用来向员工或股东保证公司是可以生存的或成功的。

1. 广告类型

广告是综合性营销传播计划中的一个不可或缺的部分，也包括公共关系和直接销售。关于做广告的地点和方式，企业有许多选择，且每个选择都有其优点和缺点。你可以自己联系不同的媒体公司，比较价格和数据，或者聘请一家专业的营销公司，这家公司并不代表任何媒体，但对所有媒体都有翔实了解。这些公司可以帮助你选择最好的广告类型和特定的供应商，使你的广告预算物超所值。

1.1 在线广告

在线广告是一种利用互联网进行宣传的形式，其目的是通过传递营销信息来吸引顾客。在线广告由广告服务器传送。在线广告包括出现在搜索引擎结果页面的相关横幅广告、按点击付费的文本广告、富媒体广告、社交网络广告、在线分类广告、广告网络和电子邮件营销，包括垃圾邮件。一种较新的在线广告形式是原生广告；如一个网站的新闻推送，可以通过减少干扰来改善用户体验。然而，一些人认为这种做法具有欺骗性。

1.2 手机及手机广告

与其他广告形式相比，手机广告是一种相对较新的广告形式，在媒体组合中占据主导地位，它使用手机、平板电脑、电子阅读器和其他可以上网的便携式电子设备。目前，移动广告的趋势包括大量使用 Twitter、Instagram、Snapchat 和 Facebook 等社交媒体。现在，这是最难破解的难题。这类广告不仅具有破坏性，而且会给顾客留下许多不良印象。如果你做了，就要把它处理好。原生广告曾一度成为进入新闻推送的好方法，但即便如此，它也因为具有欺骗性而受到审查。

1.3 平面广告

印刷品曾经是销售的一个巨大推动力，但现在营销人员使用数字广告形式取代之。然而，关于广告有一件事是肯定的，那就是，求异是件好事。当消费者对数字广告感到厌倦时，他们肯定会回归印刷产品，并享受到印刷产品带来的触感和持久性。一般来说，印刷品可以分为三大类。

1.3.1 期刊广告

如果广告是刊登在杂志、报纸或者任何定期出版物上，那它就是期刊广告。几十年来，平面广告一直是广告商及其客户的黄金标准。占据大型杂志的中间版面或报纸的封面广告，意味着有数百万人正在阅览这条信息。

1.3.2 宣传册、传单、销售点广告

虽然一些广告资料可以刊登在报纸和杂志中，但是它们通常由于很少被看到，而被视为一个单独的实体。从柜台或客户服务台上的宣传资料到精美的汽车宣传册，小型印刷媒体提供了一种更亲密、内容更丰富的吸引消费者的方式。当你拥有的信息比能塞进一个平面广告的信息还多的时候，可使用这种方法。

1.3.3 直邮广告

上述任何一项技术均可纳入“直邮”方式。它意味着你的印刷品直接邮寄给消费者，这是一种已经并将继续被低劣的营销机构滥用的技术。这些机构把精美的广告变成垃圾邮件。如果它具有创造性，且构思巧妙，并得以明智地执行，直邮可以是一个吸引客户的妙方。所以，不要将直邮方式排斥在外。

1.4 游击广告

游击广告（或市场营销）也被称为环境媒体，在过去 20 年里很引人注目。这是一个被广泛使用的术语，指任何非传统的东西，消费者通常以某种方式参与或与商品互动。这种广告形式的地点和时间都很重要。游击广告营销背后的驱动力是创意和创新，而不是巨额预算。很多时候，你会请求免除而不是允许这些广告活动，因为通过口碑和社交媒体可以传播广告信息。

1.5 广播广告

广播广告是包括电视和广播在内的大众市场传播形式。直到最近，它一直是接触大量消费者的最主要方式。广播广告在过去几年确实遭受了打击，尤其是随着数字视频录像机（DVR）的兴起和“跳过广告”技术的应用。然而，这仍然是一种很受欢迎的方式，它可以接触到数以百万计的人，特别是当美国橄榄球大赛来临的时候。

电视广告是最昂贵的广告类型之一。在热门赛事期间，电视网对商业广告播放时段收费很高。美国一年一度的“超级碗”橄榄球赛被认为是电视上最重要的活动——有超过 1.08 亿的美国观众收看，而且研究表明其中 50% 的人只收看广告。在 2014 届赛事中，32 秒的广告花费平均为 400 万美元，而 60 秒的广告则要花费 800 万美元。虚拟广告可以通过计算机图形植入常规电视节目中，它通常被插入到其他空白背景中，或者用于替换与远程电视观众无关的本地广告牌。无线电广告以无线电波的形式从发射机广播到天线，然后再广播到接收设备。播放广告的播出时间是从电视台或电视网购买的。虽然广播局限于声音，但广播广告的支持者经常把这作为一种优势。无线电是一种不断发展的媒体，可以在广播中找到，也可以在网上找到。根据阿比特伦（Arbitron）的数据，电台每周大约有 2.416 亿听众，占美国人口的 93% 以上。

1.6 户外广告

广告牌，在世界上的一些地方也被称为围板，是位于公共场所的大型建筑物，向路过的行人和驾车者展示广告。大多数情况下，它们位于有大量机动车和行人通过的主要道路上；然而，它们可以置于任何有大量观众的地方，例如在公共交通工具上和车站内、在购物中心或办公楼、在体育场等。这种被称为街头广告的形式最初在英国因广告服务商在街道公共设施和人行道上做户外广告而出名。这些广告与街头涂鸦、空中舞者和3D路面广告等产品一起将品牌信息传递到公共空间。遮蔽式户外广告将室外和室内广告结合起来，在临时基地的公共场所放置大型的移动结构（帐篷）。巨大的外部广告空间旨在对观看者产生强大的吸引力，产品推广在室内进行，其创意的装饰可以强化印象。移动广告牌通常是车载广告牌或数字屏幕。它们可以安装在专用的车辆上，而这些车辆专为在客户预先选择的路线上投放广告而建造。移动广告也可以是特别装备的货运卡车，或者在某些情况下，从飞机上散放的大横幅。

1.7 公益广告

与传统广告不同，公益广告的设计初衷是提供信息和教育，而不是销售产品或服务。公益广告传统上出现在电视和广播上，但也在网上被大力推广。

1.8 植入式广告

隐性广告是指产品或品牌嵌入娱乐和媒体中。例如，在电影中，主角可以使用某个确定品牌中的一个或其他商品，正如在电影《少数派报告》中，汤姆·克鲁斯扮演的角色约翰·安德顿侦探拥有一部手机，其右上角清楚地写有诺基亚标志，或者他的手表上刻有宝格丽标识。电影广告的另一个例子是在电影《我，机器人》中，威尔·史密斯扮演的主角多次提到他的匡威鞋，称它们为“经典”。因为电影的背景设定在遥远的未来，电影《我，机器人》和《太空炮弹》也展示未来的汽车，奥迪和梅塞德斯—奔驰的标志清楚地显示在其车头。凯迪拉克选择在电影《黑客帝国2：重装上阵》中打广告，片中出现了许多使用凯迪拉克汽车的场景。同样，欧米茄手表、福特汽车、索尼产品、宝马和阿斯顿·马丁汽车的植入式广告也出现在最近的詹姆斯·邦德系列电影中，最著名的是《皇家赌场》。在《神奇四侠：银色冲浪者的崛起》中，主要运输车辆的车头有一个大大的道奇标志。电影《银翼杀手》中也包括一些最明显的植入式广告，整部电影暂停播放了可口可乐广告。

2. 广告的功能

广告渗透到互联网、网络电视、报纸和路边的广告牌中。产品、服务和理念都是通过广告来销售的，这使企业能够吸引顾客来消费自己的产品。网络广告正在迅速取代平面广告，因为它使用方便，成本效益高，易于分发。

2.1 确定品牌

产品、服务和理念都是通过具有不同品牌形象的各个企业来销售的，而品牌形象是通过广告传播给大众的。由于广告的存在，消费者与某些品牌建立起了情感上的联系，并随着时间的流逝，对这些品牌越来越熟悉。

2.2 提供信息

广告向消费者提供必要的信息，使他们了解哪些产品可买，并在哪里可以买到。通过各种媒体门户，广告传播在市场上公开出售的产品、服务和理念的信息，产品的特色、颜色和规格，以及该产品的经销商。

2.3 说服

强有力的视觉广告能说服消费者购买商品、服务和理念，以实现其情感上的满足。说服是广告的核心使命。广告告诉你，你正在考虑的产品、服务或理念将如何改善你的生活。

《广告的社会和文化效应》一书的作者耶利米·奥沙利文认为，广告以意识形态、神话、艺术性吸引力等概念为基础。奥沙利文指出，广告将图像和理念注入产品和服务，就像产品和服务的内涵被注入图像和理念一样。

2.4　预展新趋势

预展新产品、新服务和新理念的优点会激励消费者购买这些产品，因为他们不想被排除在外。广告能让消费者了解未来的趋势和新市场。他们提供新产品、服务或理念，优惠券、折扣和试用优惠，以吸引新客户，并诱使现有客户尝试新产品。广告商向消费者预展新的或改进的产品、服务和理念，以唤醒他们想要了解前沿趋势的意识。消费者都期望拥有最新最好的产品、服务或理念，从而“赶上潮流”，而预展新趋势正是广告商利用消费者这种欲望的一种技术。

2.5　需求

《商业参考》一书中指出，广告、公共关系和促销活动所产生的需求通过分销渠道“拉动”商品或服务的销售。广告的强大功能之一是通过广告活动产生消费者对特定产品、服务和理念的需求。这些广告活动都是针对那些最有可能购买上述产品、服务和理念的消费者。产品、服务和理念根据消费者的需求批量销售。

2.6　客户群

始终如一的高质量广告增加了消费者对产品、服务或理念的忠诚度。广告试图通过增加关于品牌效益的额外信息来加强购买行为，从而维持当前的客户群。广告的目标是建立和加强与客户、潜在客户、零售商和重要利益相关者的关系。

2.7　有竞争力的定价

广告展示相对于当前市场来说具有价格竞争力的消费品，从而让消费者认识到应该花多少钱。广告让你知道正在促销的消费品是什么，下一次促销是什么时候，以及如何获得最新的优惠券或折扣，并试图确保你买到的商品物有所值。广告的目标不胜枚举，可以是短期的，也可以是长期的。短期目标与广告文案本身有关，旨在介绍某些理念，因而必须具有说服力。长期广告目标与预期效果有关。成功广告的关键是知道针对特定类型的广告进行分配。你还需要正确锁定你的目标受众，以便找到合适的消费者。

Case　Examples of Interactive Advertising

Unit 12

Text A

Services

The American Marketing Association defines services marketing as an organizational function and a set of processes for identifying or creating, communicating, and delivering value to customers and for managing customer relationship in a way that benefit the organization and stake-holders. Services are usually intangible economic activities offered by one party to another. Often time-based, services performed bring about desired results to recipients, objects, or other assets for which purchasers have responsibility. In exchange for money, time, and effort, service customers expect value from access to goods, labor, professional skills, facilities, networks, and systems; but they do not normally take ownership of any of the physical elements involved.

A service encounter can be defined as the duration in which a customer interacts with a service. The customer's interactions with a service provider typically involve face-to-face contact with service personnel, in addition to interactions with the physical elements of the service environment including the facilities and equipment.

1. Concepts of service

Classical economists believed that service work, no matter how honorable, was "unproductive". Scholars have long debated the nature of services. Some of the earliest attempts to define services focused on what makes them different from goods. Late-eighteenth and early-nineteenth century definitions highlighted the nature of ownership and wealth creation. Classical economists contended that goods were objects of value over which ownership rights could be established and exchanged. Ownership implied possession of a tangible object that had been acquired through purchase, barter or gift from the producer or previous owner and was legally identifiable as the property of the current owner. In contrast, when services were purchased, no title to goods changed hands.

1.1 Historical perspectives

Adam Smith's seminal work, *The Wealth of Nations* (1776), distinguished between the outputs of what he termed "productive" and "unproductive" labor. The former, he stated, produced goods that could be stored after production and subsequently exchanged for money or other items of value. But unproductive labor, however "honorable, ... useful, or... necessary", created services that perished at the time of production and therefore didn't contribute to wealth. French economist Jean-Baptiste Say argued that production and consumption were inseparable in services, coining the term "immaterial products" to describe them. In the 1920s, Alfred Marshall was still using the idea that services "are immaterial products". In the mid nineteenth century John Stuart Mill wrote that services are "utilities not fixed or embodied in any object, but consisting of a mere service rendered... without leaving a permanent acquisition".

1.2 Contemporary perspectives

When services marketing emerged as a separate sub-branch within the marketing discipline in the early 1980s, it was largely a protest against the dominance of prevailing product-centric view. In 1960, the US economy changed forever. In that year, for the first time in a major trading nation, more people were employed in the service sector than in manufacturing industries. Other developed nations soon followed by shifting to a service based economy. Scholars soon began to recognize that services were important in their own right, rather than as some residual category left over after goods were taken into account. This recognition triggered a change in the way services were defined. By the mid twentieth century, scholars began defining services in terms of their own unique characteristics, rather than by comparison with products. The following set of definitions shows how scholars are grappling with the distinctive aspects of service products and developing new definitions of service.

"Goods are produced: services are performed."

"A service is an activity or a series of activities which take place in interactions with a contact person or a physical machine and which provides consumer satisfaction."

"The heart of the service product is the experience of the consumer which takes place in real time... it is the interactive process itself that creates the benefits desired by the consumer."

"Services are deeds, processes and performances."

"Services are processes (economic activities) that provide time, place, form, problem-solving or experiential value to the recipient."

"The term service... is synonymous with value. A supplier has a value proposition, but value actualization takes place during the customer's usage and consumption process."

1.3 Alternative view

A recently proposed alternative view is that services involve a form of rental through which customers can obtain benefits. Customers are willing to pay for aspirational experiences and solutions that add value to their lifestyle. The term, rent, can be used as a general term to describe payment made for use of something or access to skills and expertise, facilities or networks, usually for a defined period of time, instead of buying it outright which is not even possible in many instances.

There are five broad categories within the non-ownership framework.

Rented goods services: These services enable customers to obtain the temporary right to use a physical good that they prefer not to own, e.g., boats, costumes.

Defined space and place rentals: These services enable customers to obtain use of a defined portion of a larger space in a building, vehicle or other area which can be an end in its own right, e.g., storage container in a warehouse, or simply a means to an end, e.g., table in a restaurant, seat in an aircraft.

Labor and expertise rental: People are hired to perform work that customers either choose not to do for themselves, e.g., cleaning the house, or are unable to do due to the lack of expertise, tools and skills, e.g., car repairs, surgery.

Access to shared physical environments: These environments can be indoors or outdoors where customers rent the right to share the use of the environment, e.g., museums, theme parks, gyms, golf courses.

Access to and usage of systems and networks: Customers rent the right to participate in a specified network such as telecommunications, utilities, banking or insurance, with different fees for varying levels of access.

2. Characteristics of Services

A distinctive feature of services is that production and consumption cannot be separated. Throughout the 1980s and 1990s, the so-called unique characteristics of services dominated much of the literature. The most commonly cited characteristics of services are:

Intangibility: Services are, by nature, intangible, meaning they cannot be perceived by the sense of touch, and they only exist in connection with something else, as in the goodwill of a business. This intangibility of services makes defining "great service" difficult and highly subjective, especially across different demographic groups. For example, the typical Gen-Xer was not taught manners and probably would not be concerned about someone who did not say "please" and "thank you". A Baby Boomer, on the contrary, is typically irritated by such lack of social graces. Therefore, marketers have to determine and speak to the needs of each group separately.

Inseparability: Production and consumption cannot be separated, compared with goods where production and consumption are entirely discrete processes. And personal services cannot be separated from the individual. Services are created and consumed simultaneously. The service is being produced at the same time that the client is receiving it; for example, during an online search or a legal consultation. Dentist, musicians, dancers, etc. create and offer services at the same time.

Variability: Services involve people, and people are all different. There is a strong possibility that the same enquiry would be answered slightly different by different people or even by the same person at different times. It is important to minimize the differences in performance through training, standard setting and quality assurance. The quality of services offered by firms can never be standardized.

Perishability: Services have a high degree of perishability. Unused capacity cannot be stored for future use. If services are not used today, it is lost forever. For example, spare seats in an aeroplane cannot be transferred to the next flight. Similarly, empty rooms in five-star hotels and credits not utilized are examples of services leading to economic losses. As services are activities performed for simultaneous consumption, they perish unless consumed.

Difficulty of Standardization: Because services are provided by people, and not by machines, variances in the level, quality, duration and intensity of service output occur. Judgments have to be made when providing a service. These judgments lead to a lack of standardization in the service delivery. For example, even if every employee in a call center receives identical training, some will spend more time answering the customers' questions and working to resolve problems. Additionally, each service employee has his own idea of what makes excellent service.

Purchase and Consumption Combined: With the exception of prepays and annual memberships, once a service is purchased, it is also consumed. The perishable nature of services means that relationship marketing becomes of utmost importance. Otherwise, a client can decide to use a different service provider after a less than satisfactory experience. The quality of the experience is the focus for marketers. Insurance agents and realtors focus on being trustworthy good neighbors. And, a study in the Journal of *Family Practice* entitled "Physician Behaviors that Predict Patient Trust" found that relationship strength between doctor and patient was the primary determinant of patient loyalty to their primary care provider.

The unique characteristics of services give rise to problems and challenges that are rarely paralleled in product marketing. Services are complex, multi-dimensional and multi-layered. Not only are there multiple benefits, but there are also a multiplicity of interactions between customers and organizations as well as between customers and other customers.

3. Classification of services

There are many ways to classify services. One classification considers who or what is being processed and identifies three classes of services: people processing, e.g., beauty services, child care, medical services; mental stimulus processing, e.g., education services, counselling services, life-coaching; possession processing, e.g., pet care, appliance repair, piano tuning; and information processing, e.g., financial services, data warehousing services. Another method used to classify services uses the degree of customer interaction in the service process and classifies services as high contact, e.g., hospitality, dental care, hairdressing or low contact, e.g., telecommunications, utility services.

Both economists and marketers make extensive use of the Search, Experience, Credence (SEC) classification of services. The classification scheme is based on the ease or difficulty of consumer evaluation activities and identifies three broad classes of goods.

Search goods: They are those which possess attributes that can be evaluated prior to purchase or consumption. Consumers rely on prior experience, direct product inspection and other information search activities to locate information that assists in the evaluation process. Most products fall into the search goods category, e.g., clothing, office stationery, home furnishings.

Experience goods: They are goods or services that can be accurately evaluated only after the product has been purchased and experiences. Many personal services fall into this category, e.g., restaurant, hairdresser, beauty salon, theme park, travel, holiday.

Credence claims: They are goods or services that are difficult or impossible to evaluate even after consumption has occurred. Evaluation difficulties may arise because the consumer lacks the requisite knowledge or technical expertise to make a realistic evaluation or, alternatively because the cost of information-acquisition is prohibitive or outweighs the value of the information available. Many professional services fall into this category, e.g., accountant, legal services, medical diagnosis/treatment, cosmetic surgery. These goods are called credence products because the consumer's quality evaluations depend entirely on the trust given to the product manufacturer or service provider.

While some services may possess a number of search attributes, most services are high in experience or credence properties. Empirical studies have shown that consumers' perceived risk increases along the search-experience-credence continuum. The implication is that services tend to be high involvement decisions, where the consumer invests more heavily in information search activities during the purchase decision.

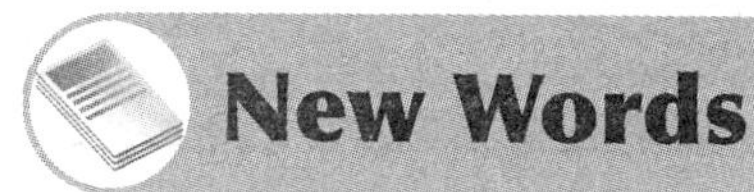

New Words

organizational [ˌɔːgənaiˈzeɪʃn] *adj.* 组织的；安排的，筹备的

intangible [ɪnˈtændʒəbl] *adj.* 无形的；不易度量的

facilities [fəˈsɪlɪtɪz] *n.* 设施，设备

personnel [ˌpɜːrsəˈnel] *n.* （组织或军队中的）全体人员，职员

honorable [ˈɒnərəbl] *adj.* 荣誉的，体面的

unproductive [ˌʌnprəˈdʌktɪv] *adj.* 效果不佳的，无益的；产量少的

highlight [ˈhaɪlaɪt] *v.* 突出，强调

contend [kənˈtend] *v.* 声称，主张，认为

possession [pəˈzeʃn] *n.* 具有，拥有

tangible [ˈtændʒəbl] *adj.* 有形的；真实的，可触摸的

barter [ˈbɑːtə] *n.* 易货贸易，实物交易

identifiable [aɪˌdentɪˈfaɪəbl] *adj.* 可识别的，可辨认的

seminal [ˈsemɪnl] *adj.* （对以后的发展）影响深远的

subsequently [ˈsʌbsɪkwəntli] *adv.* 随后，后来；接着

perish [ˈperɪʃ] *vi.* 消失；腐烂；毁灭

coin [kɔɪn] *vt.* 制造；创造，首创

immaterial [ˌɪməˈtɪriəl] *adj.* 无形体的，非物质的

embody [ɪmˈbɑːdi] *v.* 具体表现，体现，代表

permanent [ˈpɜːmənənt] *adj.* 永久的，永恒的

acquisition [ˌækwɪ'zɪʃn] *n.* 购置；获得，得到

protest ['prəʊtest] *n.* 抗议，反对

dominance ['dɑːmɪnənt] *n.* 支配，控制

residual [rɪ'zɪdʒuəl] *adj.* 剩余的，残留的

distinctive [dɪ'stɪŋktɪv] *adj.* 独特的，有特色的，与众不同的

deed [diːd] *n.* 行为；行动

synonymous [sɪ'nɑːnɪməs] *adj.* 同义的；等同于……的

actualization [ˌæktʃʊəlaɪ'zeɪʃən] *n.* 实现，现实化，真实化

alternative [ɔːl'tɜːnətɪv] *adj.* 两者择一的，供选择的

aspirational [ˌæspə'reɪʃənl] *adj.* 渴望成功的

simultaneous [ˌsaɪml'teɪniəs] *adj.* 同时发生（或进行）的

standardization ['stændədaɪzeɪʃn] *n.* 标准化，规范化

variance ['veəriəns] *n.* 变化幅度，差额

intensity [ɪn'tensəti] *n.* 紧张，剧烈，强度

identical [aɪ'dentɪkl] *adj.* 完全同样，相同的

prepay [priː'peɪ] *vt.* 预付，先付

perishable ['perɪʃəbl] *adj.* 易腐烂的，易变质的

realtor ['riːəltə] *n.* 不动产经纪人

trustworthy ['trʌstwɜːði] *adj.* 值得信任的，可信赖的

determinant [dɪ'tɜːmɪnənt] *n.* 决定因素，决定条件；决定物

multi-dimensional [ˌmʌltɪ-dɪm'enʃənəl] *adj.* 多维度的，多面向的

multi-layered [mʌltɪ-'leɪəd] *adj.* 多层的，多层次的

multiplicity [ˌmʌltɪ'plɪsəti] *n.* 多样性，多种多样

bring about 导致，引起；带来

interact with 与……相互作用

in one's own right 凭本身的条件

leave over 剩下；推迟，延期

grapple with 尽力克服；抓住

by nature 生性；本性上；就其本质

in connection with 关于；与……相连

on the contrary 相反地

social grace 社交礼仪；社交风度

standard setting 标准设置，标准制定

with the exception of 除……外

annual membership 一年会员制

service provider 服务供应商（尤指互联网服务供应商）

child care 儿童保育

mental stimulus 精神刺激

prior to 在……之前；居先

fall into 分成；属于

office stationery 办公文具，办公用品

home furnishing 家居陈设品，家居装饰

beauty salon 美容院

cosmetic surgery 整容外科（手术）

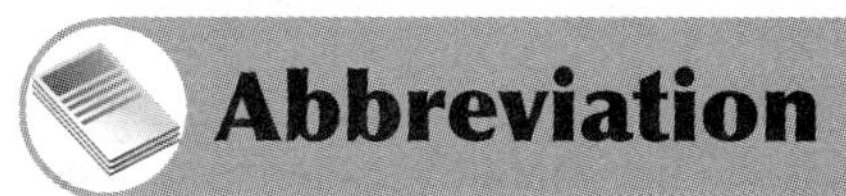

Abbreviation

SEC (Search, Experience, Credence) “搜索，体验，信任”产品属性框架

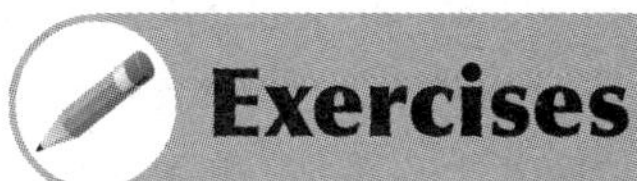

Exercises

EX. 1 Answer the following questions according to Text A.

(1) How does the American Marketing Association define services marketing?
(2) What did Adam Smith write about unproductive labor in his seminal work?
(3) How did the US economy change in 1960?
(4) What recognition triggered a change in the way services were defined?
(5) What are the five broad categories within the non-ownership framework as far as services are concerned?
(6) What is a distinctive feature of services?
(7) What are the most commonly cited characteristics of services?
(8) Why is there a lack of standardization in the service delivery?
(9) How are services classified on the basis of the degree of customer interaction in the services?
(10) What are the three broad classes of goods identified by the scheme based on the ease or difficulty of consumer evaluation activities?

EX. 2 Translate the following phrases from English into Chinese and vice versa.

(1) annual membership ____________________
(2) leave over ____________________
(3) service provider ____________________
(4) social grace ____________________
(5) standard setting ____________________
(6) 与……相互作用 ____________________
(7) 在玻璃橱窗陈列；使展现 ____________________
(8) 滥发的电邮，垃圾电邮 ____________________
(9) 易货贸易，实物交易 ____________________
(10) 无形体的，非物质的 ____________________

EX. 3 **Translate the following into Chinese.**

One of the crucial factors/problems faced by marketers is the perishability factor in services marketing. In other words services have Zero Inventory! Once sold, they stand sold and cannot be returned. Hence several times in the services industry the saying "First impression is the last impression" actually stands true. Let's take an example. A restaurant is serving food on a daily basis. One day there is a strike. Can it serve the same food on the other day? Sure. If it wants to go out of business! But otherwise, the restaurant will have to serve fresh food because the previous food prepared would have perished. Thus we can understand that services such as a doctors treatment, a hair dressers haircut, a movie or airline ticket, etc. cannot be saved for later use. They can be used only once else they perish. That's perishability in services marketing. Because of perishability, inventory is nil, demand forecasting becomes the crux of services marketing. Along with demand, creative thinking and capacity utilization is necessary. Along with this, there is the need of a strong backup plan anytime your plans backfire.

EX. 4 **Fill in the blanks with the words given below.**

tangible	uncertainty	simultaneously	credence	evaluate
participation	demonstrated	reference	purchase	discerned

The Purchase Process of Services

The intangible and inseparable aspects of services affect the consumer's evaluation of the purchase. Because services cannot be displayed, (1)________, or illustrated, consumers cannot make a prepurchase evaluation of all the characteristics of services. Similarly, because services are produced and consumed (2)________, the buyer must participate in producing the service, and that (3)________ can affect the evaluation of the service. (4)________ goods such as clothing, jewellery, and furniture have search qualities, such as color, size, and style, which can be determined before (5)________. Services such as restaurants and child care have experience qualities, which can only be (6)________ after purchase or during consumption. Finally, services provided by specialized professionals such as medical diagnosis and legal services have (7)________ qualities, or characteristics that the consumer may find impossible to (8)________ even after purchase and consumption. To reduce the (9)________ created by these qualities, service consumers turn to personal sources of information such as early adopters, opinion leaders, and (10)________ group members during the purchase decision process.

Text B

Service Marketing Mix 7Ps

Services marketing is a specialized branch of marketing. Services marketing emerged as a separate field of study in the early 1980s, following the recognition that the unique characteristics of services required different strategies compared with the marketing of physical goods.

Services marketing typically refers to both business to consumer (B2C) and business-to-business (B2B) services, and includes marketing of services such as telecommunications services, financial services, all types of hospitality, tourism leisure and entertainment services, car rental services, health care services and professional services and trade services.

Currently, more and more organizations are competing one another strategically to distinguish themselves in the area of service and quality within a market. Successful organizations strongly focus on the service paradigm with investment in people, technology, personnel policy and remuneration systems for their employees. This is very important as the behavior of the employees can have a direct influence on the quality of the service. Employees represent the face and the voice of their organization to the customers. They translate the services provision into services for the customer across all sectors.

In 1981, Bernard H. Booms and Mary J. Bitner further developed the traditional marketing mix developed by the American Professor of Marketing Jerome McCarthy into the extended marketing mix or services marketing mix. This Service Marketing Mix is also called the 7P model or the 7Ps of Booms and Bitner. This Service Marketing Mix strategy extends the original marketing mix model from four to seven elements. While Jerome McCarthy has only defined four verifiable marketing elements, the 7Ps are an extension as a result of which this services marketing mix can also be applied in service companies and knowledge intensive environments. The extended marketing mix for services is more than the simple addition of three extra Ps. Rather it also modifies the traditional mix of product, price, place and promotion for superior application to services.

1. Product

Service products are conceptualized as consisting of a bundle of tangible and intangible elements:

Core service: The basic reason for the business; that which solves consumer problems

Supplementary goods and services: Supplements or adds value to the core product and helps differentiate the service from competitors (e.g., consultation, safe-keeping, hospitality, exceptions)

Facilitating services: (sometimes called *delivery services*): Facilitate the delivery and consumption of the core service (e.g., information provision, order-taking, billing, payment methods)

Supporting services: Support the core and could be eliminated without destabilizing the core.

The distinction between supplementary and facilitating services varies, depending on the nature of the service. For instance, the provision of coffee and tea would be considered a supporting service in a bank, but would be a facilitating service in a bed and breakfast facility. Whether an element is classified as facilitating or supporting depends on the context.

2. Price

Service marketers need to consider a range of other issues in price setting and management of prices:

Price Charged: the traditional pricing decision.

Timing of Payment: Given that customers are part of the service process and that some customers remain in the process for days, months or even years (e.g., guest house, hotel stay, university tuition), decisions must be made about whether to request payment at time when the service encounter is initiated, during the encounter or on termination of an encounter. Deposits, installments and exit fees are all options that can be considered.

Mode of Payment: Given that customers enter into long-term relationships with service providers, it is possible that some patrons will expect to be able to pay on account. Payment options include: EFTPOS, direct transfer, cash/credit cheque, invoice.

Many service firms operate in industries where price is restricted by professional codes of conduct or by government influences which may have implications for pricing. It is possible to identify three broad scenarios:

Services subject to public regulation (e.g., healthcare, public transport);

Services subject to formal self-regulation (e.g., universities, schools);

Services subject to regulation of marketplace (e.g., hospitality, tourism, leisure services).

In situations where the service is subject to some type of public regulation, government departments may establish ceiling prices which effectively limit the amount that can be charged.

The concept of a social price may be more important for service marketers. A social price refers to "non-financial aspects of price". Fine identifies four types of social price: time, effort, lifestyle and psyche. In effect, this means that consumers may be more acutely aware of the opportunity costs associated with the consumption of a service. In practice, this may mean that consumers of services experience a heightened sense of temporal risk.

3. Place

In making place decisions, there are several related questions which must be asked. What is the purpose of the distribution program? Who are the customers? Who should the intermediaries be?

Purpose of Distribution: Mass distribution; selective distribution or exclusive distribution.

Number of levels in distribution channel: Direct distribution vs. multi-marketing and location decisions.

Intermediaries: Agents versus resellers; brokers and other parties; surrogate Consumers.

4. Promotion

This element comprises all the efforts the company or organization makes to stimulate the popularity of their product in the market, for instance by advertising, promotional programmes, etc. Jerome McCarthy's 4Ps marketing model is the world's most famous product marketing model. It gives a picture of a product/price mix of an organization, in combination with a promotion plan so it can approach and serve customers on the basis of well-considered distribution and customer contact channels. Jerome McCarthy's 4Ps marketing model offers marketing managers focus areas with respect to objectives and the resources to achieve those objectives.

Promotions have become a critical factor in the service marketing mix. Services are easy to be duplicated and hence it is generally the brand which sets a service apart from its counterpart. You will find a lot of banks and telecom companies promoting themselves rigorously. Why is that? It is because competition in this service sector is generally high and promotions is necessary to survive.

5. People

In Booms and Bitner's service marketing mix, "people" include people who are directly or indirectly involved in the trade of the product or service. These are mainly customer contact employees (who contact centre employees, representatives, account managers, etc.), customers, personnel and management. It is mainly the customer contact employees who are the face of the organization and they translate the quality into a service. They are the "service" providers on account of their occupation or entrepreneurship. They include, for instance, stylists, hair dressers, coaches, trainers, gardeners, lawyers, contact centre employees, etc. They deliver a physical service with a visible result.

Service companies are thoroughly aware that they must effectively manage the customer contact employees in order to monitor the quality of the service with respect to attitudes and behavior. This is very important in service companies because there might be a large variable in the performance of the customer contact employees in relation to the results of the services delivered. The quality of a service between service companies and customers (hospital intake, having a meal in a restaurant or accountancy or management consultancy services) can vary very strongly in addition to other important factors. The lack of homogeneity in services creates difficulties for service companies. Delivery of services often occurs during an interaction between a customer and contact employees. Attitude and behavior of an employee create a perception of the service as experienced by the customer (customer perception). This perception may be either positive or negative. It is even more important because it can influence customer satisfaction and in turn the customer's purchase intentions.

6. Physical Evidence

The physical evidence within the service marketing mix refers to an environment in which a service comes about from an interaction between an employee and a customer which is combined with a tangible commodity. The physical evidence includes a representation of a service for instance brochures, company stationery, business cards, reports, company website, etc. A good example is a hotel. The design, furnishing, lighting and decoration of a hotel as well as the appearance and the attitudes of the employees have a certain influence on the quality of the service and customer experience. For example, for a theme park, restaurant, or school, its "service scape" or the environment in which the service takes places (service setting) is of crucial importance when it concerns communicating about the service and the positive influencing of customer experience.

This service scape includes three physical environment dimensions that represent the relation between services and environment, namely:

Environmental conditions such as temperature, sound, smell, etc.;

Space and functions such as map, equipment, decoration, etc.;

Signs, symbols and artefacts such as signature, decoration style, personal touch, etc.

As services are intangible, customers are continuously looking for concrete clues to help them understand the nature of the service company. The more intangible the service, the more important it is to make the service around it tangible. Credit cards are a good example of tangible proof compared to the provision of (intangible) credit facilities by credit card companies and banks. In conclusion, the physical evidence serves as a visual metaphor of what the company represents, what services it facilitates and the relations between customers and employees.

Another important point for consideration: satisfied customers. Satisfied customers are the best publicity for the services or products to be delivered. The marketing strategy must be effective, in which satisfaction of existing customers can be communicated to potential customers. Social marketing is a useful tool in this respect. It is not tangible but it supplies physical evidence with the aid of, for instance, a written recommendation by a customer or user.

7. Process

The element "process" of the service marketing mix represents the activities, procedures, protocols and more by which the service in question is eventually delivered to the customer. As services are results of actions for or with customers, a process involves a sequence of steps and activities to get there.

The element "process" of the service marketing mix is an essential element within the entire service marketing mix strategy. This element comprises all activities and services in which the people involved play an important role. As a service is made up of a chain of activities, it is important to take the possible waiting period between the activities into consideration. That is why it is important that marketers take care of the communication about possible delivery times. Creating and managing effective service processes are for the existence of service companies. Managing the process factor is mainly due to the perish-ability of services which means that the services cannot be inventoried, stored for reuse or returned. For instance, airline seats that are not booked cannot be reclaimed. It is, therefore, important that the service companies manage demand as well as they possibly can.

Another distinguishing characteristic of a process in relation to a service is the evidence to be provided to the customer and this is often a standardized or customized approach based on the customer's needs and expectations. Feedback from the customer will see to the required tightening in the process with the aim to meet the customers' needs. The delivery system and the flexibility of the employees are two other key factors in the successful delivery of a service.

As services are dynamic and experiential, service companies also use a blue print method called "Service Blue Printing". This process-based method provides a better management of the service in the area of internal and external interaction, makes this transparent and ultimately this is implemented in practice.

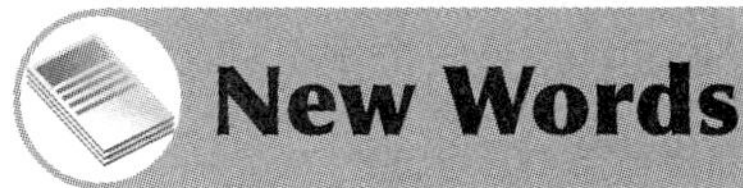

New Words

specialized ['speʃəlaɪzd] *adj.* 专业的；专门的

emerge [i'mɜːdʒ] *vi.* 出现，浮现，露出

hospitality [ˌhɒspɪ'tæləti] *n.* 服务，款待；好客，殷勤

strategically [strə'tiːdʒɪkli] *adv.* 战略上

paradigm ['pærədaɪm] *n.* 典范，范例，样式

remuneration [rɪˌmjuːnə'reɪʃn] *n.* 酬金，薪水，报酬

provision [prə'vɪʒn] *n.* 提供，供给

verifiable ['verɪfaɪəbl] *adj.* 可证实的，可核实的

intensive [ɪn'tensɪv] *adj.* 密集的，集约的

conceptualization [kən'septjuəlaɪ'zeɪʃən] *n.* 化为概念，概念化

supplementary [ˌsʌplɪ'mentəri] *adj.* 补充性的

destablize [des'teɪblaɪz] *vt.* 脱稳定化，使失去稳定性

distinction [dɪ'stɪŋkʃn] *n.* 差别，区别

tuition [tu'ɪʃn] *n.* 学费

initiate [ɪ'nɪʃieɪt] *vt.* 开始，发起；创始

termination [ˌtɜːmɪ'neɪʃn] *n.* 结束，终止

deposit [dɪ'pɑːzɪt] *n.* 押金；存款

installment [ɪn'stɔːlmənt] *n.* 分期付款

patron ['peɪtrən] *n.* 老主顾，顾客；赞助人，资助者

acutely [ə'kjuːtli] *adv.* 尖锐地；剧烈地

temporal ['tempərəl] *adj.* 暂时的；当时的

intermediary [ˌɪntə'miːdiəri] *n.* 仲裁者；调解者；中介

broker ['brəʊkə] *n.* 经纪人

surrogate ['sɜːrəgət] *n.* 代理，代理人

duplicate ['djuːplɪkeɪt] *v.* 复制

counterpart ['kaʊntəpɑːt] *n.* 职位（或作用）相当的人；对应的事物

rigorously ['rɪgərəsli] *adv.* 严厉地

representative [ˌreprɪ'zentətɪv] *n.* 销售代表，销售代理；代理

entrepreneurship [ˌɑːntrəprə'nɜːʃɪp] *n.* 企业家身份；创业精神

stylist ['staɪlɪst] *n.* 发型师

consultancy [kən'sʌltənsi] *n.* 咨询公司，专家咨询

namely ['neɪmli] *adv.* 即，也就是

artefact ['ɑːrtɪfækt] *n.* 人工制品，手工艺品

signature ['sɪgnətʃə] *n.* 签名，署名

concrete ['kɑːŋkriːt] *adj.* 确实的，具体的

publicity [pʌb'lɪsəti] *n.* （媒体的）关注，宣传，报道

protocol ['prəʊtəkɔːl] *n.* 礼仪，外交礼节；协议，规程，规约

inventory ['ɪnvəntri] *n.* （商店的）存货，库存

reclaim [rɪ'kleɪm] *v.* 收回，回收；纠正

Phrases

service marketing mix 服务行销组合	mass distribution 大量分销
tourism leisure 旅游休闲	selective distribution 选择分销
knowledge intensive environment 知识密集型环境	exclusive distribution 独家经销
delivery service 送货服务	give a picture of 把……描绘一番
exit fee 退出费	in combination with 结合
professional code 职业规范	on account of 因为，由于
be subject to 受……支配；受……影响	purchase intention 购买意向
ceiling price 价格上限	physical evidence 具体证据，物证
social price 社会定价	with the aid of 借助于
in effect 其实，实际上	a chain of 一系列（一连串）
	with the aim to 为了，旨在

Abbreviations

EFTPOS (Electronic Fund Transfers at Point-of-Sale) 销售点电子转账系统

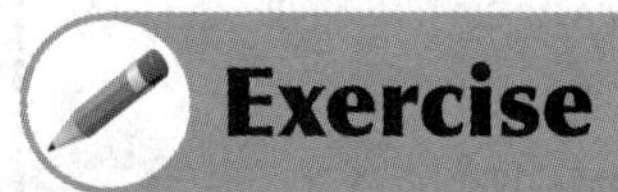

Exercise

EX. Answer the following questions according to Text B.

(1) What is the Service Marketing Mix also called?

(2) Compared with the traditional marketing mix, is the extended marketing mix for services no more than the simple addition of three extra Ps?

(3) Which type of service would the provision of coffee and tea in a bank be considered, a supporting service or a facilitating service?

(4) What are the other issues that service marketers need to consider while setting and managing price?

(5) What does a social price refer to? And what are the four types of social price identified by Fine?

(6) What questions must marketers ask while making place decisions?

(7) Why do a lot of banks and telecom companies promote themselves rigorously?

(8) Why must service companies effectively manage the customer contact employees?

(9) What are the three physical environment dimensions included in the service scape?

(10) Why is it important for service companies to manage the process factor of service?

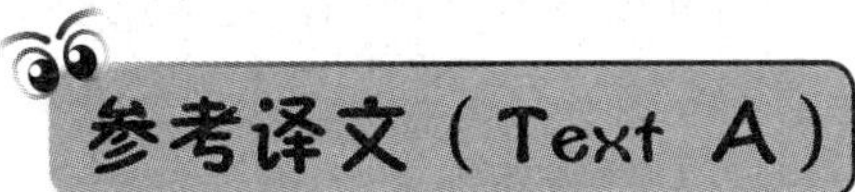

服　务

美国市场营销协会将服务营销定义为一种组织功能和一组流程，用于识别或创建、向客户传播和交付价值，并以有利于组织和利益相关者的方式管理客户关系。服务通常是一方向另一方提供的无形经济活动。执行的服务通常基于时间，为接收者、对象或购买者负责管理的其他资产带来期望的结果。作为金钱、时间和努力的交换，服务客户期望从获得商品、劳动力、专业技能、设施、访问网络和系统中获得价值；但是，他们通常不拥有所涉及的任何实物。

服务接触可以定义为客户与服务交互的持续时间。客户与服务提供者的交互通常包括与服务人员的面对面接触，以及与服务环境的实体元素（包括设施和设备）的交互。

1. 服务的概念

古典经济学家认为，服务工作，无论多么光荣，都是“非生产性的”。学者们长期以来一直在争论服务的本质。最早的一些尝试性服务定义主要集中在服务与商品的不同之处。18 世纪末和 19 世纪初的定义强调了所有权和财富创造的本质。古典经济学家认为，商品是可以建立和交换所有权的价值对象。所有权是指对有形物品的占有。该有形物品是通过从生产者或以前的所有者那里购买、易货或受赠而获得的，并且在法律上可以确认为当前所有者的财产。相比之下，当购买服务时，无商品所有权易手。

1.1　历史视角

亚当·斯密（Adam Smith）的开创性著作《国富论》区分了他所谓的“生产性”和“非生产性”劳动的产出。他说，前者生产的产品可以在生产后储存起来，然后兑换成货币或其他有价值的物品。但非生产性劳动，无论多么“光荣，……有用，还是……必要”，创造的服务在生产时就消失了，因此不能增益财富。法国经济学家让 - 巴蒂斯特·赛义德（Jean-Baptiste Say）认为，生产和消费在服务业中是不可分割的，于是创造了“非物质产品”一词来描述它们。在 20 世纪 20 年代，阿尔弗雷德·马歇尔（Alfred Marshall）仍然坚持服务“是非物质产品”这一观点。19 世纪中叶，约翰·斯图亚特·密尔（John Stuart Mill）写道，服务“不是固定的或体现在任何对象中的效用，而只是由提供的服务组成的……并不产生永久性获得”。

1.2　当代视角

20 世纪 80 年代初，当服务营销作为营销学科的一个独立分支出现时，在很大程度上对主流产品中心论的主导地位提出了抗议。1960 年，美国经济发生了永久性的变化。那一年，在一个主要贸易国内，服务业的就业人数首次超过制造业。其他发达国家很快也转向了以服务业为基础的经济。学者们很快就开始认识到，服务本身是重要的，而不是商品之后的残羹剩饭。这种认识引发了服务定义方式的更改。到了20世纪中期，学者们开始根据服务自身的独特特征来定义服务，而不是通过与产品的比较来定义。以下一组定义表明学者们如何紧扣服务产品的独特方面，并发展新的服务定义。

"生产商品，提供服务。"

"服务是在与联系人或物理机的交互过程中进行的一项活动或一系列活动，它为消费者提供满意度。"

"服务产品的核心是消费者的实时体验……正是互动过程本身创造了消费者所期望的利益。"

"服务是行为、过程和表现。"

"服务是为接受者提供时间、地点、形式、解决问题或体验价值的过程(经济活动)。"

"服务这个词……是价值的同义词。供应商有价值主张，但价值实现发生在客户的使用和消费过程中。"

1.3　其他观点

最近提出的另一种观点是，服务涉及一种租赁形式，通过这种形式，客户可以获得利益，客户愿意为那些能给他们的生活方式带来价值的理想体验和解决方案付费。租金这个术语可以作为一个通用术语来描述为使用某物或为获得某些技能和专业知识、设施或网络而支付的费用。通常是在规定的时间内支付租金，而不是直接购买，因为直接购买在很多情况下根本不可能。

在非所有权框架内租赁有五大类。

租赁商品服务：这些服务使顾客获得暂时使用某个实物商品的权利，而这个商品是他们不愿拥有的物品，如船、演出服装等。

规定空间和地点的租赁：这些服务使顾客有权使用某建筑物、车辆或其他区域中较大空间的一个特定部分，而这部分空间本身就可以达到某一目的。例如，仓库中的存储容器，或者只是一种实现目的的方式，如餐馆中的餐桌、飞机上的座位等。

劳动力和专业技能租赁：雇佣他人完成客户自身不愿做的工作，如打扫房间等，或者由于缺乏专业知识、工具和技能而无法做的工作，如汽车维修、外科手术等。

进入共享物理环境：这些环境可以是室内或室外，客户租用共享环境使用权，如博物馆、主题公园、健身房、高尔夫球场等。

进入并访问系统和网络：客户租用参与特定网络的权利，如电信、公用事业、银行或保险，而且不同参与级别，其费用也不同。

2. 服务的特点

服务的一个显著特点是生产和消费不可分割。在整个80年代和90年代，所谓的独特的服务特征主导了大部分的文献。最经常被提及的服务特点是：

无形性：从本质上讲，服务是无形的，这意味着它们不能被触觉感知，只存在于与其他事物的联系中，比如企业的商誉。服务的这种无形性使得对"优质服务"进行定义非常困难，而且非常主观，尤其是在不同的人口群体中。例如，典型的X世代人没有受过礼仪教育，可能也不会关心那些不说"请"和"谢谢"的人。相反，婴儿潮时期出生的人通常会对这种社交礼仪的缺乏感到恼怒。因此，营销人员必须确定并根据每个群体的需求说服客户。

不可分割性：生产和消费是不可分离的，而商品的生产和消费是完全分离的过程。个人服务不能与具体的某个人分开。创建和消费服务是同时发生的。在客户端接收服务的同时产生该服务。例如，在在线搜索或法律咨询期间，牙医、音乐家、舞蹈家等都在创建服务的同时提供服务。

可变性：服务涉及人员，而人与人之间有差别。针对同样的问题，不同的人，甚至是同一个人在不同的时间都很有可能做出不同的回答。重要的是通过培训、标准设置和质量保证来最大限度地缩小服务差异。企业提供的服务质量永远无法标准化。

易逝性：服务具有高度的易逝性。未利用的服务能力不能存储为将来使用。如果今天不享用服务，它将永远失去。例如，飞机上的空余座位不能转移到下一个航班。同样，五星级酒店的空房间和未使用的信贷会导致经济损失。由于服务是同时进行的消费活动，因此除非消费，否则服务将不复存在。

难以标准化：由于服务是由人而非机器提供的，因此提供的服务在水平、质量、持续时间和强度方面都会产生差异。提供服务时必须做出判断，这些判断导致服务交付缺乏标准化。例如，即使呼叫中心的每个员工都接受了相同的培训，有些员工也会花更多的时间回答客户的问题，并努力解决问题。此外，对于什么是优质服务，员工仁者见仁，智者见智。

购买和消费相结合：除了预付和年度会员制以外，一旦购买了服务，它也会被消费。服务的易逝性意味着关系营销至关重要。否则，客户在经历了不太满意的体验后，可能会决定选用另一个服务提供者。体验的质量是营销人员关注的焦点。保险代理人和房地产经纪人注重成为值得信赖的好邻居。此外，发表在《家庭实践杂志》上的一项名为"预测病人信任的医生行为"的研究发现，医生和病人之间的关系强度是决定病人对其主要护理提供者忠诚程度的主要因素。

服务的独特特性带来的问题和挑战是产品营销中很少能与之相提并论。服务是复杂、多维和多层次的。不仅存在多种利益，而且在客户和组织之间以及客户和其他客户之间还存在多种交互作用。

3. 服务分类

有许多方法可以对服务进行分类。一种分类考虑了服务对象和服务内容，并确定了三类服务：服务于人，如美容服务、儿童护理、医疗服务；服务于心智，如教育服务、辅导服务、生活辅导；服务于财产，如宠物护理、电器维修、钢琴调音；以及资讯服务，如金融服务、数据仓储服务。另一种服务分类法是利用服务过程中顾客互动的程度，并将服务分为高接触服务，如接待、牙科保健、美容；低接触服务，如电讯、公用事业服务。

经济学家和营销人员都广泛使用"搜索→体验→信用（SEC）"这一服务分类法。该分类方案基于消费者评价活动的难易程度，并确定了三类商品。

搜索类商品：顾客可以在购买或消费之前对这类商品的属性进行评估。消费者依靠以往的经验、直接的产品检查和其他信息搜索活动来确定有助于评估过程的信息。大多数产品属于搜索类商品，如服装、办公文具、家居用品。

体验类商品：只有在购买并体验产品之后，顾客才能对其属性或质量进行准确评估的商品或服务。很多个人服务都属于这一类，如餐馆、理发店、美容院、主题公园、旅游、度假等。

信用类商品：它们是即使在消费之后也很难或不可能评估的产品或服务。评估困难可能是因为消费者缺乏进行现实性评价所必需的知识或专业技术，或者是因为获取信息的成本过高或超过了现有信息的价值。许多专业服务都属于这一类，如会计、法律服务、医疗诊断/治疗、整容手术。这些商品被称为信用类产品，因为消费者的质量评估完全依赖于对产品制造商或服务提供商的信任。

虽然有些服务可能具有许多搜索属性，但大多数服务都具有较高的体验或信任属性。实证研究表明，消费者的感知风险沿着“搜索——体验——信任”这一连续体逐步增加。这意味着服务往往是高介入决策，即消费者在购买决策期间会投入更多的时间和精力搜索信息。

Case Huawei Launches Vendor-built Service Operation Center

Unit 13

Text A

O2O (Online-to-Offline) Commerce

In the past, online and offline customer experiences and interactions have collectively remained separate. Although there are cross-platform support options such as buy online and ship to store, that's not exactly what you'd call a merger between the two commerce types. Thanks to modern technologies such as mobile and in-app or location-based experiences, many businesses are now offering both options to their customers. We can effectively refer to it as online-to-offline, or O2O commerce.

1. *What is online-to-offline commerce?*

Online to offline is a phrase (commonly abbreviated to O2O) that is used in digital marketing to describe systems enticing consumers within a digital environment to make purchases of goods or services from physical businesses. Online-to-offline commerce is a business strategy that draws potential customers from online channels to make purchases in physical stores. Online-to-offline commerce, or O2O, identifies customers in the online space, such as through emails and internet advertising, and then uses a variety of tools and approaches to entice the customers to leave the online space.This type of strategy incorporates techniques used in online marketing with those used in brick-and-mortar marketing.

For starters, O2O involves engaging with your online customers in various ways to encourage or entice them to leave the digital space and enter a physical one. In other words, you're trying to push online customers to come into a local store or physical location. This is achieved by merging strategies from the two different types of commerce. You're using both online marketing and advertising techniques, in addition to brick-and-mortar style promotions.

Thus, if you want to be pedantic, instead of brick-and-mortar, you can call it click-and-mortar.

2. How does online-to-offline commerce work?

Retailers once fretted that they would not be able to compete with e-commerce companies that sold goods online, especially in terms of price and selection. Physical stores required high fixed costs (rent) and many employees to run the stores and, because of limited space, they were unable to offer such a wide selection of goods. Online retailers could offer a vast selection without having to pay for many employees and only needed access to shipping companies in order to sell their goods. Some companies that have both an online presence and an offline presence (physical stores) treat the two different channels as complements rather than competitors. The goal of online-to-offline commerce is to create product and service awareness online, allowing potential customers to research different offerings and then visit the local brick-and-mortar store to make a purchase. Techniques that O2O commerce companies may employ include in-store pick-up of items purchased online, allowing items purchased online to be returned at a physical store, and allowing customers to place orders online while at a physical store.

The rise of online-to-offline commerce has not eliminated the advantages that e-commerce companies enjoy. Companies with brick-and-mortar stores will still have customers that visit physical stores in order to see how an item fits or looks, or to compare pricing, only to ultimately make the purchase online (referred to as "showrooming"). The goal, therefore, is to attract a certain type of customer who is open to walking or driving to a local store rather than waiting for a package to arrive in the mail.

3. Online-to-offline commerce basics: The breakdown

That earlier example of buying online and shipping to store is actually a common technique used by O2O commerce companies, but it's about more than just that particular experience. Allowing items bought online to be returned or exchanged in store is another example. Another great one is setting up a digital station in-store that allows your customers to shop the online inventory from a brick-and-mortar location. It's a natural step forward for many physical and traditional retailers, especially if they hope to compete with e-commerce brands. Instead of treating the two different channels as separate entities or even competitors, you merge them to create one seamless business and customer platform. Setting up demos or product examples in your physical store and allowing customers to review the items is a great idea. In fact, there are a great many products that customers would prefer to see up close and personal before buying. IKEA, the popular Swedish furniture store, handles this swimmingly. Customers can browse products, furniture, and goods in the massive stores—which are often considered to be a maze, and then order the products online, which are shipped to their doorstep. Smaller items can be bought in-store. In this way, IKEA allows their customers to experience the best of both worlds. If you've ever been to a local store, you know how packed and chaotic it can be.

O2O is different than a traditional cross-platform experience, because in those scenarios you're generally focused on allowing your customers to simply move between different channels.

You might have one or two O2O options or practices, but that's not the majority of your business. With online-to-offline, you're effectively making it part of your regular operations, which means incorporating as many techniques and options as possible.

4. Benefits of O2O business

Obviously, O2O brings out to retailers the brand reputation. Branding is much simpler and more efficient with online capabilities like advertising, social media, mobile wallet, SMS, mobile app, push messages, combined with real-time data analytics, system integration, and AI. Take advertising as an example. A man goes online and searches for a gift for his girlfriend on Christmas Eve, right in an article giving recommendations for Christmas gift, he can see a picture of a Christmas set from a cosmetics brand. If the man clicks on the picture, he is showing his interest in the products and consequently becomes a potential customer of that brand. Those kinds of marketing tactics these days help create the brands, products or services awareness with less time and money spent.

Also, O2O business enhances customers' loyalty and increases revenue at the same time. O2O commerce follows a strategy that allows the retailer to optimize customer experience. During their shopping journey, customers are provided with online and offline benefits that they can not resist. With all the information about the brands, products or service available online, customers can make quicker and smarter decisions on what they're gonna buy. Moreover, the purchasing is much more convenient and personalized that make them feel it's so enjoyable to buy something. O2O commerce also lets retailers build up a database of customers' information including their names, age, addresses, interests and even shopping behavior. It then improves the customer engagement strategy of the brands, leading to higher level of customer loyalty. Once a company earns engagement from customers, that company will see a dramatic increase in revenue, both short-term and long-term.

One more benefit of O2O retail is that this strategy accelerates your speed to market by minimizing the time to market. Collecting customers' interest and shopping behavior online, O2O helps reduce the length of time it takes from a product being conceived until its being available for sale. For example, online channels can let a fashion brand know which items, colors or styles are the most-searched, helping them anticipate the demands of customers and avoid out-of-stock status.

5. Online-to-offline commerce trends

Now, consider Amazon's $13.7 billion purchase of Whole Foods in 2017, and you can see where the leader in online commerce is placing its bets—in physical space. Amazon will even let you pay with your Amazon Prime credit card and earn 5% rewards, the same as if you used your Amazon card to pay online. Aside from Amazon, every top-10 retailer is a brick-and-mortar operation. That's not to say that traditional retailers aren't hedging their bets. Walmart has spent mightily to bridge the gap between online users and retail locations, including its 2016 purchase of e-commerce company Jet.com. Consider that about 80% of consumers research items online before making a purchase, and one can see that the future lies in a convergence between online and offline sales.

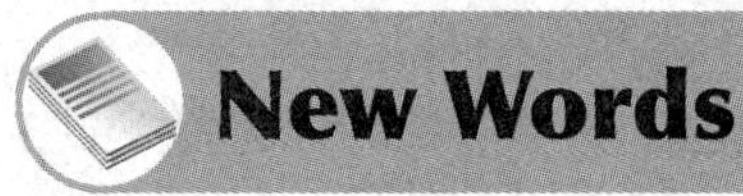

New Words

collectively [kə'lektɪvli] *adv.* 集体地，共同地
merger ['mɜːdʒə] *n.* （机构或企业的）合并，归并
exactly [ɪg'zæktli] *adv.* 精确地，准确地，确切地
phrase [freɪz] *n.* 短语，词组；习语
abbreviate [ə'briːvieɪt] *vt.* 缩略，把（词语、名称）缩写成
pedantic [pɪ'dæntɪk] *adj.* 迂腐的，学究气的
fret [fret] *v.* （使）烦恼；（使）焦急
complement ['kɒmplɪmənt] *n.* 补充物，补足物
showrooming ['ʃəʊruːmɪŋ] *n.* 展厅现象，展厅销售，陈列式商务模式
seamless ['siːmləs] *adj.* 无（接）缝的，（两部分之间）无空隙的
demo ['deməʊ] *n.* 样本唱片；演示
swimmingly ['swɪmɪŋli] *adv.* 容易地，顺利地
maze [meɪz] *n.* 迷惑；迷宫；曲径
doorstep ['dɔːrstep] *n.* 门阶
chaotic [keɪ'ɑːtɪk] *adj.* 混乱的，杂乱的；紊乱的
analytic [ˌænə'lɪtɪk] *adj.* 分析的，分析型的
recommendation [ˌrekəmen'deɪʃn] *n.* 正式建议，提议；推荐
cosmetic [kɑːz'metɪk] *n.* 化妆品，美容品
resist [rɪ'zɪst] *v.* 抵制，阻挡，反抗
database ['deɪtəbeɪs] *n.* （储存在计算机中的）数据库
accelerate [ək'seləreɪt] *v.* （使）加速，加快
project ['prɒdʒekt] *vt.* 预计
mightily ['maɪtɪli] *adv.* 强有力地；非常
convergence [kən'vɜːdʒəns] *n.* 趋同，融合

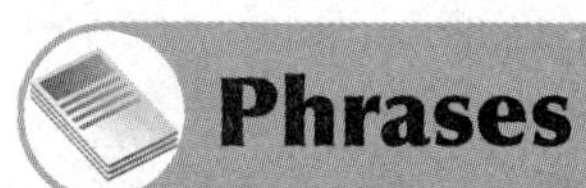

Phrases

refer to... as 把……称作，把……当作
brick-and-mortar marketing 实体市场营销
click-and-mortar marketing 虚实结合市场营销
service awareness 服务意识
up close 近距离地
mobile wallet 手机钱包
push message 推送消息
build up 建立；逐步增长；增进
place its bets 下注
hedge bets 做两手准备
bridge the gap 弥合差距，缩短差距；消除隔阂

Abbreviations

O2O (Online to Offline) 线上到线下
SMS (Short Messaging Service) 短消息业务

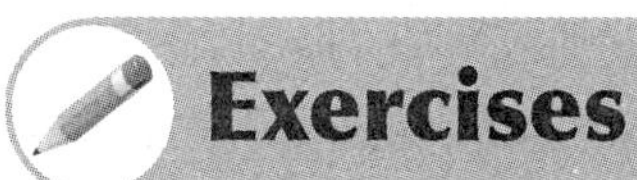

Exercises

EX. 1 Answer the following questions according to Text A.

(1) What is online to offline?
(2) What is online-to-offline commerce?
(3) What did retailers once fret?
(4) What is the goal of online-to-offline commerce?
(5) What techniques may be employed by O2O commerce companies?
(6) What should the physical and traditional retailers do if they hope to compete with e-commerce brands?
(7) In what situation is branding much simpler and more efficient?
(8) What does a database of customers' information built up by O2O retailers include?
(9) How does O2O strategy accelerate businesses' speed to market?
(10) What is the commerce trend?

EX. 2 Translate the following phrases from English into Chinese and vice versa.

1. service awareness ______________________
2. click-and-mortar marketing ______________________
3. brick-and-mortar marketing ______________________
4. bridge the gap ______________________
5. showrooming ______________________
6. 正式建议，提议；推荐 ______________________
7. 数据库 ______________________
8. 手机钱包 ______________________
9. 补充物，补足物 ______________________
10. 趋同，融合 ______________________

EX. 3 **Translate the following into Chinese.**

According to research conducted by IBM, the biggest influence on shopper behavior is still the store, even though not all purchases will take place there. Interaction with a product or service is important in shaping opinions and influencing decisions. Many customers will research online before purchasing in store, so equipping consumers with the right information will assist them in making their purchase decisions. If you fail to be online, you fail to capture that large audience who use the internet to research before heading to the stores.

Omni-channel retailing is a new movement impacting retail businesses both domestically and globally. It represents those retailers who embrace both the online and offline interactions with consumers to assist them along their buyer decision journey—including search, evaluation, the actual sale and also after-sales support. Embracing an omni-channel model will allow traditional retailers to create deeper engagement and more meaningful experiences for their shoppers—one that is hard for the pure play online retailers to emulate. This will allow you to integrate important initiatives such as in store returns for online purchases, and giving customers the ability to view in store stock levels. Empowering them with the right information, at the right time, in the right place.

EX. 4 **Fill in the blanks with the words given below.**

foreshadowed	accessed	impacted	debuted	wake
turning to	primary	expense	timely	convenience

The "Amazon Effect"

The "Amazon effect" refers to the impact created by the online, e-commerce or digital marketplace on the traditional brick and mortar business model due to the change in shopping patterns, customer expectations and a new competitive landscape.

As more and more people across the globe are (1)________ online shopping, the retail landscape continues to change rapidly. The gains for e-commerce businesses are coming at the (2)________ of brick-and-mortar retail stores, as an increasing number of shoppers are heading for their screens instead of for stores. Amazon.com Inc., which (3)________ in 1994, has maintained its lead in global online selling, and has become the poster boy for this change, giving the "Amazon Effect" its name.

Among other factors, the Amazon effect is cited as the (4)________ reason for street-based stores' declining sales, which have often (5)________ the stores' eventual closure. A WWD report cited more than 9,400 store closings in 2017, up 53% from the number that shut in the (6)________ of the Great Recession in 2008.

Beyond hitting the revenue of traditional retail stores, the Amazon effect has also led to significant changes in consumer shopping patterns. For instance, based on the (7)________ they experience on online shopping portals, today's shopper expects a lot more variety even while visiting a retail store. While it may not be possible to clearly read the contents or specifications mentioned on a small-sized pack containing an electronic gadget or cashew nuts in a retail store, the same product details can be easily (8)________ in large text on the online shopping sites. The seamless online shopping experience has also (9)________ the behavioral expectations of shoppers, as they now expect the same smoothness, (10)________ response and convenience even for services (like at a salon) that generally cannot be offered online.

Text B

Seven Ways to Optimize Online-to-Offline Marketing

In an era where online marketing is crucial to business success, it can be easy to forget to include offline marketing. However, this could prove to be a big mistake. Incorporating offline data in a marketing campaign can strengthen online marketing ROI through deeper insights into your organization's customers and their behaviors in the real world.

Most modern-day marketers understand this. They know that customers switch between physical and digital worlds freely while they move through the buyer's journey. This makes Online-to-Offline—also known as O2O—marketing an effective way for businesses to reach customers at all touch points to drive engagement and sales.

In Online-to-Offline (O2O) commerce, companies treat their online and offline marketing channels as complementary instead of competitive. Some examples include:

Click and collect—where customers buy products online and then pick them up in-store;

Online shopping during a physical visit;

Returning items purchased online to a physical store.

A testament to the importance of O2O was demonstrated in Amazon's acquisition of Whole Foods. Amazon invested over $13 billion in the acquisition because they understood an undeniable reality about consumers: Despite all the fascination with devices and digital services, most sales still happen in physical stores. 76% of consumers who search for products or services in their local area end up visiting a store within a day, with many of these visits resulting in purchases. Spotify estimates show that over 80% of retail sales will happen in stores to 2021, and possibly beyond. These stats make it clear that an effective marketing campaign can not afford to overlook offline strategies.

An IBM study shed light on how today's consumers expect an exciting and engaging shopping experience in stores, similar to the one offered online. In spite of this, almost 90% of brands aren't set up to cater to these demands. Consequently, many brands are falling behind, leaving customers unsatisfied with the service and experience they get in physical stores.

There are numerous ways to enhance the customer experience by utilizing digital technology on site to make shopping a more enjoyable time for consumers—and a more profitable campaign for marketers. Let's look at 7 ways businesses can optimize their online and offline marketing activities.

1. Permit online activities to happen offline

One of the biggest trends in retail is click-and-collect shopping, with more than 70% of customers taking advantage of the ability to order items online and collect them in a nearby store.

This simple marketing technique feeds directly into the consumer's desire for instant gratification, which is now the norm, thanks to services like Netflix and Uber that make it easier to get what we want without waiting. This encourages more customers to visit physical retail locations, which then increases the chances of impulsive buys.

2. Harness the potential of immersive technology

As shoppers also are getting more tech savvy, they expect businesses to provide better shopping experiences that integrate available technology, starting with boosting convenience by simplifying purchasing, delivery, return, and refund processes. For instance, enabling ePOS systems or mobile payments using mPOS, or pay-in-aisle technology to facilitate a speedy, cashless checkout.

With the growth of using mobile phones, it is also important to design the shopping experiences with mobile-first and "phygical" (physical-digital) mentality. Leverage voice and facial recognition, Augmented Reality (AR) and Virtual Reality (VR) to boost interactive shopping experiences, allowing shoppers to engage whenever and wherever they want.

Using the same example of Nordstrom's opt-in-app, this app also allows customers to reserve items to try on in-store later. Furthermore, its functions also include taking photos of any items to find similar ones using AI power, as well as scanning to learn more about stock availability and reviews.

One of the other great technology integrations that your business can deploy is Quick Response (QR) code. They can be displayed on screens and printed on receipts to give customers access to information. They can also be used to connect with loyalty programmes, or to bookmark items that they like.

3. Improve personalization with data insights

Living in the digital age, shoppers become more skeptical and practical when it comes to their shopping experience. They start to show less and less interest and trust in traditional marketing campaigns.

As 80% of consumers are more likely to buy from businesses that cater to their exact interests, and strive to meet their exact demand, personalisation counts for a lot. In other words, to move, engage, and forge a bond with customers, retailers need to be more real and inclusive in the way they do marketing.

One way to do this is by using customer data gathered online to improve the offline shopping experience. Nordstrom, one of American's biggest fashion retailers, has introduced data-driven personalised experiences at their retail stores. One of their unique techniques is an opt-in-app that delivers the online profile of shoppers who are in store to that specific store's sales assistants, so that the sales assistants can help create a better shopping experience for the customers.

4. Prioritize mobile-first

We all know that mobile devices aren't going anywhere. Moreover, they are quickly becoming the dominant force, with consumers opting for their devices over desktops. Statistics show that Americans spend upwards of 4.5 hours on their smartphones every day, and 80% of millennials sleep with their phone nearby.

What might be surprising is that this obsession with mobile devices does not spell the end of offline marketing. Forrester reports that annual sales for mobile phones have soared north of $60 billion, but that number is relatively small compared to the $1 trillion in offline sales that is directly influenced by mobile phone use. While the landscape is changing, brands can track the changes and evolve with them so that it's possible to connect with customers at various touch points, both online and offline.

Trip Advisor is an example of a brand that has made their app available offline, allowing customers to benefit from their services even when internet connectivity is not an option.

Businesses can also leverage the love of mobile by using beacon technology in their stores, transmitting messages to customer's devices as they move around the store. 71% of retailers can use beacons to track customer buying patterns and then analyse and adapt their marketing to offer a better service.

5. Link KPIs for online and offline marketing

Companies need to make big decisions on their budgets, investments, and marketing strategy, all of which must ensure the highest possible ROI. By choosing to only look at online operations and omit offline avenues, it will be significantly more difficult to achieve your marketing goals

More companies are realizing the value of aligning their KPIs for online and offline marketing, with studies showing that 47% of companies now focus using their offline marketing to boost online traffic and engagement. Conversely, 68% of companies are using their online marketing to drive brand loyalty—a traditional goal of offline marketing. 65% of companies use online marketing activities to encourage offline engagement.

Although e-commerce teams and in-store staff tend to work as separate units, companies can align their sales and marketing initiatives so that everyone and everything are geared to working towards the same goals.

6. Be Flexible with your campaign

It's not always easy to determine the best keywords to target or the most important KPIs to set when measuring the success of any marketing campaign.

In the digital landscape, the state of retail is dramatically changing, which affects both online and offline marketing. Many factors change, including:

Our customers and their desires;

The company skillset and experience;

Performance capabilities;

Competitors and their strategies; and

Our knowledge of our own companies.

As a result, it's impossible to just set and forget your KPIs. There is no such thing as a perfect set. When companies want to optimize their online and offline campaign, it is important to consider this and think about which KPIs to change or retire.

7. Develop offline and online SEO

For many companies, offline SEO is somewhat of a mystery. Many make the error of disregarding SEO in offline marketing, believing it has no impact on your online performance.

When customers find a company through organic search, it's clear that online SEO is working well. This translates to higher expectations for offline interactions as consumers approach physical stores confidently based on user reviews, social proof, and a good online presence.

Just as SEO must market to people, not machines, companies must ensure their offline service is consumer-centric. It should reflect your online SEO, building upon the value and connections that your online marketing has developed.

Alignment is the key to the success of modern marketing. It's easy to discount the impact of offline activities on your online operations. With digital transformation being such a major focus for many businesses, it's understandable that many companies are choosing to focus heavily on online marketing. However, despite the drive towards digitalization, companies must remember that they are still selling to humans. People care about making a connection with brands and seek out enjoyable experiences. In many cases, that means going to physical stores to do their shopping.

Marketers need to look for ways in which their online and offline channels can complement each other so that their marketing campaigns are aligned. By using new technology such as data insights, store apps and beacons, companies can increase personalization efforts and communicate with their customer base offline. They can also take advantage of the prevalence of mobile users and work on satisfying the overarching desire for a faster and better service.

Companies that build on traditional principles and adopt a customer-centric approach will be able to build a stronger reputation, both online and offline, which will breed the customer loyalty needed to make their marketing campaign more successful.

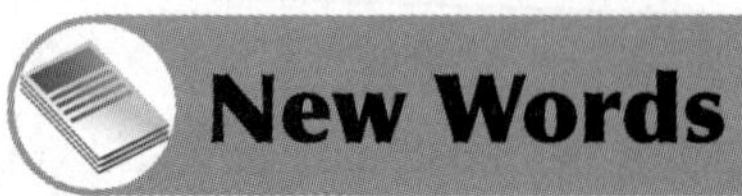

era ['ɪrə] *n.* 时代，年代	testament ['testəmənt] *n.* 证据；证明
complementary [ˌkɑːmplɪ'mentri] *adj.* 互补的，补充的	demonstrate ['demənstreɪt] *vt.* 证明；演示，示范

undeniable [ˌʌndɪ'naɪəbl] *adj.* 不可否认的，确凿的

fascination [ˌfæsɪ'neɪʃn] *n.* 极大的吸引力；入迷，着迷

stat [stæt] *n.* 统计

overlook [ˌoʊvər'lʊk] *vt.* 忽略；未注意到

gratification [ˌgrætɪfɪ'keɪʃn] *n.* 满足，满意；快感

impulsive [ɪm'pʌlsɪv] *adj.* 凭冲动行事的，易冲动的

harness ['hɑːnɪs] *vt.* 控制，利用

simplify ['sɪmplɪfaɪ] *vt.* 简化，使简单

integration [ˌɪntɪ'greɪʃn] *n.* 结合；整合，一体化

bookmark ['bʊkmɑːk] 给……设置书签

personalization ['pɜːsənəlaɪzeɪʃən] *n.* 人格化；个性化

skeptical ['skeptɪkl] *adj.* 怀疑的，心存疑惑的

count [kaʊnt] *vi.* 重要，有价值

forge [fɔːdʒ] *vi.* 建立；锻造；伪造

inclusive [ɪn'kluːsɪv] *adj.* 包含……在内的；包罗广泛的

prioritize [praɪ'ɔːrətaɪz] *vt.* 按重要性排列；划分优先顺序

millennial [mɪ'lenɪəl] *n.* 千禧一代

obsession [əb'seʃn] *n.* 痴迷，着魔；困扰

soar [sɔː] *vi.* 急升，猛增

option ['ɑːpʃn] *n.* 选择，选择权；可选择的事物

transmit [træns'mɪt] *vt.* 传送，输送；发射

omit [ə'mɪt] *vt.* 忽略；漏掉；删除

align [ə'laɪn] *vt.* 使结盟；使一致

initiative [ɪ'nɪʃətɪv] *n.* 倡议；首创精神

gear [gɪə] *v.* （使）适合；使准备好

skillset [skɪlset] *n.* 技能组

disregard [ˌdɪsrɪ'gɑːd] *vt.* 不顾；漠视，不理会

discount ['dɪskaʊnt] *v.* 认为……不重要，低估；打折扣

digitalization [ˌdɪdʒɪtəlaɪ'zeɪʃən] *n.* 数字化

prevalence ['prevələns] *n.* 流行

overarching [ˌəʊvə'ɑːtʃɪŋ] *adj.* 非常重要的，首要的

breed [briːd] *v.* 养育；引起，产生

Phrases

click-and-collect shopping “线上购物，线下提货”购物方式

physical store 实体店

shed light on 阐明，解释；将……弄明白

in spite of 尽管；不管，不顾

cater to 迎合，投合

fall behind 落后，跟不上

on site 在现场，临场

feed into 注入（流入，装进）

instant gratification 即时满足，即时满意；及时行乐

facial recognition 面部识别

count for a lot 有很大价值或重要性

north of 比……更多，超过

beacon technology 信标技术

customer buying pattern 顾客购买模式

be geared to 适应……的需要；面向
translate to 把……转化成……
build upon 基于；把……建立于
make a connection with 与……联系
seek out 找出；挑出
customer base 客户集合
build a reputation 树立名声，建立声誉

Abbreviations

ROI (Return on Investment) 投资回报率
IBM (International Business Machines) 美国国际商用机器公司
ePOS (electronic Point of Sale) 电子支付系统
mPOS (mobile Point of Sale) 便携式支付系统
AI (Artificial Intelligence) 人工智能
AR (Augmented Reality) 增强现实
VR (Virtual Reality) 虚拟现实
QR Code (Quick Response Code) 由 Denso 公司研制的一种二维码符号
KPI (Key Performance Indicator) 关键绩效指标
SEO (Search Engine Optimization) 搜索引擎优化

Exercise

EX. Answer the following questions according to Text B.

(1) How do companies treat their online and offline marketing in O2O commerce?
(2) What is one of the biggest trends in retail?
(3) What are the functions of Nordstrom' s opt-in-app?
(4) What is one of Nordstrom's unique techniques?
(5) What might be surprising in terms of mobile devices?
(6) How do most retailers use beacon technology to leverage the love of mobile devices?
(7) According to studies, what is the percentage of companies using their online marketing to drive brand loyalty?
(8) What are the changing factors of retail in the digital landscape?
(9) What should the offline service be like since SEO must market to people, not machines?
(10) What is the key to the success of modern marketing?

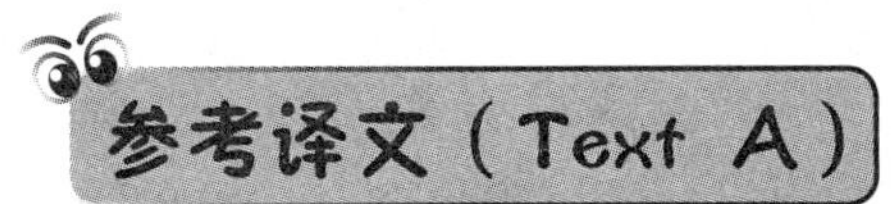

线上到线下商务

过去，线上和线下的客户体验和互动总的来说是分开的。尽管有多种跨平台支持选择，比如线上购买和线下发货到商店，但这确实不是两种商务类型的合并。由于有了移动和应用软件或基于位置的体验等现代技术，许多企业现在都向客户提供两种选择。我们可以有效地将其称之为线上到线下，或 O2O 商务。

1. 什么是线上到线下商务?

线上到线下（Online to offline) 是一个用于数字营销中的短语 (通常缩写为 O2O)，是在数字环境中吸引消费者从实体企业购买商品或服务的系统。线上到线下商务是一种商业策略，它从在线渠道吸引潜在客户到实体店购物。O2O 是通过电子邮件、网络广告等方式，在网络空间中识别顾客，然后利用各种工具和手段，诱使顾客离开网络空间。这种策略将在线营销和实体营销中使用的技术结合起来。

O2O 通过各种方式与在线客户互动，以鼓励或吸引他们离开数字空间，进入实体空间。换句话说，你试图推动在线客户进入本地商店或实体店，通过合并两种不同类型的商业策略可以实现这一点。除了实体形式的促销之外，你还可以使用在线营销和广告技术。因此，如果想显得有学问的话，可以称之为虚实结合体店，而不是实体店。

2. 线上到线下商务是如何运作的?

零售商曾经担心，他们将无法与在线销售商品的电子商务公司竞争，尤其是在价格和选择方面。实体店需要高昂的固定成本（租金）和许多员工来经营，由于空间有限，他们无法提供广泛的商品选择。然而，在线零售商可以提供大量的商品选择，他们不需要雇佣许多员工，只需要联系货运公司就可以销售商品。一些同时拥有在线和线下业务（实体店）的公司将这两个不同的渠道视为互补，而非竞争对手。线上到线下商务的目标是在网上创造产品和服务意识，让潜在客户研究不同的产品，然后光顾当地的实体店进行购买。O2O 商务企业可能采用的技术包括：在线购物、店内提货，允许线上购买的商品在实体店退货，以及允许顾客在实体店在线下单。

线上到线下商务的兴起并没有消除电子商务公司所具有的优势，仍然会有顾客光顾实体店。他们为了看一件商品是否合身，好看，或者为了比较价格，最终在网上购买（这被称作“展厅现象”或“先逛店后网购”)。因此，线上到线下的目标是吸引特定类型的顾客，他们愿意步行或开车去当地的商店，而不是等待收取邮寄的包裹。

3. 线上到线下商务模式基本原理分析

在线购物和送货上门实际上是 O2O 商业公司使用的一种常见技术，但这不仅仅是一种特定的体验。另一种做法是允许网上购买的商品在商店里退换。还有一个很棒的方法是建立一个店内数字站点，让客户可以在实体店购买在线商品。对于许多实体零售商和传统零售商来说，这自然是一个进步，尤其是如果他们希望与电子商务品牌竞争的话。你必须将这两个不同的渠道合并为一个无缝的业务和客户平台，而不是将它们视为单独的实体甚至竞争对手。在实体店中展示产品样品，并允许客户查看商品，这是一个好主意。事实上，顾客在购买前更喜欢近距离亲自查看大量的商品。颇受欢迎的瑞典家具商店宜家就很好地处理了这一问题。顾客可以在大型商店中随意观看产品、家具和商品——这些大型商店通常被认为是一个迷宫——然后在网上订购产品，这些产品会被送到顾客的家门口。较小的商品可以在商店里买到。通过这种方式，宜家让顾客拥有两种最佳体验。如果你曾经去过当地的商店，你就会知道那里是多么的拥挤和混乱。

O2O 与传统的跨平台体验不同，因为在跨平台场景中，你通常专注于让客户只在不同的渠道之间移动。你可能有一两个 O2O 业务选择或实践，但那并不是你的主要业务。通过线上到线下模式，你可以有效地将其作为常规操作的一部分，这意味着要包含尽可能多的技术和商品选项。

4. O2O 业务的好处

显然，O2O 给零售商带来了品牌声誉。通过在线功能，如广告、社交媒体、手机钱包、短信服务（SMS）、移动应用程序、推送消息等，再结合实时数据分析、系统整合和人工智能等技术，品牌推广将更简化、更高效。以广告为例。一名男子在圣诞前夜上网为女友挑选圣诞礼物，就在一篇推荐圣诞礼物的文章中，他看到了一张某化妆品品牌圣诞套装的图片。如果他点击了该图片，就表示他对该产品感兴趣，从而成为该品牌的潜在客户。如今，这类营销策略有助于以更少的时间和花费打造品牌、产品或服务意识。

O2O 业务在提高客户忠诚度的同时也增加了收入。O2O 商业遵循的策略是让零售商优化客户体验。在他们的购物之旅中，顾客享有了线上和线下好处，且无法抗拒。由于线上提供了所有关于品牌、产品或服务的相关信息，顾客可以就购买事宜做出更快、更明智的决定。此外，购物更加方便和个性化，从而让顾客觉得购物是一件如此令人愉快的事。O2O 商业还可以让零售商建立一个顾客信息数据库，包括他们的姓名、年龄、地址、兴趣甚至购物行为，从而完善顾客对品牌的参与策略，提高顾客忠诚度。一旦一家公司赢得了顾客的关注，该公司的短期和长期收入都将大幅增长。

O2O 零售的另一个好处是，这种策略通过减少投放市场的时间来加快投放市场的速度。通过收集顾客的兴趣和在线购物行为信息，O2O 有助于缩短产品从构思到上市的时间。例如，在线渠道可以让一家时装品牌企业知道哪些商品、颜色或款式是顾客搜索最多的，从而帮助公司预测顾客的需求，避免缺货情况发生。

5. 线上到线下商业趋势

现在，想想亚马逊在 2017 年以 137 亿美元收购全食超市，你就会发现，在线商务的领头企业把赌注都押在了实体空间。亚马逊甚至会让你用亚马逊优惠信用卡支付，并获得 5% 的奖励，就像你用亚马逊卡在线支付一样。除了亚马逊，每一家排名前十的零售商都是实体店。这并不是说传统零售商没有对冲他们的赌注。沃尔玛已投入巨资弥合在线用户和零售场所之间的差距，包括 2016 年收购电子商务公司 Jet.com。考虑到约 80% 的消费者在购买前会在网上搜索有关商品的信息，我们可以看到，未来的趋势将是线上和线下销售相融合。

Alibaba Leading the Way in Merging Online and Offline Shopping